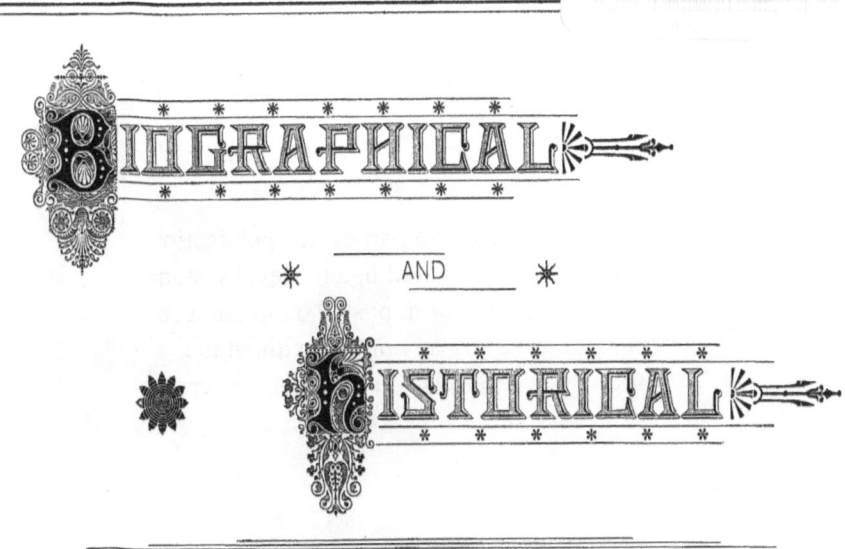

BIOGRAPHICAL AND HISTORICAL MEMOIRS

HISTORY OF ARKANSAS.

SOUTHERN HISTORICAL PRESS, INC.
Book Publishers

This volume was reproduced from
An 1889 edition located in the
O.C. Bailey Library
Hendrix College
Conway, Arkansas

All rights reserved. No part of this publication
may be reproduced, stored in a retrieval system,
transmitted in any form, posted on to the web
in any form or by any means without the
prior written permission of the publisher.

Please direct all correspondence and orders to:

www.southernhistoricalpress.com
or
SOUTHERN HISTORICAL PRESS, Inc.
PO Box 1267
375 West Broad Street
Greenville, SC   29601
southernhistoricalpress@gmail.com

Originally published: Nashville, 1889
Reprinted with New Material by:
Southern Historical Press, Inc.
Greenville, SC
New Material Copyright 1978 by
The Rev. Silas Emmett Lucas, Jr.
Easley, SC
ISBN #0-89308-078-0
All rights Reserved.
Printed in the United States of America

Preface.

THIS beautiful volume has been prepared in response to the popular demand for the preservation of local history and biography. The method of preparation followed is the most successful and the most satisfactory yet devised—the most successful in the enormous number of volumes circulated, and the most satisfactory in the general preservation of personal biography and family record, conjointly with local history. The number of volumes now being distributed seems fabulous. Careful estimates place the number circulated in Ohio at 50,000 volumes; Pennsylvania, 60,000; New York, 75,000; Indiana, 40,000; Illinois, 40,000; Iowa, 30,000; Missouri, 25,000; Kansas, 20,000; Tennessee, 20,000; Kentucky, 25,000; Georgia, 20,000; Alabama, 20,000; Virginia, 25,000, and all the other States at the same proportionate rate. There have already been distributed in Arkansas, including this edition, over 8,000 volumes, and about one-half of the State is yet untouched.

The design of the present extensive biographical and historical research in all the States is to gather and preserve in attractive form, while fresh with the evidences of truth, the enormous fund of perishing occurrence. The phenomenal success of the enterprise is shown in the enormous number of volumes circulated—more than 1,000,000 in the last fifteen years.

Special care was employed and great expense incurred to render the volume accurate. In all cases the personal sketches were submitted by mail to the subjects, for revision and correction, and in most instances were improved and returned. The better element of all classes was given representation, thus placing in permanent form, for all time, a work of general merit. Nothing promised is omitted. The publishers with pride call special attention to the superb mechanical execution of the volume. They warmly thank their friends for the success of their difficult enterprise.

October, 1890.

THE PUBLISHERS.

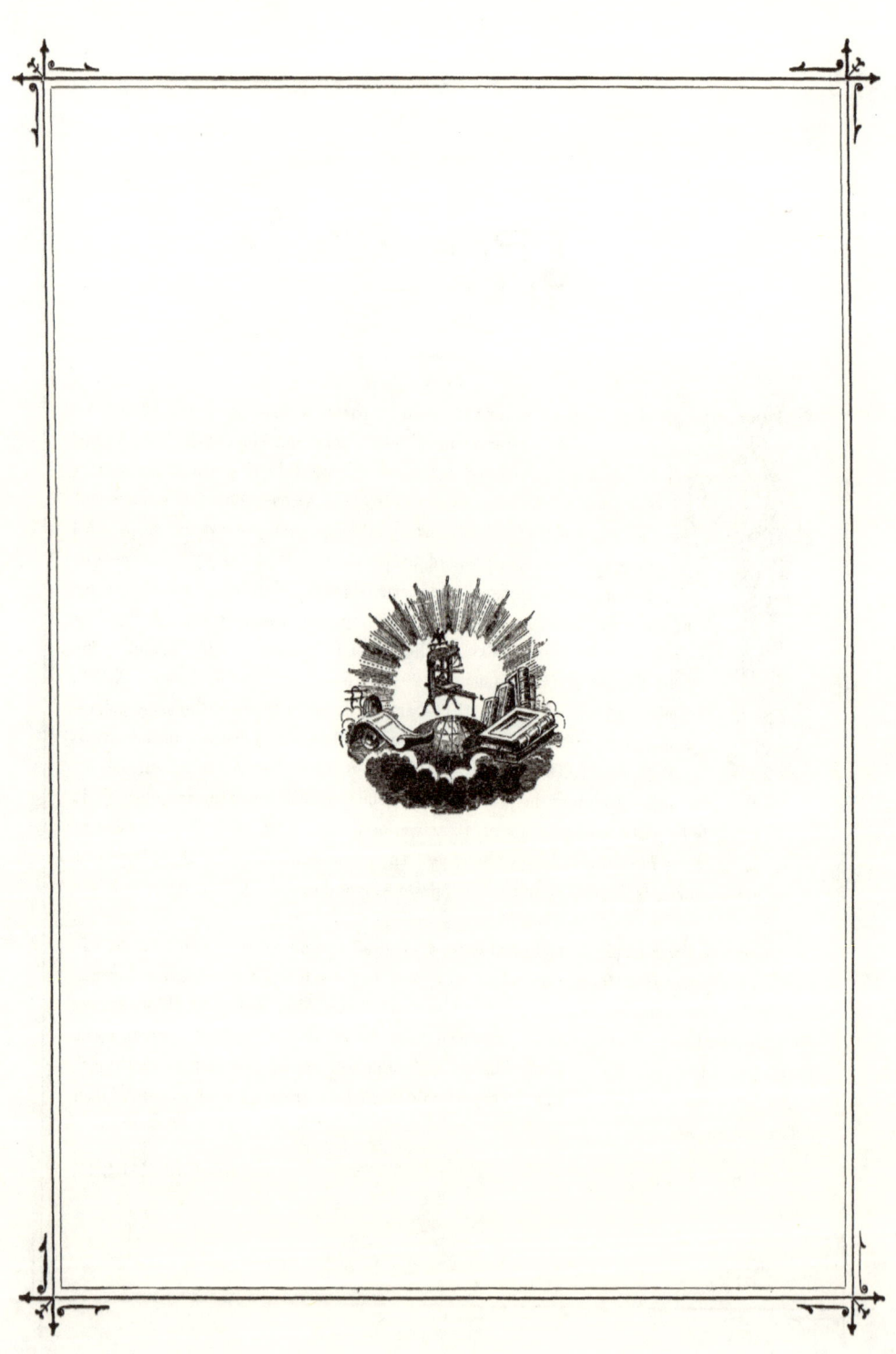

CHAPTER I.

Geology—Importance of Geologic Study—Area and Climate—Boundaries—Principal Streams of the State—The Mountain Systems—The Great Springs—Diversity of Soils—Caves—The Mines, Their Wonderful Deposits and Formations.................................9-18

CHAPTER II.

Archæology—Remains of Flint Arrow and Spear Heads, and Stone and Other Ornaments—Evidences of Prehistoric People along the Mississippi—Mounds, etc., in Other Portions of the State—Local Archæologists and Their Work—The Indians—Tribal and Race Characteristics—The Arkansas Tribes—The Cession Treaties—The Removal of the Cherokees, Creeks and Choctows—An Indian Alarm—Assassination of the Leaders, etc., etc...................................19-23

CHAPTER III.

Discovery and Settlement—De Soto in Arkansas—Marquette and Joliet—La Salle, Hennepin and Tonti—French and English Schemes of Conquest and Dreams of Power—Louisiana—The "Bubble" of John Law—The Early Viceroys and Governors — Proprietary Change of Louisiana — French and Spanish Settlers in Arkansas—English Settlers—A Few First Settlers in the Counties—The New Madrid Earthquake—Other Items of Interest...................................24-34

CHAPTER IV.

Organization—The Viceroys and Governors—The Attitude of the Royal Owners of Louisiana—The District Divided—The Territory of Arkansas Formed from the Territory of Missouri—The Territorial Government—The First Legislature—The Seat of Government—Other Legislative Bodies—The Duello—Arkansas Admitted to Statehood—The Constitutional Conventions—The Memorable Reconstruction Period—Legislative Attitude on the Question of Secession—The War of the Governors, etc., etc.................................34-44

CHAPTER V.

Advancement of the State—Misconceptions Removed—Effects of Slavery upon Agriculture—Extraordinary Improvements Since the War—Important Suggestions —Comparative Estimate of Products—Growth of the Manufacturing Interests—Wonderful Showing of Arkansas—Its Desirability as a Place of Residence—State Elevations.................................45-52

CHAPTER VI.

Politics—Importance of the Subject—The Two Old Schools of Politicians — Triumph of the Jacksonians — Early Prominent State Politicians — The Great Question of Secession—The State Votes to Join the Confederacy—Horror of the War Period—The Reconstruction Distress—The Baxter-Brooks Embroglio.....................52-55

CHAPTER VII.

Societies, State Institutions, etc.—The Ku Klux Klan—Independent Order of Odd Fellows—Ancient, Free and Accepted Masons—Grand Army of the Republic—Bureau of Mines—Arkansas Agricultural Associations—State Horticultural Society—The Wheel—The State Capital—The Capitol Building—State Libraries—State Medical Society—State Board of Health—Deaf Mute Institute — School for the Blind — Arkansas Lunatic Asylum—Arkansas Industrial University—The State Debt.................................56-64

CHAPTER VIII.

The Bench and Bar—An Analytic View of the Profession of Law—Spanish and French Laws—English Common Law—The Legal Circuit Riders—Territorial Law and Lawyers—The Court Circuits—Early Court Officers—The Supreme Court—Prominent Members of the State Bench and Bar—The Standard of the Execution of Law in the State.................................65-73

CHAPTER IX.

The Late Civil War—Analytical View of the Troublous Times—Passage of the Ordinance of Secession—The Call to Arms—The First Troops to take the Field—Invasion of the State by the Federal Army—Sketch of the Regiments—Names of Officers—Outline of Field Operations—Cleburne and Yell—Extracts from Private Memoranda—Evacuation of the State—Re-occupation —the War of 1812—The Mexican War—Standard of American Generalship.................................73-81

CONTENTS.

CHAPTER X.

Public Enterprises—The Real Estate Bank of Arkansas—State Roads and Other Highways—The Military Roads—Navigation within the State from the Earliest Times to the Present—Decadence of State Navigation—Steamboat Racing—Accidents to Boats—The Rise and Growth of the Railroad Systems—A Sketch of the Different Lines—Other Important Considerations..............82-87

CHAPTER XI.

The Counties of the State—Their Formation and Changes of Boundary Lines, etc.—Their County Seats and Other Items of Interest Concerning them—Defunct Counties—New Counties—Population of all the Counties of the State at every General Census........................87-92

CHAPTER XII.

Education—The Mental Type Considered—Territorial Schools, Laws and Funds—Constitutional Provisions for Education—Legislative Provisions—Progress since the War—The State Superintendents — Statistics — Arkansas Literature—The Arkansaw Traveler........93-97

CHAPTER XIII.

The Churches of Arkansas—Appearance of the Missionaries—Church Missions Established in the Wilderness—The Leading Protestant Denominations—Ecclesiastical Statistics—General Outlook from a Religious Standpoint 98-101

CHAPTER XIV.

Names Illustrious in Arkansas History—Prominent Mention of Noted Individuals—Ambrose H. Sevier—William E. Woodruff—John Wilson—John Hemphill—Jacob Barkman—Dr. Bowie—Sandy Faulkner—Samuel H. Hempstead—Trent, Williams, Shinn Families, and Others—The Conways—Robert Crittenden—Archibald Yell—Judge David Walker—Gen. G. D. Royston—Judge James W. Bates.............................102-112

History of Arkansas.

CHAPTER I.

GEOLOGY—IMPORTANCE OF GEOLOGIC STUDY—AREA AND CLIMATE—BOUNDARIES—PRINCIPAL STREAMS OF THE STATE—THE MOUNTAIN SYSTEMS—THE GREAT SPRINGS—DIVERSITY OF SOILS—CAVES—THE MINES, THEIR WONDERFUL DEPOSITS AND FORMATIONS.

> Such blessings Nature pours,
> O'erstocked mankind enjoys but half her stores.—*Young.*

THE matter of first importance for every civilized people to know is the economic geology of the country they inhabit. The rocks and the climate are the solution in the end of all problems of life, as they are the prime sources from which all that human beings can possess comes. The measure of each and every civilization that has adorned the world is in exact degree with the people's knowledge of the natural laws and the environments about them.

The foundation of civilization rests upon the agriculturists, and nothing can be of more importance to this class than some knowledge of what materials plants are composed, and the source from whence they derive existence; the food upon which plants live and grow; how they are nourished or destroyed; what plant food is appropriated by vegetation itself, without man's aid or intervention, through the natural operations in constant action. The schools will some day teach the children these useful and fundamental lessons, and then, beyond all peradventure, they will answer very completely the lately pr pounded question: "Are the public schools a failure?" The knowledge of the elementary principles of the geology of this country is now the demand of the age, made upon all nations, in all climes.

The character of vegetation, as well as the qualities of the waters and their action upon vegetable and animal life, is primarily determined by the subjacent rocks on which the soil rests. Earth and air are but the combinations of the original gases, forming the solids, liquids and the atmosphere surrounding the globe. The soil is but the decomposed rocks—their ashes, in other words, and hence is seen the imperative necessity of the agriculturist understanding something of the rocks which lie beneath the land he would successfully cultivate. He who is educated in the simple fundamental principles of geology—a thing easier to learn than is the difference in the oaks and pines of the forest—to him there is a clear comprehension of the life-giving qualities stored in the surface rocks, as well as a knowledge of the minerals to be found in their company. A youth so educated possesses incomparable advantages over his school companion in the start of life, who has concentrated his energies on the classics or on metaphysical subjects, whether they enter the struggle for life as farmers, stock raisers, miners or craftsmen. It is as much easier to learn to analyze a rock, mineral or soil, than to learn a Greek verb, as the one is more valuable to know than the other. All true knowledge is the acquirement of that which may aid in the race of life, an education that is so practical that it is always helpful and useful.

The geology of Arkansas, therefore, so far as given in this chapter, is in fact but the outline of the physical geography of one of the most interesting localities of the continent, and is written wholly for the lay reader, and attempted in a manner that will reach his understanding.

Within the boundary lines of the State are 53,045 square miles, or 33,948,800 acres. It has 3,868,800 more acres of land than the State of New York, and multiplies many times the combined natural resources of all the New England States. It has 2,756 miles of navigable rivers.

It had a population in 1880, as shown by the census, of 802,525. Of these there were 10,350 foreigners and 210,666 colored. In 1820 the Territory had a population of 14,255; in 1830, of 30,338; in 1840, of 97,554; in 1850, of 209,897; in 1860, of 435,450; in 1870, of 481,471. (This was the Civil War decade.) In 1885 the population had advanced about 200,000 over the year 1880, or was near 1,000,000. In 1887 it reached the figures of 1,260,000, or an increase of more than a quarter of a million in two years, and there is reason to believe this increased ratio will pass beyond the two million mark in the next census. At least, an increase of one hundred per cent in the ten years is indicated. Keeping in mind that there are no great populous cities in the State, it will be known that this has been that healthy increase of population which gives glowing promises for the future of the State. Here the agricultural districts, and the towns and cities, have kept even pace, while in some of the leading States of the Mississippi Valley the great cities have grown while the rural population has markedly decreased. These are serious problems to reflective minds in those States where the cities are overgrowing and the country is declining. Happily, Arkansas is troubled with no such indications of the disturbed natural distribution of its people. The State, since it emerged from the dark and evil days of civil war and reconstruction, has not only not been advertised in regard to its natural resources, but has been persistently slandered. The outside world, more than a generation ago, were plausibly led to believe the energy of its citizens was justly typified in the old senseless ballad, "The Arkansaw Traveler," and the culture and refinement of its best people are supposed to be told in the witty account of Judge Halliburton's "First Piano in Arkansas." The ruined hopes, the bankrupted fortunes and the broken hearts that are the most recent history of the Western deserts, form some of the measure the poor people are paying for the deceptions in this regard that have been practiced upon them. These silly but amusing things have had their effect, but they were pleasant and harmless, compared to the latest phase of pretexts for persistent publications of the cruelest falsehoods ever heaped upon the heads of innocent men. But, in the end, even this will do good; it is to be seen now among the people. It will put the people of the State upon their mettle, resulting, if that is not already the fact, in giving it the most orderly, law abiding, peaceful and moral people of any equal district of the Union.

The State is in the central southern portion of the great Mississippi Valley, and in climate, soil, rocks, minerals and water may well be designated as the capital of this "garden and granary of the world," with resources beneath the surface that are not, taken all together, surpassed on the globe. Its eastern line is the channel of the Mississippi River "beginning at the parallel 36° of north latitude, thence west with said parallel to the middle of the main channel of the St. Francois (Francis) River; thence up the main channel of said last mentioned river to the parallel of 36° 30' of north latitude; thence west with the last mentioned parallel, or along the southern line of the State of Missouri, to the southwest corner of said State; thence to be bounded on the west to the north bank of Red River, as designated by act of Congress and treaties, existing January 1, 1837, defining the western limits of the Territory of Arkansaw, and to be bounded west across and south of Red River by the boundary line of the State of Texas as far as the northwest corner of the State of Louisiana; thence easterly with the northern boundary line of said last named State to the middle of the main channel of the Mississippi River; thence up the middle of the main channel of said last mentioned river, including an island in said river known as Belle Point Island, and all other land as originally surveyed and included as a part of the Territory, or State of Arkansas, to the 36° of north latitude, to the place of beginning."*

The State includes between its north and south boundary lines the country lying between parallel of latitude 33° north, and parallel of latitude 36° 30′ north, and between its east to west lines the country between longitude 90° and a little west of longitude 94° 30′. Its geographical position on the continent assures the best conditions of temperature, salubrity and rainfall, this being shown by the absence of the intense heat and the cold storms of the higher latitudes and the drouths of the west.

From the meteorological reports it is learned that the average rainfall in the State during June, July and August is sixteen inches, except a narrow belt in the center of the State, where it is eighteen inches, and a strip on the western portion of the State, where it is from eight to fourteen inches. Accurate observations covering fifteen years give an average of seventy-five rainy days in the year.

Of twenty-three States where are reported 134 destructive tornadoes, four were in Arkansas.

The annual mean temperature of Los Angeles, Cal., is about 1° less than that of Little Rock.

The watershed of the State runs from the north of west to the southeast, from the divide of the Ozark Mountain range, except a few streams on the east side of the State, which flow nearly parallel with the Mississippi River, which runs a little west of south along the line of the State. North of the Ozark divide the streams bear to a northerly direction.

Of the navigable rivers within its borders the Arkansas is navigable 505 miles; Bartholomew Bayou, 68 miles; Black River, 147 miles; Current River, 63 miles; Fourche La Favre River, 73 miles; Little Missouri River, 74 miles; Little Red River, 48 miles; Little River, 98 miles; Mississippi River, 424 miles; Ouachita River, 134 miles; Petit Jean River, 105 miles; Red River, 92 miles; Saline River, 125 miles; St. Francis River, 180 miles; White River, 619 miles.

These streams flow into the Mississippi River and give the State an unusual navigable river frontage, and they run so nearly in parallel lines to each other and are distributed so equally as to give, especially the eastern half and the southwest part of the State, the best and cheapest transportation facilities of any State in the Union. These free rivers will in all times control the extortions of transportation lines that are so oppressive to the people of less favored localities.

The Arkansas River passes diagonally across the center of the State, entering at Fort Smith, and emptying into the Mississippi at Napoleon.

South of this the main stream is the Ouachita River and its tributaries; the Saline River, which divides nearly equally the territory between the Arkansas and Ouachita Rivers; and the Little Missouri on the southwest, which divides the territory between the Ouachita and Red Rivers. North of the Arkansas, and about equally dividing the ter-

---

* The above descriptive boundary lines are in the authoritative language of the State Constitutional Convention. To understand the south and west lines necessitates a reference to the treaties and acts of Congress. The following would simplify the descriptive part of the west and south lines: Beginning at the southwest corner of Missouri, or in the center of Section 19, Township 21, Range 34 west of the fifth principal meridian line, thence in a straight line south, bearing a little east to strike the east line of Section 4, Township 8 north, Range 32 west; thence in a straight line south, bearing a little west to where the line strikes Red River in Section 14, Township 13 south, Range 33 west; thence along said river to the southwest corner of Section 7, Township 14 south, Range 28 west; thence south to the northwest corner of the northeast quarter of Section 18, Township 20 south, Range 28 west; thence east along the 33° of latitude to the middle of the channel of the Mississippi River; thence up said river to the place of beginning. The State lines run with the lines of latitude and the meridional lines, and not with the government survey lines.

ritory between the Mississippi and the Arkansas Rivers, is White River, running nearly southeast. Its main tributary on the west is Little Red River, and on the northeast Black River, which enters the State from Missouri, and flows southwesterly and empties into the White at Jacksonport, Jackson County. Another important tributary is Cache River, which flows a little west of south from Clay County, emptying into the White near Clarendon.

Eel River is in the northeast corner of the State and partially drains Craighead County. Eleven Points, Currant, Spring and Strawberry Rivers are important tributaries of Black River. St. Francis River flows from Missouri, and from 36° 30' north latitude to 36° north latitude it forms the boundary line between Missouri and Arkansas, and continuing thence south empties into the Mississippi a few miles above Helena.

Main Fork of White River rises in Madison County and flows northwest in and through Washington County into Benton County; thence northeast into Missouri, returning again to Arkansas in Boone County. Big North Fork of White River rises in the south central part of Missouri, flows southward, and forms its junction in Baxter County, Ark. La Grue River is a short distance south of White River; it rises in Prairie County and joins the White in Desha County. Middle Fork of Saline River rises in Garland County and flows southeast. Rolling Fork of Little River rises in Polk and passes south through Sevier County. Cassatot River also rises in Polk and passes south through Sevier County. Clear Fork of Little Missouri rises in Polk County and passes southeast. East Fork of Poteau River rises in Scott County and runs nearly due west into the Indian Territory. L'Auguille River rises in Poinsett County and flows through Cross, St. Francis and Lee Counties, and empties into the St. Francis within a few miles of the mouth of the latter. Big Wattensaw River rises in Lonoke County and runs east into Prairie County, and empties into White River. Muddy Fork of Little Missouri River rises in Howard County and runs southeast. Yache Grass River runs north through Sebastian County and empties into the Arkansas River east of Fort Smith. Terre Noir River runs from northwest to the southeast in Clark County and empties into Ouachita River. Sulphur Fork of Red River enters the State from Texas, about the center of the west line of Miller County, and running a little south of east empties into Red River. Sabine River flows south through the central southern portions of the State, and empties into the Ouachita River near the south line of the State.

There are numerous creeks forming tributaries to the streams mentioned, equally distributed over the State, which are fully described in the respective counties. Besides these water-courses mention should properly be made of the nineteen bayous within the State's borders.

The Ozark Mountains pass through the northern portion of Arkansas, from west to east, and form the great divide in the watersheds of the State. Rich Mountains are in the central western part, and run east from its west line, forming the dividing line between Scott and Polk Counties, and also between Scott and Montgomery Counties, and run into Yell County.

South and east of the Rich Mountains are the Silver Leaf Mountains, also running east and west from Polk County, through Montgomery to Garland County. These are the mountain formations seen about Hot Springs. Sugar Loaf Mountain is in Cleburne County, and receives its name from its peculiar shape. It is in the northern central part of the State. Another mountain of the same name, containing the highest point in the State, is in Sebastian County, and extends into the Indian Territory. Boston Mountains are in the northwestern part of the State, running east and west in Washington, Crawford and other counties. These include the main mountainous formations. There are many points in these ranges that have local names.

It would require volumes to give a complete account of the variety of the innumerable springs which burst forth with their delicious waters— warm, hot and cold, salt, mineral and medicated. The fame of some of the medical, and the Hot Springs of Arkansas, are known throughout the civilized world, and pilgrims from all nations come to be washed and healed in them. They were known to and celebrated by the pre-historic peoples of America; and the migrating buffaloes, ages and ages ago, came annually from the land of the Dakotas to the spring waters of Arkansas. The instincts of the wild beasts antedate the knowledge of man of the virtues and values of the delicious waters so bountifully given to the State. Nearly all over its territory is one wonder after another, filling every known range of springs and spring waters, which, both in abundance of flow and in medicinal properties, mock the world's previous comprehension of the possibilities of nature in this respect.

When De Soto, in June, 1542, discovered the Mississippi River and crossed into (now) Arkansas, and had traveled north into the territory of Missouri, he heard of the "hot lakes" and turned about and arrived in time where is now Hot Springs. Even then, to the aborigines, this was the best-known spot on the continent, and was, and had been for centuries, their great sanitarium. The tribes of the Mississippi Valley had long been in the habit of sending here their invalids, and even long after they were in the possession of the whites it was a common sight to see the camp of representatives of many different tribes. The whites made no improvement in the locality until 1807. Now there is a flourishing city of 10,000 inhabitants, and an annual arrival of visitors of many thousands. The waters, climate, mountain air and grand scenery combine to make this the great world's resort for health and pleasure seekers, and at all seasons of the year. The seasons round, with rarest exceptions, are the May and October months of the North.

In the confined spot in the valley called Hot Springs there are now known seventy-one springs. In 1860 the State geologist, D. D. Owen, only knew of forty. Others will no doubt be added to the list. These range in temperature from 93° to 150° Fahrenheit. They discharge over 500,000 gallons of water daily. The waters are clear, tasteless and inodorous; they come from the sides of the ridge pure and sparkling as the pellucid Neva; holding in solution, as they rush up hot and bubbling from nature's most wonderful alembic, every valuable mineral constituent. In the cure, especially of nearly all manner of blood and chronic diseases, they are unequaled, and their wonders have become mainly known to all the world by the living and breathing advertisements of those who have proven in their own persons their wonderful curative powers. To reach Hot Springs and be healed, is the hope and aspiration of the invalid, when all other remedies have failed. And it is but just now that the pleasure seeker, the tourist, the scientist, and the intelligence and culture of the world are beginning to understand that this is one of the world's most inviting places to see and enjoy.

But the marvels of the district are not confined to the immediate locality of Hot Springs. Here is indeed a wide district, with a quantity and variety of medical springs that are simply inapproachable on the globe. Going west from Hot Springs are systems of springs running into Montgomery County a distance of forty miles. As continued discoveries of other springs in Hot Springs are being made, and as these widely distributed outlying springs are comparatively of recent disclosure, it may be assumed that for many years to come new and valuable springs will become celebrated.

In Carroll County, in the northwest part of the State, are Eureka Springs, only second to Hot Springs in the wide celebrity of fame as healing waters. They, too, may well be considered one of the world's wonders. There are forty-two of these springs within the corporate limits of the city that has grown up about them. They received no public notice until 1879, when with a bound they became advertised to the world. Their wonderful cures, especially in cases of rheumatism, cancer, dyspepsia and other, if not nearly all, chronic diseases, have bordered on the marvelous, if not the miraculous.

In White County are the noted White Sulphur Springs, at Searcy, and the sulphur and chalybeate springs, known as the Armstrong and the Griffin Springs, and the medical springs—Blanchard Springs—in Union County; the Ravenden Springs, in Randolph County, and the Sugar Loaf

Springs, in Cleburne County; the very recently discovered Lithia Springs, near Hope, in Hempstead County, pronounced by a leading medical journal, in its January issue, 1889, to be the most remarkable discovery of this class of medical waters of this century. These are some of the leading springs of the State which possess unusual medicinal properties. By a glance at the map it will be seen they are distributed nearly equally all over its territory. Simply to catalogue them and give accompanying analyses of the waters would make a ponderous volume of itself. In the above list have been omitted mention of the fine Bethseda Springs in Polk County, or the fine iron and chalybeate springs near Magnolia; Bussey's Springs, near Eldorado, Union County; Butler's Saline Chalybeate Springs, in Columbia County; the double mineral spring of J. I. Holdernist, in Calhoun County; a large number of saline chalybeate springs in Township 10 south, Range 23 west, in Hempstead County, called Hubbard's Springs; or Crawford's Sulphur Springs; or those others in Section 16, Township 12 south, Range 10 west; or Murphy's or Leag's Mineral Springs, all in Bradley County; or Gen. Royston's noted chalybeate springs in Pike County, and still many others that are known to possess mineral qualities, though no complete examination of them has yet been made.

Special mention should not be omitted of the Mountain Valley Springs, twelve miles northwest of Hot Springs. The fame of these springs has demanded the shipment of water, lately, to distant localities in vast and constantly increasing quantities. The knowledge of them is but comparatively recent, and yet their wonderful healing qualities are already widely known.

Innumerable, apparently, as are the health springs of Arkansas, they are far surpassed by the common springs found nearly all over the State.

Mammoth Spring is in Fulton County, and is unrivaled in the country. The water boils up from an opening 120 feet in circumference, and flows uninterruptedly at the rate of *9,000 barrels a minute*. From the compression of so large an amount of carbonic acid held in solution, the whole surface of this water basin is in a continual state of effervescence. Spring River, a bold stream, is produced by this spring, and gives an unlimited amount of water power.

The general division of the surface of the State is uplands and lowlands. It is a timber State, with a large number of small prairies. East and near Little Rock is Lonoke Prairie, and other small prairies are in the southwest part. In its northeast portion are some large strips of prairie, and there are many other small spots bare of timber growths, but these altogether compose only a small portion of the State's surface.

The variety and excellence of soils are not surpassed by any State in the Union. The dark alluvial prevails in nearly all the lowlands, while on many sections of the uplands are the umber red soils of the noted tobacco lands of Cuba. About two-thirds of the State's surface shows yellow pine growth, the great tall trees standing side by side with the hardwoods, walnut, maple, grapevines, sumac, etc. A careful analysis of the soils and subsoils of every county in the State by the eminent geologist, Prof. D. D. Owen, shows this result: The best soils of Iowa, Wisconsin and Minnesota are inferior to the best soils of Arkansas in fertilizing properties. The following reports of State geologists tell the story:

	Ark.	Minn.	Iowa.	Wis.
Organic and Volatile Matter	14,150	6,334	6,028	6,580
Alumnia	8,715	5,585	3,288	4,610
Carbonate Lime	21,865	690	940	665

In fertilizing qualities the only comparative results to the Arkansas soils are found in the blue limestone districts of Central Kentucky.

Analysis of the soils shows the derivative geological formation of soils, and their agricultural values; their losses by cultivation, and what soils lying convenient will repair the waste. Arkansas County, the mother of counties in the State, lying in the southeast, shows the tertiary formations. Benton County, at the opposite northwest corner, has the subcarboniferous. The tertiary is found in Newton County; Clark, Hempstead and Sevier show the cretaceous; Conway, Crawford, Johnson, Ouachita, Perry, Polk, Pope, Prairie, Pulaski, Scott, Van Buren, White, Garland and Montgomery, the novaculite, or whetstone grit; Greene, Jackson, Poinsett and Union, the quaternary. In addition to Benton, given above, are Independence, Madison, Monroe, Searcy and Washington, subcarboniferous. The lower silurian is represented in Fulton, Izard, Lawrence, Marion and Randolph. These give the horizons of the rock formations of the State. The State has 28,000,000 acres of woodland—eighty-one and one-half per cent of her soil. Of this twenty-eight per cent is in cleared farms.

If there be drawn a line on the map, beginning a few miles west of longitude 91°, in the direction of Little Rock, thence to the north boundary line of Clark County, just west of the Iron Mountain Railroad, then nearly due west to the west line of the State, the portion north of this line will be the uplands, and south the lowlands. The uplands correspond with the Paleozoic, and lowlands with the Neozoic.

The granitic axis outbursts in Pulaski, Saline, Hot Springs, Montgomery, Pike and Sevier Counties, and runs from the northeast to the southwest through the State. In Northern Arkansas the disturbance shows itself in small faults, gentle folds and slightly indurated shales; but nearer the granite axis, greater faults, strata with high dip and talcose slate, intersected with quartz and calcite veins, become common. These disturbances are intimately connected with, and determine to some extent, the character of the mineral deposits of the State. The veins along the granite axis were filled probably with hot alkaline waters depositing the metalliferous compounds they contained.

Almost every variety of land known to the agriculturist can be found, and, for fertility, the soils of the State are justly celebrated. Composed as they are of uplands and lowlands, and a variety of climate, they give a wide range of products. In the south and central portions are produced the finest cotton in the markets, while the uplands yield fruits in abundance and variety. No place in the great valley excels it in variety of garden vegetables, small and orchard fruits, grasses, grains, and other field crops. Among agriculturists in Arkansas, truly cotton has been king. It is grown upon lands that would produce a hundred bushels of corn to the acre. All over the State a bale of cotton to the acre is the average—worth at this time $50. Per acre it is about the same labor to raise as corn. In the varied and deep rich soils of the State are produced the vegetation—fruits, vegetables and plants—of the semi-tropic regions, and also the whole range of the staple products of the north. Cereals, fruits and cotton grow as well here as anywhere. In the uplands will some day be raised grapes and tobacco that will be world famous.

That portion of the hilly lands in Clay, Greene, Craighead, Poinsett, St. Francis, Lee and Phillips Counties, known as Crowley's ridge, has a soil and vegetable growth distinctive from any other portion of the State. Its principal forest growth is yellow poplar, which is found in immense size. With this timber are the oak, gum, hickory, walnut, sugar and maple. The soil is generally of a light yellowish or gray color, often gravelly, very friable and easily cultivated, producing abundant crops of cotton, corn, oats, clover, timothy and red top, and is most excellent for fruits.

The prevailing soil is alluvial, with more or less diluvial soils. The alluvial soils, especially along the streams, are from three to thirty feet deep, and these rich bottoms are often miles in width. There are no stronger or more productive lands than these anywhere, and centuries of cultivation create no necessity for fertilizers.

The swamp lands or slashes as a general thing lie stretched along between the alluvial lands and second bottoms. They are usually covered with water during the winter and spring, and are too wet for cultivation, though dry in the summer and fall. They can be easily reclaimed by draining.

The second bottoms are principally on the eastern side of the State, extending from the slashes to the hills. The soil is mostly gray color, sometimes yellowish, resting upon a subsoil of yellowish or mulatto clay. The rich, black lands prevail largely in Hempstead, Little River, Sevier, Nevada, Clark, Searcy, Stone, Izard and Independence Counties.

In the mountainous range of the Ozarks, in Independence County, are remarkable cave formations. They are mostly nitre caves and from these and others in the southeast and west of Batesville, the Confederacy obtained much of this necessity. Near Cushman, Independence County, are the wonderful caves. The extent and marvelous beauty of formations are in the great arched room, the "King's Palace." This cave has been explored for miles under the earth, and many wonders and beauties are seen on every hand. On the side of the mouth of one of the caves in this vicinity a strong spring leaps from the mountain's side and into the cave, and the rumbling of the rushing waters beneath the earth can be heard quite a distance. The notable saltpetre caves are in Marion, Newton, Carroll, Independence, Washington and Benton Counties.

There are gold mines in Arkansas, yet no remarkable finds that is, no marvelous wonders have as yet been uncovered. The universal diffusion of milky quartz in veins, seams and beds, as well as all the other geological tokens which lead on to fortune, are recent discoveries, and the intelligent gold hunters are here in abundance. Who can tell what the future may have in store? But should no rich paying gold fields ever be found, still in the resources of the State are ores of silver, antimony, zinc, iron, lead, copper, manganese, marble, granite, whet and honestone, rock-crystal, paints, nitre earths, kaolin, marls, freestone, limestone, buhr and grindstone and slate, which may well justify the bold assertion of that eminent geologist, Prof. D. D. Owen, in 1860, after carefully looking over the State, "that Arkansas is destined to rank as one of the richest mineral States in the Union." Its zinc ores compare favorably with those of Silesia, and its argentiferous galena far exceeds in percentage of silver the average of such ores of other countries. Its novaculite (whetstone) rock can not be excelled in fineness of texture, beauty of color, and sharpness of grit. Its crystal mountains for extent, and their products for beauty, brilliancy and transparency, have no rivals in the world. Its mineral waters are in variety and values equalled only by its mineral products.

Anticipating the natural questions as to why the mines of Arkansas are not better developed, it will be sufficient to condense to the utmost Prof. Owen's words in reference to the Bellah mine in Sevier County: "It is the same vein that is found in Pulaski County, and runs northeast and southwest nearly through the State. Some years ago the Bellah mine was explored and six shafts were sunk. Three of the principal shafts were about thirty feet deep. The work was done under the supervision of Richard W. Bellah, afterward of Texas. There was a continuous vein, increasing in thickness as far as he went. On the line other shafts were sunk from six to twelve feet deep, all showing the ore to be continuous. About five tons of ore were taken out. A portion of this was sent to Liverpool, England, to be tested, and the statement in return was 'seventy-three per cent lead, and 148 ounces of silver to the ton.'" Mr. Bellah wrote to Prof. Owen: "I am not willing to lease the mines; but I will sell for a reasonable price, provided my brother and sister will sell at the same. I have put the price upon the mines, and value it altogether [460 acres of land] at $10,000." Such was the condition of affairs at this mine when the war came. Substantially, this is the ante-bellum history of the Arkansas mining interests. Prof. Owen reports picking up from the debris of these deserted shafts ore that analyzed seventy-three per cent lead and fifty-two and one-half ounces of silver to the ton of lead.

That these rich fields should lie fallow-ground through the generations can now be accounted for only from the blight of slavery upon the enterprise and industry of people, the evils of a great civil war, and the natural adaptation of the soil and slavery to the raising of cotton.

On the line of this vein, in Saline County, from very superficial explorations, were discovered veins bearing argentiferous lead and copper.

Lead is found in about every county in Northern Arkansas. These are a continuation of the Missouri lead ores. The richest argentiferous lead ores reported are in Pulaski, Saline, Montgomery, Polk, Pike, Ashley and Sevier Counties, being found in the quartz and calcite gangues. It is associated in the north of the State with zinc, copper, and with antimony in Sevier County.

One of the latest discoveries is the value of the antimony mines of Polk and Sevier Counties. A mine is being worked successfully for antimony, and the increase of silver is improving as the shaft goes down. At any hour in the progress of the work, according to the opinions of the best scientific mining experts, this shaft may reach one of the noted silver deposits of the world. In the Jeff Clark antimony mine, at a distance of 100 feet down, was found a rich pocket of silver. In every particular, so far, this mine is a transcript of that of the noted Comstock mine. The Comstock mine showed silver on the surface; so did the Sevier County mine; then it passed down 100 feet, following a vein of antimony; so has the Sevier mine; then in each has silver been found.

There is an unchanging law which governs the rock and mineral formations. Nature never lies, and there is no doubt that the Arkansas mineral belt, through Montgomery, Polk, Howard and Sevier Counties, will prove to be one of the richest mining districts of the world.

The antimony mine has been quite successfully worked the past two years. The Bob Wolf mine, Antimony Bluff mine, and Stewart Lode are being profitably worked. Capital and the facilities for reducing ores by their absence are now the only drawback to the mineral products of the State.

Iron is found native in the State only in meteorites. The magnatite ore is found plentiful in Magnet Cove. Lodestones from this place are shipped abroad, and have a high reputation. This is one of the best iron ores, and the scarcity of fuel and transportation in the vicinity are the causes of its not being worked. The limonite iron ore is the common ore of all Northern Arkansas; immense deposits are found in Lawrence, where several furnaces are operated. In the southern part of the State is the bog iron ore. The brown hematite is found in Lawrence, Randolph, Fulton and other counties. Workable veins of manganese are found in Independence County. This valuable ore is imported now from Spain; it is used in making Spiegel iron.

Bituminous and semi-anthracite coal is found in the true coal measures of the uplands of Arkansas. That of the northwest is free from sulphur. The semi-anthracite is found in the valley of the Arkansas River. These coal fields cover 10,000 acres. There are four defined coal horizons—the subconglomerate, lower, middle and upper. The coal fields of this State belong to the lowest—the subcarboniferous—in the shale or millstone grit less than 100 feet above the Archimedes limestone. In the Arkansas Valley these veins aggregate over six feet. The veins lie high in the Boston Mountains, dipping south into the Arkansas Valley. Shaft mining is done at Coal Hill, Spadra and many other points. It is shipped down the river in quantities to New Orleans.

Aluminum, corundum, sapphire, oriental ruby, topaz and amethysts are found in Howard and Sevier Counties. Strontianite is found in Magnet Cove—valuable in the purification of sugar. In the synclinal folds of Upper Arkansas common salt is easily obtained. Good salt springs are in Sevier County, also in Dallas and Hot Springs Counties. Chalcedony, of all colors, cornelian, agates, novaculite, honestone, buhrstone, varieties of granite, eight kinds of elegant marble, sandstones, white, gray, red, brown and yellow, are common in the grit horizon; flagstones, roofing and pencil slates, talc, kaolin, abound in Saline, Washington, St. Francis and Greene Counties. The potter's clay of Miller, Saline and Washington is extensively worked. "Rock oil" has been discovered in large pockets in Northwest Arkansas.

In the development of its mineral resources the State is still in its infancy, so much so, indeed, that what will prove yet to be the great sources of wealth are not even now produced as a commercial commodity. In some respects this is most remarkable. For instance, Arkansas might supply the world, if necessity required, with lime and cement, can produce the best of each at the least cost, and yet practically all these consumed are imported here from other States. Years ago Prof.

D. D. Owen called attention to the valuable marls in the southwest part of the State, but the great beds lie untouched and cotton planters send off for other fertilizers. So also of the great beds of gypsum that lie uncovered and untouched. The outside world wants unlimited supplies of kaolin, fire-clays and such other clays as the State possesses in inestimable quantities, and yet the thrifty people seem to be oblivious of the fact that here is the way to easy sources of wealth.

People can live here too easily it seems. In this way only can a reason be found for not striking boldly out in new fields of venture, with that vigor of desperation which comes of stern and hard necessity. Where nature is stubborn and unyielding, man puts forth his supremest efforts.

Magnet Cove probably furnishes more remarkable formations than any other district in the world. The "Sunk Lands" in the northeast part of the State, the result of the disturbance of the New Madrid earthquake 1811-12, present features of interest to both lay and scientific investigators. The curious spectacle of deep lakes, beneath which can be seen standing in their natural position the great forest trees, is presented; and instead of the land animals roving and feeding among them are the inhabitants of the deep waters.

The natural abutments of novaculite rocks at Rockport, on the Ouachita River, with the proper outlying rocks on the opposite side of the river, are a very interesting formation.

Cortes Mountain, Sebastian County, as seen from Hodges Prairie presents a grand view. The bare hard rock looks as though the waves in their mighty swells had been congealed and fixed into a mountain. It is 1,500 feet high. Standing Rock, Board Camp Creek, Polk County, is a conspicious and interesting landmark. It rises from out the crumbling shales, like an artificial piece of masonry, to the height of ninety feet.

The Dardanello Rock as seen from the Arkansas River, opposite Morristown, is composed of ferruginous substance, and the great column dips at an angle of 40° toward the river. From one point on the southeast is the wonderful Dardanelle Profile. All the features of the face, with a deep-cut mouth slightly open as if in the act of listening to what one is going to say to it, and the outlines of the head, neck and shoulders, are faithfully produced. Its faithfulness of detail and heroic proportions are its strong characteristics.

Sandstone Dam across Lee Creek, Crawford County, is a curious instance of nature's perfect engineering. The formation here possesses as much interest to the scientist as the noted Natural Bridge.

Investigations of the Mammoth Spring lead to the conclusion that it has underground connection with Havell's Valley, Mo; that here the waters from many springs, some rising to the surface and others not rising, are as the head of a vast funnel, which pour down the subterranean channel and, finally meeting obstructions to further progress, are forced up through the solid rock and form the Mammoth Spring, a navigable subterranean river in short, whose charts no bold seaman will ever follow.

North of Big Rock are the traces of a burnt out volcano, whose fires at one time would have lighted up the streets of Little Rock even better than the electric lights now gleaming from their high towers.

The track of the awful cataclysm, once here in its grand forces, is all that is left; the energies of nature's greatest display of forces lost in the geological eons intervening.

CHAPTER II.

Archaeology—Remains of Flint Arrow and Spear Heads and Stone and Other Ornaments—Evidences of Pre-historic People Along the Mississippi—Mounds, etc., in Other Portions of The State—Local Archaeologists and their Work—The Indians—Tribal and Race Characteristics—The Arkansas Tribes—The Cession Treaties—The Removal of the Cherokees, Creeks and Choctaws—An Indian Alarm—Assassination of the Leaders, etc., etc.

> Some lazy ages, lost in sleep and ease,
> No actions leave to busy chronicles;
> Such whose superior felicity but makes
> In story chasms, in epochas mistakes.—*Dryden.*

IN the long gone ages, reaches of time perhaps only to be measured by geological periods, races of men have been here, grown, flourished, declined and passed away, many not even leaving a wrack behind; others transmitting fossil traces, dim and crumbling, and still later ones, the successors of the earlier ones, who had no traditions of their predecessors, have left something of the measure of their existence in the deftly cut flints, broken pottery, adobe walls, or great earthworks standing in the whilom silent wilderness as mute and enduring monuments to their existence; man, races, civilizations, systems of religion passing on and on to that eternal silence—stormfully from the inane to the inane, the great world's epic that is being forever written and that is never writ.

Arkansas is an inviting field for the investigation of the archaeologist, as well as the geologist. Races of unknown men in an unknown time have swarmed over the fair face of the State. Their restless activities drove them to nature's natural storehouses and the fairest climes on the continent. Where life is easiest maintained in its best form do men instinctively congregate, and thus communities and nations are formed. The conditions of climate and soil, rainfall and minerals are the controlling factors in the busy movements of men. These conditions given, man follows the great streams, on whose bosom the rudest savages float their canoes and pirogues.

Along the eastern part of the State are the most distinct traces of prehistoric peoples, whose hieroglyphics, in the form of earthworks, are the most legible to the archaeologist. Here, earthworks in greatest extent and numbers are found, indicating that this section once swarmed with these barbaric races of men.

In Lonoke County, sixteen miles southeast of Little Rock, and on the Little Rock & Altheimer branch of the St. Louis, Arkansas & Texas Railroad, is a station called Toltec. It is located on the farm of Mr. Gilbert Knapp, and is near Mounds Lake. This lake is either the line of what was a horse-shoe bend in Arkansas River long ago, or is the trace of a dead river. The lake is in the form of a horse-shoe, and covers a space of about three miles. The horse-shoe points east of north, and the heels to the southwest. Here is a great field of large and interesting mounds and earthworks. A little east of the north bend of the lake are two great mounds—one square and the other cone shaped. The cone shaped is the larger and taller, and is supposed to have been 100 feet high, while the other was about seventy-five feet in elevation. About them to the north and east are many small mounds, with no apparent fixed method in their location. These have all been denuded of their timber and are in cultivation, except the larger one above mentioned. Upon this is a growth of heavy timber, elms, hickory, and oaks with as high as 500 rings, and standing on an alluvial soil from eight to fifteen feet deep. These large mounds are enclosed with an earth wall starting out from the bank of the lake, and circling at a considerable distance and returning to the lake, and keeping nearly an equal distance from the larger mound. The sloping base of each mound reaches the base and overlaps or mingles with the base of its neighbor. Around this big wall was once an outside ditch. The humus on the smaller mounds shows, in cultivation, a stronger and deeper alluvial soil than the surrounding land.

There are evidences in these mounds that while they were built by one nation, for objects now problematical, they have been used by other succeeding peoples for other and different purposes, much after the manner that are now found farmers with well-kept gardens on the tops of the mounds, or stately residences, or on others growing cotton and corn. In them human and animal bones are seen, and there are indications that, while they were built for purposes of worship or war, when the builders passed away more than one race of their successors to the country used them as convenient burial grounds. They were skillful stone workers and potters, and their mason's tools are frequently met with. Nearly every implement of the stone age is found in and about the mounds.

Mr. Knapp, who has given the subject considerable intelligent study, is so convinced that these works were made by the Toltec race that he has named the new station in honor of that people. On the line of this earth-wall mentioned are two deep pools that never are known to become dry.

East of Toltec thirty or more miles, in Lonoke Prairie, are mounds that apparently belong to the chain or system which runs parallel with the river, through the State. The small mounds or barrows, as Jefferson termed the modern Indian burial places, are numerous, and distributed all over Arkansas.

What is pronounced a fortified town is found in well marked remains on St. Francis River. It was discovered by Mr. Savage, of Louisville. He reports "parts of walls, built of adobe brick and cemented." On these remains he detected trees growing numbering 800 rings. He reports the brick made of clay and chopped or twisted straw, and with regular figures. A piece of first-class engineering is said to be traced here in a sap-mine, which had passed under the walls of the fortification.

The bones and pottery and tools and arms of the prehistoric peoples of Arkansas are much more abundant than are found in any other spot in the United States.

Mrs. Hobbs, living four miles southeast of Little Rock, has a very complete collection of the antiquities of the State. It is pronounced by antiquarians as one of the most valuable in the country. The Smithsonian Institute has offered her every inducement to part with her collection, but she has refused. It is hoped the State will some day possess this treasure, and suitably and permanently provide for its preservation.

When the white man discovered and took possession of North America, he found the red man and his many tribes here, and under a total misapprehension of having found a new continent, he named this strange people Indians. The new world might have been called Columbia, and the people Columbians. Again, instead of being sparse tribes of individuals fringing the shores of the Atlantic Ocean there were 478 tribes, occupying nearly the whole of the north half of this western hemisphere; some in powerful tribes, like the Iroquois; some were rude agricultural and commercial peoples, some living in houses of logs or stone, permanent residents of their localities; others warriors and hunters only, and still others migratory in their nature, pirates and parasites. One characteristic strongly marked them all—a love of liberty and absolute freedom far stronger than the instinct of life itself. The Indian would not be a slave. Proud and free, he regarded with contempt the refinements of civilization. He breathed the same free air as did the eagle of the crags, and would starve before he would do manual work, or, as he believed, degrade himself in doing aught but paint himself, sing his war songs and go forth to battle, or pursue the wild game or meet the savage wild beasts in their paths and slay them in regular combat. To hunt, fish and fight was the high mission of great and good men to his untutored mind, while the drudgery of life was relegated to the squaws and squaw-men. His entire economic philosophy was simply the attainment of his desires with the least exertion. In a short time he will have filled his earthly mission, and passed from the stage of action, leaving nothing but a dim memory. From their many generations of untold numbers has come no thought, no invention, no action that deserves to survive them a day or an hour. The Indians of to-day, the few that are pure blood, are but the remnants, the useless refuse of a once numerous people, who were the undisputed possessors of a continent, but are now miserable, ragged and starving beggars at the back doors of their despoilers, stoically awaiting the last final scene in the race tragedy. And, like the cheerful sermon on the tombstone, who shall say that white civilization, numbers and power, will not in the course of time, and that not far distant, be the successors of the residue of wretches now representing the red race? "I was once as you are, you will soon be as I am." A grim philosophy truly, but it is the truth of the past, and the great world wheels about much now as it has forever.

What is now Arkansas has been the possession of the following Indian tribes; no one tribe, it seems, occupied or owned the territory in its entirety, but their possessions extended into the lines, covering a portion of the lands only, and then reaching many degrees, sometimes to the north, south and west: The Osages, a once numerous tribe, were said to own the country south of the Missouri River to Red River, including a large portion of Arkansas. The Quapaws, also a powerful nation, were the chief possessors, and occupied nearly the whole of the State, "time out of mind;" the Cherokees were forced out of Georgia and South Carolina, and removed west of the Mississippi River in 1836; the Hitchittees were removed from the Chattahouchee River to Arkansas. They speak the Muskogee dialect—were 600 strong when removed; the Choctaws were removed to the west, after the Cherokees. In 1812 they were 15,000 strong.

The Quapaws, of all the tribes connected with Arkansas, may be regarded as the oldest settlers, having possessed more of its territory in well defined limits than any of the others. In the early part of the eighteenth century they constituted a powerful tribe. In the year 1720 they were decimated by smallpox; reduced by this and other calamities, in 1820, one hundred years after, they were found scattered along the south side of the Arkansas River, numbering only 700 souls. They never regained their former numerical strength or warlike importance, but remained but a band of wretched, ragged beggars, about whose hunting grounds the white man was ever lessening and tightening the lines.

January 5, 1819, Gov. Clark and Pierre Chouteau made a treaty with the tribe by which was ceded to the United States the most of their territory. The descriptive part of the treaty is in the following words: "Beginning at the mouth of the Arkansas River; thence extending up the Arkansas to the Canadian Fork, and up the Canadian Fork to its source; thence south to the big Red River, and down the middle of that river to the Big Raft; thence in a direct line so as to strike the Mississippi River, thirty leagues in a straight line, below the mouth of the Arkansas, together with all their claims to lands east of the Mississippi River and north of the Arkansas River. With the exception and reservation following, that is to say, that tract of country bounded as follows: Beginning at a point on the Arkansas River opposite the present Post of Arkansas, and running thence a due southwest course to the Washita River; thence up that river to the Saline Fork, to a point from whence a due north course would strike the Arkansas River at the Little Rock, and thence down the right bank of the Arkansas to the place of beginning." In addition to this a tract was reserved north of the Arkansas River, which the treaty says is indicated by "marks on the accompanying map." This west line of the Quapaw reservation struck the river about where is now Rock Street.

In November, 1824, Robert Crittenden, the first Territorial secretary, effected a treaty with the Quapaws, at Harrington's, Ark., which ceded the above reservation and forever extinguished all title of that tribe to any portion of Arkansas. The tribe was then removed to what is now the Indian Territory.

The other original occupants or claimants to the Arkansas Territory were the Osages. Of these there were many tribes, and in 1830 numbered 4,000 strong, but mostly along the Osage River. Their claim lapped over, it seems, all that portion of the Quapaw lands lying north of the Arkansas River.

The title of the Osages was extinguished to what is now Arkansas by a treaty of November 10, 1808, made at Fort Clark, on the Missouri River. By this treaty they ceded all the country east of a line running due south from Fort Clark to the Arkansas River, and down said river to its confluence with the Mississippi River. These Indians occupied only the country along the Missouri and Osage Rivers, and if they were ever on what they claimed as their southern boundary, the Arkansas River, it was merely on expeditions.

About 1818, Georgia and South Carolina commenced agitating the subject of getting rid of the Indians, and removing them west. They wanted their lands and did not want their presence. At first they used persuasion and strategy, and finally force. They were artful in representing to the Indians the glories of the Arkansas country, both for game and rich lands. During the twenty years of agitating the subject Indians of the tribes of those States came singly and in small bands to Arkansas, and were encouraged to settle anywhere they might desire north of the Arkansas River, on the Osage ceded lands. The final act of removal of the Indians was consummated in 1839, when the last of the Cherokees were brought west. Simultaneous with the arrival of this last delegation of Indians an alarm passed around among the settlers that the Indians were preparing to make a foray on the white settlements and murder them all. Many people were greatly alarmed, and in some settlements there were hasty preparations made to flee to places of safety. In the meantime the poor, distressed Cherokees and Choctaws were innocent of the stories in circulation about them, and were trying to adjust themselves to their new homes and to repair their ruined fortunes. The Cherokees were the most highly civilized of all the tribes, as they were the most intelligent, and had mingled and intermarried with the whites until there were few of pure blood left among them. They had men of force and character, good schools and printing presses, and published and edited papers, as well as their own school books. These conditions were largely true, also, of the Chickasaws. The Cherokees and Chickasaws were removed west under President Jackson's administration. The Cherokees were brought by water to Little Rock, and a straight road was cut out from Little Rock to the corner of their reservation, fifteen miles above Batesville, in Independence County, over which they were taken. Their southeast boundary line was a straight line, at the point designated above Batesville, to the mouth of Point Remove Creek.

The history of the removal of the Cherokee Indians (and much of the same is true of the removal of the Chickasaws and Creeks), is not a pleasant chapter in American history. The Creeks of Florida had waged war, and when conquered Gen. Scott removed them beyond the Mississippi River. When the final consummation of the removal of the Cherokees was effected, it was done by virtue of a treaty, said to have been the work of traitors, and unauthorized by the proper Indian authorities. At

CHAPTER II.

Archaeology—Remains of Flint Arrow and Spear Heads and Stone and Other Ornaments—Evidences of Pre-historic People Along the Mississippi—Mounds, etc., in Other Portions of The State—Local Archaeologists and their Work—The Indians—Tribal and Race Characteristics—The Arkansas Tribes—The Cession Treaties—The Removal of the Cherokees, Creeks and Choctaws—An Indian Alarm—Assassination of the Leaders, etc., etc.

> Some lazy ages, lost in sleep and ease,
> No actions leave to busy chronicles;
> Such whose superior felicity but makes
> In story chasms, in epochas mistakes.—*Dryden.*

IN the long gone ages, reaches of time perhaps only to be measured by geological periods, races of men have been here, grown, flourished, declined and passed away, many not even leaving a wrack behind; others transmitting fossil traces, dim and crumbling, and still later ones, the successors of the earlier ones, who had no traditions of their predecessors, have left something of the measure of their existence in the deftly cut flints, broken pottery, adobe walls, or great earthworks standing in the whilom silent wilderness as mute and enduring monuments to their existence; man, races, civilizations, systems of religion passing on and on to that eternal silence—stormfully from the inane to the inane, the great world's epic that is being forever written and that is never writ.

Arkansas is an inviting field for the investigation of the archæologist, as well as the geologist. Races of unknown men in an unknown time have swarmed over the fair face of the State. Their restless activities drove them to nature's natural storehouses and the fairest climes on the continent. Where life is easiest maintained in its best form do men instinctively congregate, and thus communities and nations are formed. The conditions of climate and soil, rainfall and minerals are the controlling factors in the busy movements of men. These conditions given, man follows the great streams, on whose bosom the rudest savages float their canoes and pirogues.

Along the eastern part of the State are the most distinct traces of prehistoric peoples, whose hieroglyphics, in the form of earthworks, are the most legible to the archæologist. Here, earthworks in greatest extent and numbers are found, indicating that this section once swarmed with these barbaric races of men.

In Lonoke County, sixteen miles southeast of Little Rock, and on the Little Rock & Altheimer branch of the St. Louis, Arkansas & Texas Railroad, is a station called Toltec. It is located on the farm of Mr. Gilbert Knapp, and is near Mounds Lake. This lake is either the line of what was a horse-shoe bend in Arkansas River long ago, or is the trace of a dead river. The lake is in the form of a horse-shoe, and covers a space of about

CHAPTER III.

Discovery and Settlement—De Soto in Arkansas—Marquette and Joliet—La Salle, Hennepin and Tonti—French and English Schemes of Conquest and Dreams of Power—Louisiana—The "Bubble" of John Law—The Early Viceroys and Governors—Proprietary Change of Louisiana—French and Spanish Settlers in Arkansas—English Settlers—A Few First Settlers in the Counties—The New Madrid Earthquake—Other Items of Interest.

> Hail, memory, hail! In thy exhaustless mine
> From age to age unnumbered treasures shine!
> Thought and her shadowy brood thy call obey,
> And place and time are subject to thy sway.—*Rogers.*

FERDINAND DE SOTO, the discoverer of the Mississippi, was the first civilized white man to put foot upon any part of what is now the State of Arkansas. He and his band of adventurous followers had forged their way over immense obstacles, through the trackless wastes, and in the pleasant month of June, 1541, reached the Mississippi River at, as is supposed, Chickasaw Bluffs, a short distance below Memphis. He had sailed from San Lucan in April, 1538, with 600 men, twenty officers and twenty-four priests. He represented his king and church, and came to make discoveries for his master in Florida, a country undefined in extent, and believed to be the richest in the world.

His expedition was a daring and dangerous one, and there were but few men in the tide of time who could have carried it on to the extent that did this bold Spaniard. The worn and decimated band remained at the Chickasaw Bluffs to rest and recuperate until June 29, then crossing the river into Arkansas, and pushing on up the Mississippi River, through brakes and swamps and slashes, until they reached the higher prairie lands that lead toward New Madrid; stopping in their north course at an Indian village, Pacaha, whose location is not known. De Soto sent an expedition toward the Osage River, but it soon returned and reported the country worthless.* He then turned west and proceeded to the Boston Mountains, at the head-waters of White River; then bending south, and passing Hot Springs, he went into camp for the winter on the Ouachita River, at Autamqua Village, in Garland County. In the spring he

---

*It is proper to here state the fact that some local investigators, and others who have studied the history of De Soto's voyaging through Arkansas, do not believe that he reached and discovered the river as high up as Memphis. They think he approached it a short distance above the mouth of Red River, and from that point made his detour around to Red River. Others in the State, who have also studied the subject thoroughly, find excellent evidence of his presence in Arkansas along the Mississippi, particularly in Mississippi County. See "History of Mississippi County, Ark." After examining the testimony carefully I incline to the account as given in the context as being the most probable.—Ed.

floated down the river, often lost in the bayous and overflows of Red River, and finally reached again the Mississippi. Halting here he made diligent inquiries of the Indians as to the mouth of the great stream, but they could give him no information. In June, one year from the date of his discovery, after a sickness of some weeks, he died. As an evidence of his importance to the expedition his death was kept a secret, and he was buried at night, most appropriately, in the waves of the great river that gave his name immortality. But the secrecy of his death was of no avail, for there was no one who could supply his place, and with his life closed the existence, for all practical purposes, of the expedition. Here the interest of the historian in De Soto and his companions ceases. He came not to possess the beautiful country, or plant colonies, or even extend the dominions of civilization, but simply to find the fabled wealth in minerals and precious stones, and gather them and carry them away. Spain already possessed Florida, and it was all Florida then, from the Atlantic to the boundless and unknown west.

The three great nations of the old world had conquered and possessed—the Spaniards Florida, the English Virginia and New England, and the French the St. Lawrence. The feeblest of all these colonizers or conquerors were the English, and they retained their narrow foothold on the new continent with so little vigor that for more than a century and a half they knew nothing of the country west of them save the idle dreams and fictions of the surrounding savages. The general world had learned little of De Soto's great western discoveries, and when he was buried in the Mississippi all remained undisturbed from the presence or knowledge of civilized men for the period of 132 years.

Jacques Marquette, a French Jesuit priest, had made expeditions along the Northern lakes, proselyting among the Indian tribes. He had conceived the idea that there was a great western river leading to China and Japan. He was joined in his ambition to find this route, and the tribes along it, by Joliet, a man fired with the ambition and daring of the bold explorer. These two men, with five employes, started on their great adventure May 17, 1673. They found the Upper Mississippi River and came down that to the mouth of the Arkansas River, thence proceeding up some distance, it is supposed to near where is Arkansas Post. Thus the feet of the white man pressed once more the soil of this State, but it was after the lapse of many years from the time of De Soto's visit. Marquette carried into the newly discovered country the cross of Christ, while Joliet planted in the wilderness the tri-colors of France. France and Christianity stood together in the heart of the great Mississippi Valley; the discoverers, founders and possessors of the greatest spiritual and temporal empire on earth. From here the voyagers retraced their course to the Northern lakes and the St. Lawrence, and published a report of their discoveries.

Nine years after Marquette and Joliet's expedition, Chevalier de La Salle came from France, accompanied by Henry de Tonti, an Italian, filled with great schemes of empire in the new western world; it is charged, by some historians of that day, with no less ambition than securing the whole western portion of the continent and wresting Mexico from the Spaniards. When Canada was reached, La Salle was joined by Louis Hennepin, an ambitious, unscrupulous and daring Franciscan monk. It was evidently La Salle's idea to found a military government in the new world, reaching with a line of forts and military possession from Quebec, Canada, to at least the Gulf, if not, as some have supposed, extending through Mexico. He explored the country lying between the Northern lakes and the Ohio River. He raised a force in Canada and sailed through Green Bay, and, sending back his boat laden with furs, proceeded with his party to the head waters of the Illinois River and built Fort Creve Cœur. He detached Hennepin with one companion and sent him to hunt the source of the Mississippi. He placed Tonti in command of Creve Cœur, with five men, and himself returned to Canada in the latter part of 1681, where he organized a new party with canoes, and went to Chicago; crossing the long portage from there to the Illinois River, he floated down that stream to the Mississippi and on to the Gulf of Mexico, discovering the mouth of the Mississippi River April 5, 1682, and three days after, with becoming pomp and ceremony, took possession, in the name of France, of the territory, and named it Louisiana, in honor of his king, Louis XIV. The vast region thus acquired by France was not, as it could not be, well defined, but it was intended to embrace, in addition to much east of the Mississippi River, all the continent west of that current.

After this expedition La Salle returned to France, fitted out another expedition and set sail, ostensibly to reach the mouth of the Mississippi River and pass up that stream. He failed to find the river, and landed his fleet at Metagordo Bay, Texas, where he remained two years, when with a part of his force he started to reach Canada via Fort St. Louis, but was assassinated by one of his men near the Trinity River, Texas, March 19, 1687, and his body, together with that of his nephew, was left on the Texas prairie to the beasts and buzzards. La Salle was a born commander of men, a great explorer, with vast projects of empire far beyond the comprehension of his wretched king, or the appreciation of his countrymen. Had he been supported by a wise and strong government, France would never, perhaps, have been dispossessed of the greatest inter-continental colonial empire on earth—from the Alleghanies to the Rocky Mountains. This was, in fact, the measure of the territory that La Salle's expedition and military possession gave to France. The two great ranges of mountains, the north pole and South America, were really the boundary lines of Louisiana, of which permanent ownership belonged forever to France, save for the weakness and inefficiency of that *bete noire* of poor, beautiful, sunny France—Louis XIV. In the irony of fate the historian of to-day may well write down the appellation of his toadies and parasites, as the *grand monarque*. La Salle may justly be reckoned one of the greatest founders of empire in the world, and had poor France had a real king instead of this weak and pompous imbecile, her tri-colors would have floated upon every breeze from the Alleghanies to the Pacific Ocean, and over the islands of more than half of the waters of the globe.

The immensity of the Louisiana Territory has been but little understood by historians. It was the largest and richest province ever acquired, and the world's history since its establishment has been intimately connected with and shaped by its influence. Thus the account of the Territory of Louisiana is one of the most interesting chapters in American history.

Thirteen years after the death of La Salle, 1700, his trusty lieutenant, Tonti, descended the Mississippi River from the Illinois, with a band of twenty French Illinois people, and upon reaching Arkansas Post, established a station. This was but carrying out La Salle's idea of a military possession by a line of forts from Canada to the Gulf. It may be called the first actual and intended permanent possession of Arkansas. In the meantime, Natchez had become the oldest settled point in the Territory, south of Illinois, and the conduct of the commandant of the canton, Chopart, was laying the foundations for the ultimate bloody massacre of that place, in November, 1729. The Jesuit, Du Poisson, was the missionary among the Arkansans. He had made his way up the Mississippi and passed along the Arkansas River till he reached the prairies of the Dakotahs.

The Chickasaws were the dreaded enemy of France; it was they who hurried the Natchez to that awful massacre; it was they whose cedar bark canoes, shooting boldly into the Mississippi, interrupted the connections between Kaskaskia and New Orleans, and delayed successful permanent settlements in the Arkansas. It was they who weakened the French empire in Louisiana. They colleagued with the English, and attempted to extirpate the French dominion in the valley.

Such was Louisiana more than half a century after the first attempt at colonization by La Salle. Its population may have been 5,000 whites and half that number of blacks. Louis XIV had fostered it by giving it over to the control of Law and his company of the Mississippi, aided by boundless but transient credit. Priests and friars dispersed through tribes from Biloxi to the Dakotahs, and propitiated the favor of the savages. But still the valley of the Mississippi remained a wilderness. All its patrons—though among them it counted kings and high ministers of state—had not accomplished for it in half a century a tithe of that prosperity which, within the same period, sprung naturally from the benevolence of William Penn to the peaceful settlers on the Delaware.

It required the feebleness of the *grand monarque* to discover John Law, the father of inflated cheap money and national financial ruin. In September, 1717, John Law's Company of the West was granted the commerce and control of Louisiana. He arrived at New Orleans with 800 immigrants in August of that year. Instead of coming up the Mississippi, they landed at Dauphine Island to make their way across by land. The reign of John Law's company over Louisiana was a romance or a riot of folly and extravagance. He was to people and create a great empire on cheap money and a monopoly of the slave trade. For fourteen years the Company of the West controlled Louisiana. The bubble burst, the dreams and illusions of ease and wealth passed away, and but wretched remnants of colonies existed, in the extremes of want and suffering. But, after all, a permanent settlement of the great valley had been made. A small portion of these were located at Arkansas Post, up the Arkansas River and on Red River, and like the most of the others of Law's followers, they made a virtue of necessity and remained because they could not get away.

John Law was an Englishman, a humbug, but a magnificent one, so marked and conspicuous in the world's history that his career should have taught the statesmen of all nations the simple lesson that debt is not wealth, and that every attempt to create wealth wholly by legislation is sure to be followed by general bankruptcy and ruin.

The Jesuits and fur-traders were the founders of Illinois; Louis XIV and privileged companies were the patrons of Southern Louisiana, while the honor of beginning the work of colonizing the southwest of our republic belongs to the illustrious Canadian, Lemoine D'Iberville. He was a worthy successor of La Salle. He also sought to find the mouth of the Mississippi, and guided by floating trees and turbid waters, he reached it on March 2, 1699. He perfected the line of communication between Quebec and the Gulf; extended east and west the already boundless possessions of France; erected forts and carved the lilies on the trees of the forests; and fixed the seat of government of Louisiana at Biloxi, and appointed his brother to command the province. Under D'Iberville, the French line was extended east to Pascagoula River; Beinville, La Sueur, and St. Denys had explored the west to New Mexico, and had gone in the northwest beyond the Wisconsin and the St. Croix, and reached the mouth of and followed this stream to the confluence of the Blue Earth. D'Iberville died of yellow fever at Havana, July 9, 1706, and in his death the Louisiana colony lost one of its most able and daring leaders. But Louisiana, at that time, possessed less than thirty families of whites, and these were scattered on voyages of discovery, and in quest of gold and gems.

France perfected her civil government over Louisiana in 1689, and appointed Marquis de Sanville, royal viceroy. This viceroy's empire was as vast in territory as it was insignificant in population—less than 300 souls.* By regular appointments of viceroys the successions were maintained (including the fourteen years of Law's supremacy) until by the treaty of Fontainbleau, November 3, 1762, France was stripped of her American possessions, and Canada and the Spanish Florida; everything east of the Mississippi except the island of New Orleans was given to England, and all Louisiana, including New Orleans west of the Mississippi River and south of the new southern boundary line of Canada, was given to Spain, in lieu of her Florida possessions. Hence, it was November 3, 1762, that what is now Arkansas passed from the dominion of France to that of Spain.

The signing of this treaty made that day the most eventful one in the busy movements of the

---

* The title of France to the boundless confines of Louisiana were confirmed by the treaty of Utrecht. The contentions between England and France over the Ohio country, afterward, are a part of the annals of the general history of the country.

human race. It re-mapped the world, gave the English language to the American continent, and spread it more widely over the globe than any that had before given expression to human thought, the language that is the *alma mater* of civil liberty and religious independence. Had France permanently dominated America, civil liberty and representative government would have been yet unborn. The dogmatic tyranny of the middle ages, with all its intolerance and war, would have been the heritage of North America.

Thus re-adjusted in her domain, Louisiana remained a province of Spain until October 1, 1800, when the Little Corporal over-ran Spain with his victorious legions, and looted his Catholic majesty's domains. Napoleon allowed his military ambition to dwarf his genius, and except for this curious fact, he was the man who would have saved and disenthralled the French mind, and have placed the Gaul, with all his volcanic forces, in an even start in the race of civilization with the invincible and cruel Anglo-Saxon. He was the only man of progressive genius that has ever ruled poor, unfortunate France. The treaty of St. Ildefonso, secretly transferring Louisiana from Spain again into the possession of France, was ratified March 24, 1801. Its conditions provided that it was to remain a secret, and the Spanish viceroy, who was governor of Louisiana, knew nothing of the transfer, and continued in the discharge of his duties, granting rights, creating privileges and deeding lands and other things that were inevitable in breeding confusions, and cloudy land titles, such as would busy the courts for a hundred years, inflicting injustice and heavy burdens upon many innocent people.

In 1802 President Jefferson became possessed of the secret that France owned Louisiana. He at once sent James Monroe to Paris, who, with the resident minister, Mr. Livingston, opened negotiations with Napoleon, at first only trying to secure the free navigation of the Mississippi River, but to their great surprise the Emperor more than met them half way, with a proposal to sell Louisiana to the United States. The bargain was closed, the consideration being the paltry sum of $15,000,000.

This important move on the great chess-board of nations occurred April 30, 1803. The perfunctory act of lowering the Spanish ensign and hoisting the flag of France; then lowering immediately the tri-colors and unfurling the stars and stripes, it is hoped never to be furled, was performed at St. Louis March 9, 1804. Bless those dear old, nation-building pioneers! These were heavy drafts upon their patriotic allegiance, but they were equal to the occasion, and ate their breakfasts as Spaniards, their dinners as Frenchmen, and suppers as true Americans.

The successful class of immigrants to the west of the Mississippi were the French Canadians, who had brought little or nothing with them save the clothes on their backs, and an old flintlock gun with which to secure game. They colonized after the French mode of villages and long strips of farms, and a public commons. They propitiated the best they could the neighboring Indian tribes, erected their altars, hunted, and frolicked, and were an honest, simple-minded and just people, but little vexed with ambitious pride or grasping avarice. The mouth of the Arkansas River was the attractive point for immigrants on their way to the Arkansas Territory, and they would ascend that stream to Arkansas Post. There were not 500 white people in the Territory of (now) Arkansas in 1803, when it became a part of the United States. In 1810 the total population was 1,062. So soon as Louisiana became a part of the United States, a small but never ceasing stream of English speaking people turned their faces to the west and crossed the "Father of Waters." Those for Arkansas established Montgomery Point, at the mouth of White River, making that the transfer place for all shipments inland. This remained as the main shipping and commercial point for many years. By this route were transferred the freights for Arkansas Post. The highway from Montgomery Point to the Post was a slim and indistinct bridle path. The immigrants came down the Cumberland and Tennessee Rivers to the Ohio in keelboats and canoes, and were mostly from Tennessee; beckoned to this fair and rich kingdom by its sunny clime, its mountains and rivers, and its productive valleys, all enriched with a flora and fauna surpassing the dream of a pastoral poem.

The French were the first permanent settlers of Arkansas, and descendants of these people are still here. Many bearing the oldest French names have attained to a position among the most eminent of the great men of the trans-Mississippi. Sometimes the names have become so corrupted as to be unrecognizable as belonging to the early illustrious stock. The English-speaking people speaking French names phonetically would soon change them completely, The Bogys and Lefevres, for instance, are names that go back to the very first settlements in Arkansas. "Lefevre" on the maps is often spelled phonetically thus: "Lafaver." Representatives of the Lefevre family are yet numerous in and about Little Rock, and in other portions of the State.

Peter L. Lefevre and family were among the very first French settlers, locating in the fall of 1818 on the north side of the river on Spanish Grant No. 497, about six miles below Little Rock. His sons were Peter, Enos, Francis G., Ambrose, Akin, Leon and John B., his daughter being Mary Louise. All of these have passed away except the now venerable Leon Lefevre, who resides on the old plantation where he was born in the year 1808. For eighty one years the panorama of the birth, growth and the vicissitudes of Arkansas have passed before his eyes. It is supposed of all living men he is the oldest representative surviving of the earliest settlers; however, a negro, still a resident of Little Rock, also came in 1818.

The first English speaking settlers were Tennesseeans, Kentuckians and Alabamians. The earliest came down the Mississippi River, and then penetrating Arkansas at the mouths of the streams from the west, ascended these in the search for future homes. The date of the first coming of English speaking colonists may be given as 1807, those prior to that time being only trappers, hunters and voyagers on expeditions of discovery, or those whose names can not now be ascertained.

South Carolina and Georgia also gave their small quotas to the first pioneers of Arkansas. From the States south of Tennessee the route was overland to the Mississippi River, or to some of its bayous, and then by water. A few of these from the Southern States brought considerable property, and some of them negro slaves, but not many were able to do this. The general rule was to reach the Territory alone and clear a small piece of ground, and as soon as possible to buy slaves and set them at work in the cotton fields.

In 1814 a colony of emigrants, consisting of four families, settled at Batesville, then the Lower Missouri Territory, now the county seat of Independence County. There was an addition of fifteen families to this colony the next year. Of the first was the family of Samuel Miller, father of (afterward) Gov. William R. Miller; there were also John Moore, the Magnesses and Beans. All these families left names permanently connected with the history of Arkansas. In the colony of 1815 (all from Kentucky) were the brothers, Richard, John, Thomas and James Peel, sons of Thomas Peel, a Virginian, and Kentucky companion of Daniel Boone. Thomas Curran was also one of the later colonists from Kentucky, a relative of the great Irishman, John Philpot Curran. In the 1815 colony were also old Ben Hardin—hero of so many Indian wars—his brother, Joab, and William Griffin, Thomas Wyatt, William Martin, Samuel Elvin, James Akin, John Reed, James Miller and John B. Craig.

Alden Trimble, who died at Peel, Ark., in April, 1889, aged seventy-four years, was born in the Cal Hogan settlement, on White River, Marion County, June 14, 1815. This item is gained from the obituary notice of his death, and indicates some of the very first settlers in that portion of the State.

Among the oldest settled points, after Arkansas Post, was what is now Arkadelphia, Clark County. It was first called Blakelytown, after Adam Blakely. He had opened a little store at the place, and about this were collected the first settlers, among whom may now be named Zack Davis, Samuel Parker and Adam Highnight. The Blakelys and the names given above were all located in that settlement in the year 1810. The next year came John Hemphill, who was the first to discover and utilize the valuable waters of the salt springs of that place. He engaged in the successful manufacture of salt, and was in time succeeded by his son-in-law, Jonathan O. Callaway. Jacob Barkman settled in Arkadelphia in 1811. He was a man of foresight and enterprise, and soon established a trade along the river to New Orleans. He commenced navigating the river in canoes and pirogues, and finally owned and ran in the trade the first steamboat plying from that point to New Orleans. He pushed trade at the point of settlement, at the same time advancing navigation, and opened a large cotton farm.

In Arkansas County, among the early prominent men who were active in the county's affairs were Eli I. Lewis, Henry Scull, O. H. Thomas, T. Farrelly, Hewes Scull, A. B. K. Thetford and Lewis Bogy. The latter afterward removed to Missouri, and has permanently associated his name with the history of that State. In a subsequent list of names should be mentioned those of William Fultony, James Maxwell and James H. Lucas, the latter being another of the notable citizens of Missouri.

Carroll County: Judges George Campbell and William King, and John Bush, T. H. Clark, Abraham Shelly, William Nooner, Judge Hiram Davis, W. C. Mitchell, Charles Sneed, A. M. Wilson, Elijah Tabor, William Beller, M. L. Hawkins, John McMillan, M. Perryman, J. A. Hicks, N. Rudd, Thomas Callen, W. E. Armstrong.

Chicot County: John Clark, William B. Patton, Richard Latting, George W. Ferribee, Francis Rycroft, Thomas Knox, W. B. Duncan, J. W. Boone, H. S. Smith, James Blaine, Abner Johnson, William Hunt, J. W. Neal, James Murray, B. Magruder, W. P. Reyburn, J. T. White, John Fulton, Judge W. H. Sutton, J. Chapman, Hiram Morrell, Reuben Smith, A. W. Webb.

In Clark County, in the earliest times, were W. P. L. Blair, Colbert Baker, Moses Graham, Mathew Logan, James Miles, Thomas Drew, Daniel Ringo, A. Stroud, David Fisk and Isaac Ward.

Clay County: John J. Griffin, Abraham Roberts, William Davis, William H. Mack, James Watson, J. G. Dudley, James Campbell, Singleton Copeland, C. H. Mobley.

Conway County: Judge Saffold, David Barber, James Kellam, Reuben Blunt, James Barber, James Ward, Thomas Mathers, John Houston, E. W. Owen, Judge B. B. Ball, J. I. Simmons, T. S. Haynes, B. F. Howard, William Ellis, N. H. Buckley, James Ward, Judge Robert McCall, W. H. Robertson, L. C. Griffin, Judge W. T. Gamble, D. D. Mason, George Fletcher and D. Harrison.

Craighead County: Rufus Snoddy, Daniel O'Guinn, Yancey Broadway, Henry Powell, D. R. Tyler, Elias Mackey, William Q. Lane, John Hamilton, Asa Puckett, Eli Quarles, William Puryear.

In Crawford County were Henry Bradford, Jack Mills, G. C. Pickett, Mark Beane, J. C. Sumner, James Billingsley.

Crittenden County: J. Livingston, W. D. Ferguson, W. Goshen, William Cherry, Judge D. H. Harrig, O. W. Wallace, S. A. Cherry, Judge Charles Blackmore, S. R. Cherry, John Tory, F. B. Read, Judge A. B. Hubbins, H. O. Oders, J. H. Wathen, H. Bacon.

Fulton County: G. W. Archer, William Wells, Daniel Hubble, Moses Brannon, John Nichols, Moses Steward, Enos C. Hunter, Milton Yarberry, Dr. A. C. Cantrell.

Greene County: Judge L. Brookfield, L. Thompson, James Brown, J. Sutfin, G. Hall, Charles Robertson, Judge W. Hane, Judge George Daniel, G. L. Martin, J. Stotts, James Ratchford, Judge L. Thompson, H. L. Holt, J. L. Atkinson, J. Clark, H. N. Reynolds, John Anderson, Benjamin Crowley, William Pevehouse, John Mitchell, Aaron Bagwell, A. J. Smith, Wiley Clarkson, William Hatch.

In Hempstead County: J. M. Steward, A. S. Walker, Benjamin Clark, A. M. Oakley, Thomas Dooley, D. T. Witter, Edward Cross, William McDonald, D. Wilburn and James Moss.

Hot Springs County: L. N. West, G. B. Hughes, Judge W. Durham, G. W. Rogers, T. W. Johnson, J. T. Grant, J. H. Robinson, H. A. Whittington, John Callaway, J. T. Grant, Judge G. Whittington, L. Runyan, R. Huson, J. Bankson, Ira Robinson, Judge A. N. Sabin, C. A. Sabin, W. W. McDaniel, W. Dunham, A. B. McDonald, Joseph Lorance.

Independence County: R. Searcy, Robert Bean, Charles Kelly, John Reed, T. Curran, John Bean, I. Curran, J. L. Daniels, J. Redmon, John Ruddell, C. H. Pelham, Samuel Miller, James Micham, James Trimble, Henry Engles, Hartwell Boswell, John H. Ringgold.

Izard County: J. P. Houston, John Adams, Judge Mathew Adams, H. C. Roberts, Jesse Adams, John Hargrove, J. Blyeth, William Clement, Judge J. Jeffrey, Daniel Jeffrey, A. Adams, J. A. Harris, W. B. Carr, Judge B. Hawkins, B. H. Johnson, D. K. Loyd, W. H. Carr, A. Creswell, H. W. Bandy, Moses Bishop, Daniel Hively, John Gray, William Powell Thomas Richardson, William Seymour.

Jackson County: Judge Hiram Glass, J. C. Saylors, Isaac Gray, N. Copeland, Judge E. Bartley, John Robinson, A. M. Carpenter, Judge D. C. Waters, P. O. Flynn, Hall Roddy, Judge R. Ridley, G. W. Cromwell, Sam Mathews, Sam Allen, Martin Bridgeman, John Wideman, Newton Arnold, Joseph Haggerton, Holloway Stokes.

Jefferson County: Judge W. P. Hackett, J. T. Pullen, Judge Creed Taylor, Peter German, N. Holland, Judge Sam C. Roane, William Kinkead, Thomas O'Neal, E. H. Roane, S. Dardenne, Sam Taylor, Judge H. Bradford, H. Edgington, Judge W. H. Lindsey, J. H. Caldwell.

Johnson County: Judge George Jameson, Thomas Jenette, S. F. Mason, Judge J. P. Kessie, A. Sinclair, William Fritz, W. J. Parks, R. S. McMicken, Augustus Ward, Judge J. L. Cravens, A. M. Ward, M. Rose, A. L. Black, W. A. Anderson, Judge J. B. Brown, A. Sinclair, William Adams, W. M. H. Newton.

Lafayette County: Judge Jacob Buzzard, Jesse Douglass, Joshua Morrison, I. W. Ward, J. T. Conway, W. E. Hodges, J. Morrison, George Dooley, J. M. Dorr, J. P. Jett, W. B. Conway, W. H. Conway, T. V. Jackson, G. H. Pickering, Judge E. M. Lowe, R. F. Sullivan, James Abrams.

Lawrence County: Joseph Hardin, Robert Blane, H. Sandford, John Reed, R. Richardson, J. M. Kuykendall, H. R. Hynson, James Campbell, D. W. Lowe, Thomas Black, John Rodney, John Spotts, William J. Hudson, William Stuart, Isaac Morris, William B. Marshall, John S. Ficklin.

Madison County: Judge John Bowen, H. B. Brown, P. M. Johnson, H. C. Daugherty, M. Perryman, T. McCuiston.

In Miller County: John Clark, J. Ewing, J. H. Fowler, B. English, C. Wright, G. F. Lawson, Thomas Polk, George Wetmore, David Clark, J. G. Pierson, John Morton, N. Y. Crittenden, Charles Burkem, George Collum, G. C. Wetmore, D. C. Steele, G. F. Lawton and Judge G. M. Martin.

Mississippi County: Judge Edwin Jones, J. W. Whitworth, E. F. Loyd, S. McLung, G. C. Barfield, Judge Nathan Ross, Judge John Troy, J. W. Dewitt, J. C. Bowen, Judge Fred Miller, Uriah Russell, T. L. Daniel, J. G. Davis, Judge Nathan Ross, J. P. Edrington, Thomas Sears, A. G. Blackmore, William Kellums, Thomas J. Mills, James Williams, Elijah Buford, Peter G. Reeves.

Monroe County: Judge William Ingram, J. C. Montgomery, James Eagan, John Maddox, Lafayette Jones, Judge James Carlton, M. Mitchell, J. R. Dye, J. Jacobs, R. S. Bell.

Phillips County: W. B. R. Horner, Daniel Mooney, S. Phillips, S. M. Rutherford, George Seaborn, H. L. Biscoe, G. W. Fereby, J. H. McKenzie, Austin Hendricks, W. H. Calvert, N. Righton, B. Burress, F. Hanks, J. H. McKeal, J. K. Sandford, S. S. Smith, C. P. Smith, J. H. McKenzie, S. C. Mooney, I. C. P. Tolleson, Emer Askew, P. Pinkston, Charles Pearcy, J. B. Ford, W. Bettiss, J. Skinner, H. Turner and M. Irvin.

Pike County: Judge W. Sorrels, D. S. Dickinson, John Hughes, J. W. Dickinson, Judge W. Kelly, Isaac White, J. H. Kirkhan, E. K. Williams, Henry Brewer.

Poinsett County: Judges Richard Hall and William Harris, Drs. Theophilus Griffin and John P. Hardis, Harrison Ainsworth, Robert H. Stone, Benjamin Harris.

Pope County: Judge Andrew Scott, Twitty

Pace, H. Stinnett, W. Garrott, W. Mitchell, Judge S. K. Blythe, A. E. Pace, J. J. Morse, F. Heron, Judge Thomas Murray, Jr., S. M. Hayes, S. S. Hayes, R. S. Witt, Judge Isaac Brown, R. T. Williamson, W. W. Rankin, Judge J. J. Morse, J. B. Logan, W. C. Webb.

Pulaski County: R. C. Oden, L. R. Curran, Jacob Peyatte, A. H. Renick, G. Greathouse, M. Cunningham, Samuel Anderson, H Armstrong, T. W. Newton, D. E. McKinney, S. M. Rutherford, A. McHenry, Allen Martin, J. H. Caldwell, Judge S. S. Hall, J. Henderson, William Atchison, R. N. Rowland, Judge David Rorer, J. K. Taylor, R. H. Callaway, A. L. Langham, Judge J. H. Cocke, W. Badgett, G. N. Peay, J. C. Anthony, L. R. Lincoln, A. Martin, A. S. Walker, Judge R. Graves, J. P. and John Fields, J. K. Taylor, W. C. Howell, J. Gould, Roswell Beebe, William Russell, John C. Peay.

Randolph County: Judge P. R. Pittman, B. J. Wiley, William Black, R. Bradford, J. M. Cooper, B. J. Wiley, B. M. Simpson, John Janes, James Campbell, Samuel McElroy, Edward Mattix, Thomas S. Drew, R. S. Bettis, James Russell.

St. Francis County: Andrew Roane, William Strong, S. Crouch, Judge John Johnson, T. J. Curl, G. B. Lincecum, William Lewis, Judge William Strong, Isaac Mitchell, David Davis, Isaac Forbes, Judge William Enos, N. O. Little, W. G. Bozeman, H. M. Carothers, Judge R. H. Hargrove, H. H. Curl, Cyrus Little.

Saline County: Judge T. S. Hutchinson, Samuel Caldwell, V. Brazil, C. Lindsey, A. Carrick, Judge H. Prudden, G. B. Hughes, Samuel Collins, J. J. Joiner, J. R. Conway, R. Brazil, E. M. Owen, George McDaniel, C. P. Lyle.

Scott County: Judge Elijah Baker, S. B. Walker, James Riley, J. R. Choate, Judge James Logan, G. Marshall, Charles Humphrey, W. Cauthorn, G. C. Walker, T. J. Garner, Judge Gilbert Marshall, W. Kenner.

Searcy County: Judge William Wood, William Kavanaugh, E. M. Hale, Judge Joseph Rea, William Ruttes, Joe Brown, V. Robertson, T. S. Hale, Judge J. Campbell.

Sevier County: Judge John Clark, R. Hartfield, G. Clark, J. T. Little, Judge David Foran, P. Little, William White, Charles Moore, A. Hartfield, Judge J. F. Little, Henry Morris, Judge Henry Brown, George Halbrook, Judge R. H. Scott, S. S. Smith.

Sharp County: John King, Robert Lott, Nicholas Norris, William Morgan, William J. Gray, William Williford, Solomon Hudspeth, Stephen English, John Walker, L. D. Dale, John C. Garner, R. P. Smithee, Josiah Richardson, Judge A. H. Nunn, William G. Matheny.

Union County: John T. Cabeen, John Black, Jr., Judge John Black, Sr., Benjamin Gooch, Alexander Beard, Thomas O'Neal, Judge G. B. Hughes, John Cornish, John Hogg, Judge Hiram Smith, J. R. Moore, John Henry, John Stokeley, Judge Charles H. Seay, W. L. Bradley, Judge Thomas Owens.

Van Buren County: Judge J. L. Laferty, P. O. Powell, N. Daugherty, Philip Wail, L. Williams, Judge J. B. Craig, Judge J. M. Baird, J. McAllister, Judge William Dougherty, A. Morrison, George Counts, A. Caruthers, W. W. Trimble, R. Bain, J. O. Young, George Hardin, A. W. McRaines, Judge J. C. Ganier.

Washington County: L. Newton, Lewis Evans, John Skelton, Judge Robert McAmy, B. H. Smithson, Judge John Wilson, James Marrs, V. Caruthers, James Coulter, J. T. Edmonson, Judge J. M. Hoge, James Crawford, John McClellan, Judge W. B. Woody, W. W. Hester, Judge John Cureton, L. C. Pleasants, Isaac Murphy, D. Callaghan, Judge Thomas Wilson, W. L. Wallace and L. W. Wallace.

White County: Judge Samuel Guthrie, P. W. Roberts, P. Crease, Michael Owens, M. H. Blue, S. Arnold, J. W. Bond, William Cook, J. Arnold, Milton Saunders, James Bird, Samuel Beeler, James Walker, Martin Jones, Philip Hilger, James King, L. Pate, John Akin, Reuben Stephens, Samuel Guthrie.

Woodruff County: Rolla Gray, Durant H. Bell, John Dennis, Dudley Glass, Michael Haggerdon, Samuel Taylor, James Barnes, George Hatch, John Teague, Thomas Arnold and Thomas Hough.

The above were all prominent men in their localities during the Territorial times of Arkansas. Many of them have left names and memories intimately associated with the history of the State. They were a part of those pioneers "who hewed the dark, old woods away," and left a rich inheritance, and a substantial civilization, having wealth, refinement and luxuries, that were never a part of their dreams. They were home makers as well as State and Nation builders. They cut out the roads, opened their farms, bridged the streams, built houses, made settlements, towns and cities, rendering all things possible to their descendants; a race of heroes and martyrs pre-eminent in all time for the blessings they transmitted to posterity; they repelled the painted savage, and exterminated the ferocious wild beasts; they worked, struggled and endured that others might enjoy the fruits of their heroic sacrifices. Their lives were void of evil to mankind; possessing little ambition, their touch was the bloom and never the blight. Granted, cynic, they builded wiser than they knew, yet they built, and built well, and their every success was the triumphant march of peace. Let the record of their humble but great lives be immortal!

The New Madrid earthquake of 1811-12, commencing in the last of December, and the subterranean forces ceasing after three months' duration, was of itself a noted era, but to the awful display of nature's forces was added a far more important and lasting event, the result of the silent but mighty powers of the human mind. Simultaneously with the hour of the most violent convulsions of nature, the third day of the earthquake, there rode out at the mouth of the Ohio, into the lashed and foaming waters of the Mississippi, the first steamboat that ever ploughed the western waters—the steamer "Orleans," Capt. Roosevelt. So awful was the display of nature's energies, that the granitic earth, with a mighty sound, heaved and writhed like a storm-tossed ocean. The great river turned back in its flow, the waves of the ground burst, shooting high in the air, spouting sand and water; great forest-covered hills disappeared at the bottom of deep lakes into which they had sunk; and the "sunk lands" are to this day marked on the maps of Southeast Missouri and Northeast Arkansas. The sparse population along the river (New Madrid was a flourishing young town) fled the country in terror, leaving mostly their effects and domestic animals.

The wild riot of nature met in this wilderness the triumph of man's genius. Where else on the globe so appropriately could have been this meeting of the opposing forces as at the mouth of the Ohio and on the convulsed bosom of the Father of Waters? How feeble, apparently, in this contest, were the powers of man; how grand and awful the play of nature's forces! The mote struggling against the "wreck of worlds and crush of matter." But, "peace be still," was spoken to the vexed earth, while the invention of Fulton will go on forever. The revolving paddle-wheels were the incipient drive-wheels, on which now ride in triumph the glories of this great age.

The movement of immigrants to Arkansas in the decade following the earthquake was retarded somewhat, whereas, barring this, it should and would have been stimulated into activity by the advent of steamboats upon the western rivers. The south half of the State was in the possession of the Quapaw Indians. The Spanish attempts at colonizing were practical failures. His Catholic majesty was moving in the old ruts of the feudal ages, in the deep-seated faith of the "divinity of kings," and the paternal powers and duties of rulers. The Bastrop settlement of "thirty families," by a seigniorial grant in 1797, had brought years of suffering, disappointment and failure. This was an attempt to found a colony on the Ouachita River, granting an entire river and a strip of land on each side thereof to Bastrop, the government to pay the passage of the people across the ocean and to feed and clothe them one year. To care for its vassals, and to provide human breeding grounds; swell the multitudes for the use of church and State; to "glorify God" by repressing the growing instincts of liberty and the freedom of thought, and add subjects to the possession and powers of these gilded toads, were the essence of the oriental schemes for peopling the new world. Happily for mankind they failed, and the wild beasts returned to care for their young in safety and await the coming of the real pioneers, they who came bringing little or nothing, save a manly spirit of self-reliance and independence. These were the successful founders and builders of empire in the wilderness.

CHAPTER IV.

Organization.—The Viceroys and Governors—The Attitude of the Royal Owners of Louisiana—The District Divided—The Territory of Arkansas Formed from the Territory of Missouri—The Territorial Government—The First Legislature—The Seat of Government—Other Legislative Bodies—The Deullo—Arkansas Admitted to Statehood—The Constitutional Conventions—The Memorable Reconstruction Period—Legislative Attitude on the Question of Secession—The War of the Governors, etc., etc.

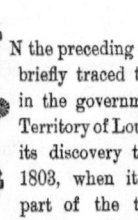

IN the preceding chapter are briefly traced the changes in the government of the Territory of Louisiana from its discovery to the year 1803, when it became a part of the territory of the United States. Discovered by the Spanish, possessed by the French, divided and re-divided between the French, Spanish and English; settled by the Holy Mother Church, in the warp and woof of nations it was the flying shuttle-cock of the great weaver in its religion as well as allegiance for 261 years. This foundling, this waif of nations, was but an outcast, or a trophy chained to the triumphal car of the victors among the warring European powers, until in the providence of God it reached its haven and abiding home in the bosom of the union of States.

As a French province, the civil government of Louisiana was organized, and the Marquis de Sanville appointed viceroy or governor in 1689.

UNDER FRENCH RULE.

Robert Cavelier de La Salle (April 9, formal)	1682–1688
Marquis de Sanville	1689–1700
Bienville	1701–1712
Lamothe Cadillac	1713–1715
De L'Epinay	1716–1717
Bienville	1718–1723
Boisbriant (ad interim)	1724
Bienville	1732–1741
Baron de Kelerec	1753–1762
D'Abbadie	1763–1766*

UNDER SPANISH RULE.

Antonio de Ulloa	1767–1768
Alexander O'Reilly	1768–1769
Louis de Unzaga	1770–1776
Bernando de Galvez	1777–1784
Estevar Miro	1785–1787
Francisco Luis Hortu, Baron of Carondelet	1789–1792
Gayoso de Lemos	1793–1798
Sebastian de Cosa Calvo y O'Farrell	1798–1799
Juan Manual de Salcedo	1800–1803

From the dates already given it will be seen that the official acts of Salcedo during his entire

* Louisiana west of the Mississippi, although ceded to Spain in 1762, remained under French jurisdiction until 1766.

term of office, under the secret treaty of Ildefonso, were tainted with irregularity. Thousands of land grants had been given by him after he had in fact ceased to be the viceroy of Spain. The contracting powers had affixed to the treaty the usual obligations of the fulfillment of all undertakings, but the American courts and lawyers, in that ancient spirit of legal hypercritical technicalities, had given heed to the vicious doctrine that acts in good faith of a *de facto* governor may be treated as of questionable validity. This was never good law, because it was never good sense or justice.

The acts and official doings of these vice-royalties in the wilderness present little or nothing of interest to the student of history, because they were local and individual in their bearing. It was the action of the powers across the waters, in reference to Canada and Louisiana, that in their wide and sweeping effects have been nearly omnipotent in shaping civilization.

Referring to the acquisition of Canada and the Louisiana east of the Mississippi River, Bancroft says that England exulted in its conquest;* enjoying the glory of extended dominion in the confident expectation of a boundless increase of wealth. But its success was due to its having taken the lead in the good old struggle for liberty, and it was destined to bring fruits, not so much to itself as to the cause of freedom and mankind.

France, of all the States on the continent of Europe the most powerful, by territorial unity, wealth, numbers, industry and culture, seemed also by its place marked out for maritime ascendency. Set between many seas it rested upon the Mediterranean, possessed harbors on the German Ocean, and embraced between its wide shores and jutting headlands the bays and open waters of the Atlantic; its people, infolding at one extreme the offspring of colonists from Greece, and at the other the hardy children of the Northmen, being called, as it were, to the inheritance of life upon the sea. The nation, too, readily conceived or appropriated great ideas and delighted in bold resolves. Its travelers had penetrated farthest into the fearful interior of unknown lands; its missionaries won most familiarly the confidence of the aboriginal hordes; its writers described with keener and wiser observation the forms of nature in her wildness, and the habits and languages of savage man; its soldiers, and every lay Frenchman in America owed military service, uniting beyond all others celerity with courage, knew best how to endure the hardships of forest life and to triumph in forest warfare. Its ocean chivalry had given a name and a colony to Carolina, and its merchants a people to Acadia. The French discovered the basin of the St. Lawrence; were the first to explore and possess the banks of the Mississippi, and planned an American empire that should unite the widest valleys and most copious inland waters in the world. But over all this splendid empire in the old and the new world was a government that was medieval—mured in its glittering palaces, taxing its subjects, it would allow nothing to come to the Louisiana Territory but what was old and worn out. French America was closed against even a gleam of intellectual independence; nor did all Louisiana contain so much as one dissenter from the Roman Church.

"We have caught them at last," exultingly exclaimed Choiseul, when he gave up the Canadas to England and the Louisiana to Spain. "England will ere long repent of having removed the only check that could keep her colonies in awe. * * * She will call on them to support the burdens they have helped to bring on her, and they will answer by striking off all dependence," said Vergennes.

These keen-witted Frenchmen, with a penetration far beyond the ablest statesmen of England, saw, as they believed, and time has confirmed, that in the humiliation and dismemberment of the territory of France, especially the transfer to England of Canada, they had laid the mine which some day would destroy the British colonial system, and probably eventuate in the independence of the American colonies. The intellect of France was keeping step with the spirit of the age; it had been excluded of course from the nation's councils, but saw what its feeble

---

*Bancroft, vol. iv.-457; Gayarre's Histoire de la Louisiane, vol. ii.-121.

government neither could see nor prevent, that the distant wilderness possessed a far greater importance on the world's new map than was given it by the gold and gems it was supposed to contain; and that the change of allegiance of the colonies was the great step in the human mind, as it was slowly emerging from the gloom and darkness of the middle ages. Thus it was that the mere Territory of Louisiana, before it was peopled by civilized man, was playing its important part in the world's greatest of all dramas.

The first official act of our government, after the purchase of Louisiana, was an act of Congress, March 26, 1804, dividing Louisiana into two districts, and attaching the whole to Indiana Territory, under the government of William Henry Harrison. The division in Louisiana was by a line on the thirty-third parallel; the south was named the District of Orleans; that north of it was named the District of Louisiana. This is now the south line of the State of Arkansas.

In 1805 the District of Louisiana was erected into the Territory of Louisiana. It was however a territory of the second class and remained under the government and control of Indiana Territory until 1812.

By act of June 4, 1812, the name of Louisiana Territory was changed and became the Missouri Territory, being made a territory of the first class, and given a territorial government. Capt. William Clark, of the famous Lewis and Clark, explorers of the northwest, was appointed governor, remaining as such until 1819, when Arkansas Territory was cut off from Missouri.

The act of 1812, changing the District of Louisiana to Missouri Territory, provided for a Territorial legislature consisting of nine members, and empowered the governor to lay off that part where the Indian title had been extinguished into thirteen counties. The county of New Madrid, as then formed, extended into the Arkansas territorial limits, "down to the Mississippi to a point directly east of the mouth of Little Red River; thence to the mouth of Red River; thence up the Red River to the Osage purchase," etc. In other words it did not embrace the whole of what is now Arkansas.

December 13, 1813, the County of Arkansas, Missouri Territory, was formed, and the county seat was fixed at Arkansas Post.*

Besides Arkansas County, Lawrence County was formed January 15, 1815, and Clark, Hempstead and Pulaski Counties, December 15, 1818.

Missouri neglected it seems to provide a judicial district for her five southern or Arkansas counties. Therefore Congress, in 1814, authorized the President to appoint an additional judge for Missouri Territory, "who should hold office four years and reside in or near the village of Arkansas,"—across the river from Arkansas Post.

March 2, 1819, Congress created the Territory of Arkansas out of the Missouri Territory. It was only a territory of the second class, and the machinery of government consisted of the governor and three judges, who constituted the executive, judicial and legislative departments, their official acts requiring the consent of Congress. President Monroe appointed James Miller, governor; Robert Crittenden, secretary; Charles Jouett, Andrew Scott and Robert P. Letcher, judges of the superior court. The act designated Arkansas Post as the temporary seat of government. In the absence of the Governor, Robert Crittenden, "acting governor," convened the first session of the provisional government on August 3, 1819. The act continued the new territory under the laws of Missouri Territory. The five counties designated above as formed prior to the division of Arkansas, had been represented in the Missouri Territorial legislature. Elijah Kelly, of Clark County, was a representative, and he rode on horseback from his home to St. Louis. The session was probably not a week in length, and the pay and mileage little or nothing.

This first Territorial legislature appointed a treasurer and auditor, provided a tax for general purposes, and divided the five counties into two judicial circuits: First, Arkansas and Lawrence Counties; Second, Pulaski, Clark and Hempstead Counties.

---

*During the latter part of the eighteenth century, something of the same municipal division was made, and called "Arkansas Parish," the name being derived from an old Indian town called Arkansea.

HISTORY OF ARKANSAS.

April 21, 1820, Congress passed an act perfecting the Territorial organization, and applying the same provisions to Arkansas that were contained in the act creating Missouri into a Territory of the first class.

The first legislative body elected in Arkansas convened at Arkansas Post, February 7 to 24, 1820. In the council were: President, Edward McDonald; secretary, Richard Searcy; members, Arkansas County, Sylvanus Phillips; Clark County, Jacob Barkman; Hempstead County, David Clark; Lawrence County, Edward McDonald; Pulaski County, John McElmurry. In the house of representatives: Speaker, Joseph Hardin (William Stephenson was first elected, served one day and resigned, on account of indisposition); J. Chamberlain, clerk; members, Arkansas County, W. B. R. Horner, W. O. Allen; Clark, Thomas Fish; Hempstead, J. English, W. Stevenson; Lawrence, Joseph Hardin, Joab Hardin; Pulaski, Radford Ellis, T. H. Tindall. This body later adjourned to meet October following, continuing in session until the 25th.

At this adjourned session the question of the removal of the Territorial seat of government from Arkansas Post to "the Little Rock," came up on a memorial signed by Amos Wheeler and others. "The Little Rock" was in contradistinction to "the Rocks," as were known the beautiful bluffs, over 200 feet high, a little above and across the river from "the Little Rock." In 1820 Gov. Miller visited the Little Rock—Petit Rocher—with a view to selecting a new seat of government. The point designated was the northeast corner of the Quapaw west line and Arkansas River. Immediately upon the formation of the Territory, prominent parties began to look out for a more central location for a capital higher up the river, and it was soon a general understanding that the seat of government and the county seat of Pulaski County, the then adjoining county above Arkansas County on the river, would be located at the same place. A syndicate was formed and Little Rock Bluff was pushed for this double honor. The government had not yet opened the land to public entry, as the title of the Quapaws had just been extinguished. These parties resorted to the expedient of locating upon the land "New Madrid floats," or claims, under the act of February 17, 1815, which authorized any one whose land had been "materially injured" by the earthquake of 1811 to locate the like quantity of land on any of the public lands open for sale. Several hundred acres were entered under these claims as the future town site. The county seat of Pulaski County was, contrary to the expectation of the Little Rock syndicate, located at Cadron, near the mouth of Cadron Creek, where it enters the Arkansas River.

On the 18th day of October, 1820, the Territorial seat of government was removed from the Post of Arkansas to the Little Rock, the act to take effect June 1, 1821. The next Territorial legislature convened in Little Rock, October 1 to 24, 1821. The council consisted of Sam C. Roane, president, and Richard Searcy, secretary. In the house William Trimble was speaker, and A. H. Sevier, clerk.

The third legislature met October 6 to 31, 1823. Sam C. Roane was president of the council, and Thomas W. Newton, secretary; while T. Farrelly was speaker, and D. E. McKinney, clerk of the house.

The fourth legislature was held October 3 to November 3, 1825. Of the council, the president was Jacob Barkman; secretary, Thomas W. Newton. Of the house, Robert Bean was speaker; David Barber, clerk.

The fifth Territorial legislature was held October 1 to 31, 1827, and a special session held October 6 to October 28, 1828; E. T. Clark served as president of the council, and John Clark, secretary; J. Wilson was speaker of the house, and Daniel Ringo, clerk.

In the sixth legislature, Charles Caldwell was president of the council, and John Caldwell, secretary; John Wilson was speaker of the house, and Daniel Ringo, clerk.

The seventh legislature held October 3 to November 7, 1831, had Charles Caldwell as president of the council, and Absalom Fowler, secretary; William Trimble was speaker of the house, and G. W. Ferebee, secretary.

In the eighth legislature, October 7 to November 16, 1833, John Williamson was president of the council and William F. Yeomans, secretary; John Wilson was speaker of the house, and James B. Keatts, clerk.

The ninth legislature met October 5 to November 16, 1835. The president of the senate was Charles Caldwell; secretary, S. T. Sanders. John Wilson was speaker of the house and L. B. Tully, clerk.

This was the last of the Territorial assemblies. James Miller was succeeded as governor by George Izard, March 4, 1825, and Izard by John Pope, March 9, 1829. William Fulton followed Pope March 9, 1835, and held the office until Arkansas became a State.

Robert Crittenden was secretary of State (nearly all of Miller's term "acting governor"), appointed March 3, 1819, and was succeeded in office by William Fulton, April 8, 1829; Fulton was succeeded by Lewis Randolph, February 23, 1835.

George W. Scott was appointed Territorial auditor August 5, 1819, and was succeeded by Richard C. Byrd, November 20, 1829; Byrd was followed by Emzy Wilson, November 5, 1831; and the latter by William Pelham, November 12, 1833, his successor being Elias N. Conway, July 25, 1835.

James Scull, appointed treasurer August 5, 1819, was succeeded by S. M. Rutherford, November 12, 1833, who continued in office until the State was formed.

The counties in 1825 had been increased in number to thirteen: Arkansas, Clark, Conway, Chicot, Crawford, Crittenden, Lawrence, Miller, Hempstead, Independence, Pulaski, Izard and Phillips. The territory was divided into four judicial circuits, of which William Trimble, Benjamin Johnson, Thomas P. Eskridge and James Woodson Bates were, in the order named, the judges. The delegates in Congress from Arkansas Territory were James W. Bates, 1820-23; Henry W. Conway, 1823-29; Ambrose H. Sevier, 1829-36.

The Territorial legislature, in common with all other legislatures of that day, passed some laws which would have been much better not passed, and others that remained a dead letter on the books. Among other good laws which were never enforced was one against duelling. In 1825 Whigs and Democrats allowed party feelings to run high, and some bloody duels grew out of the heat of campaigns.

Robert Crittenden and Henry W. Conway fought a duel October 29, 1827. At the first fire Conway fell mortally wounded and died a fortnight thereafter.

December 4, 1837, John Wilson, who, it will be noticed, figured prominently in the preceding record of the Territorial assemblies, was expelled from the house of representatives, of which body he was speaker, for killing J. J. Anthony.

A constitutional convention, for the purpose of arranging for the Territory to become a State in the Union, was held in Little Rock, in January, 1836. Its duty was to prepare a suitable constitution and submit it to Congress, and, if unobjectionable, to have an act passed creating the State of Arkansas. John Wilson was president, and Charles P. Bertrand, secretary, of the convention. Thirty-five counties were represented by fifty-two members.

June 15, 1836, Arkansas was made a State, and the preamble of the act recites that there was a population of 47,700.

The first State legislature met September 12 to November 8, 1836, later adjourning to November 6, 1837, and continued in session until March 5, 1838. The president of the senate was Sam C. Roane; secretary, A. J. Greer; the speaker of the house was John Wilson (he was expelled and Grandison D. Royston elected); clerk, S. H. Hempstead.

The second constitutional convention, held January 4 to January 23, 1864, had as president, John McCoy, and secretary, R. J. T. White. This convention was called by virtue of President Lincoln's proclamation. The polls had been opened chiefly at the Federal military posts, and the majority of delegates were really refugees from many of the counties they represented. It simply was an informal meeting of the Union men in response to the President's wish, and they mostly made their own credentials. The Federal army occupied the

Arkansas River and points north, while the south portion of the State was held by the Confederates. It is said the convention on important legal questions was largely influenced by Hon. T. D. W. Yonly, of Pulaski County. The convention practically re-enacted the constitution of 1836, abolished slavery, already a fact, and created the separate office of lieutenant-governor, instead of the former *ex-officio* president of the senate. The machinery of State government was thus once more in operation. The convention wisely did its work and adjourned.

The next constitutional convention was held January 7 to February 18, 1868. Thomas M. Bowen was president, and John G. Price, secretary. The war was over and the Confederates had returned and were disposed to favor the constitution which they found the Unionists had adopted in their absence, and was then in full force in the State. Isaac Murphy (Federal) had been elected governor under the constitution of 1864, and all the State offices were under control of the Unionists. His term as governor would expire in July, 1868.

This convention made sweeping changes in the fundamental laws. The most prominent were the disfranchisement of a large majority of the white voters of the State, enfranchising the negroes, and providing for a complex and plastic system of registration. This movement, and its severe character throughout, were a part of the reconstruction measures emanating from Congress. Arkansas was under military rule and the constitution of 1864, and this condition of affairs, had been accepted by the returned conquered Confederates. But the Unionists, who had fled to the Federal military posts for protection, were generally eager to visit their vanquished enemies with the severest penalties of the law. A large part of the intelligence and tax-payers of the State were indiscriminately excluded from the polls, and new voters and new men came to the front, with grievances to be avenged and ambitions to be gratified. The unusual experiment of the reversal of the civic conditions of the ex-slaves with their former masters was boldly undertaken. Impetuous men now prevailed in the name of patriotism, the natural reflex swing of the pendulum—the anti-climax was this convention of reconstruction to the convention of secession of 1861. The connection between these two conventions—1861-1868—is so blended that the convention of '61 is omitted in its chronological order, that the two may be set properly side by side.

March 4, 1861, a State convention assembled in Little Rock. The election of delegates was on February 18, preceding. The convention met the day Abraham Lincoln was inducted into office as president of the United States. The people of Arkansas were deeply concerned. The conservative minds of the State loved the Union as sincerely as they regretted the wanton assaults that had been made upon them by the extremists of the North. The members of that convention had been elected with a view to the consideration of those matters already visible in the dark war-clouds lowering upon the country. The test of the union and disunion sentiment of that body was the election of president of the convention. Judge David Walker (Union) received forty votes against thirty-five votes for Judge B. C. Totten. Hon. Henry F. Thomasson introduced a series of conservative resolutions, condemning disunion and looking to a convention of all the States to "settle the slavery question" and secure the perpetuation of the Union. The resolutions were passed, and the convention adjourned to meet again in May following. This filled the wise and conservative men of the State with great hopes for the future. But, most unfortunately, when the convention again met war was already upon the country, and the ordinance of secession was passed, with but one negative vote. The few days between the adjournment and re-assembling of the convention had not made traitors of this majority that had so recently condemned disunion. The swift-moving events, everywhere producing consternation and alarm, called out determined men, and excitement ruled the hour.

The conventions of 1861 and 1868—secession and reconstruction! When the long-gathering cloud-burst of civil war had passed, it left a century's trail of broken hearts, desolated homes, ruined lives, and a stream of demoralization overflowing the beautiful valleys of the land to the mountain tops. The innocent and unfortunate negro was the stumbling-block at all times. The convention of 1861 would have founded an empire of freedom, buttressed in the slavery of the black man; the convention of 1868 preferred to rear its great column of liberty upon the ashes of the unfortunate past; in every era the wise, conservative and patriotic sentiment of the land was chained and bound to the chariot-wheels of rejoicing emotion. Prudence and an intelligent insight into the future alone could prevent men from "losing their reason."

The constitution of 1868, as a whole, was not devoid of merit. It opened the way for an age of internal improvements, and intended the establishment of a liberal public free school system, and at the same time provided safeguards to protect the public treasury and restrain reckless extravagance.

Then the legislatures elected under it, the State officers, and the representatives in the upper and lower Congress, were in political accord with the dominant party of the country. Gen. Grant was president; Powell Clayton, governor; Robert J. L. White, secretary of State; J. R. Berry, auditor, and Henry Page, treasurer. The first legislature under the constitution of 1868 passed most liberal laws to aid railroads and other internal improvements, and provided a system of revenue laws to meet the new order of affairs. During 1869 to 1871 railroad aid and levee bonds to the amount of $10,419,773.74 were issued. The supreme court of the State in after years declared the railroad aid, levee and Halford bonds void, aggregating $8,604,773.74. Before his term of governor had expired, Gov. Clayton was elected United States senator (1871–77), and in 1873 Hon. Stephen W. Dorsey was elected to a like position.

The climax and the end of reconstruction in Arkansas will always be an interesting paragraph in the State's history. Elisha Baxter and Joseph Brooks were the gubernatorial candidates at the election of 1872. Both were Republicans, and Brooks was considered one of the most ardent of that party. Baxter was the nominee of the party and on the same ticket with Grant, who was candidate for president. Brooks was nominated on a mixed ticket, made up by disaffected Republicans, but on a more liberal platform toward the Democrats than the regular ticket. On the face of the first returns the Greeley electors and the Brooks ticket were in the majority, but when the votes were finally canvassed, such changes were made, from illegal voting or bulldozing it was claimed, as to elect the Grant and Baxter tickets. Under the constitution of 1868, the legislature was declared the sole judge of the election of State officers. Brooks took his case before that body at its January term, 1873—at which time Baxter was inaugurated—but the assembly decided that Baxter was elected, and, whether right or wrong, every one supposed the question permanently settled.

Brooks however, went before the supreme court (McClure being chief justice), that body promptly deciding that the legislature was by law the proper tribunal, and that as it had determined the case its action was final and binding. Baxter was inaugurated in January, 1873; had been declared elected by the proper authorities, and this had been confirmed by the legislature, the action of the latter being distinctly approved by the supreme court. The adherents of Brooks had supposed that they were greatly wronged, but like good citizens all acquiesced. Those who had politically despised Brooks—perhaps the majority of his voters—had learned to sympathize with what they believed were his and their mutual wrongs. Baxter had peacefully administered the office more than a year, when Brooks went before Judge John Whytock, of the Pulaski circuit court, and commenced *quo warranto* proceedings against Baxter. The governor's attorneys filed a demurrer, and the case stood over. Wednesday, April 15, 1874, Judge Whytock, in the absence of Baxter's attorneys, overruled the demurrer, giving judgment of ouster against Baxter, and instantly Brooks, with an officer, hastened to the State house, demanded the surrender of the office, and arrested Baxter. Thus a stroke of the pen by a mere circuit court judge *in banc* plunged the State into tumult.

Couriers sped over the city, and the flying news gave the people a genuine sensation. Indeed, not only Baxter but the State and the nation received a great surprise.

As soon as Baxter was released, though only under arrest a few minutes, he fled to St. John's College, in the city, and from this headquarters called for soldiers, as did Brooks from the State house, and alas, poor Arkansas! there were now again two doughty governors beating the long roll and swiftly forming in the ranks of war. Brooks converted the State house and grounds into a garrison, while Baxter made headquarters at the old Anthony Hotel, and the dead-line between the armed foes was Main Street. Just in time to prevent mutual annihilation, though not in time to prevent bloodshed, some United States soldiers arrived and took up a position of armed neutrality between the foes.

If there can be anything comical in a tragedy it is furnished just here in the fact that, in the twinkling of an eye, the adherents and voters of the two governors had changed places, and each was now fighting for the man whom he had opposed so vehemently. And in all these swift changes the supreme court had shown the greatest agility. By some remarkable legerdemain, Brooks, who was intrenching himself, had had his case again placed before the supreme court, and it promptly reversed itself and decided that the circuit court had jurisdiction. The wires to Washington were kept hot with messages to President Grant and Congress. The whole State was in dire commotion with "mustering squadrons and clattering cars." The frequent popping of picket guns was in the land; a steamboat, laden with arms for Baxter, was attacked and several killed and many wounded. Business was again utterly prostrated and horrors brooded over the unfortunate State; and probably the most appalling feature of it all was that in the division in the ranks of the people the blacks, led by whites, were mostly on one side, while the whites were arrayed on the other. Congress sent the historical Poland Committee to investigate Arkansas affairs. President Grant submitted all legal questions to his attorney-general.

The President, at the end of thirty days after the forcible possession of the office, sustained Baxter—exit Brooks. The end of the war, the climax of reconstruction in Arkansas, had come. Peace entered as swiftly as had war a few days before. The sincerity and intensity of the people's happiness in this final ending are found in the fact that when law and order were restored no one was impeached, no one was imprisoned for treason.

The report of the Poland Committee, 1874, the written opinion of Attorney-General Williams, the decision of the Arkansas supreme court by Judge Samuel W. Williams, found in Vol. XXIX of Arkansas Reports, page 173, and the retiring message of Governor Baxter, are the principal records of the literature and history of the reign of the dual governors. The students of law and history in coming time will turn inquiring eyes with curious interest upon these official pages. The memory of "the thirty days" in Arkansas will live forever, propagating its lessons and bearing its warnings; the wise moderation and the spirit of forbearance of the people, in even their exulting hour of triumph, will be as beacon lights shining out upon the troubled waters, transmitting for all time the transcendent fact that in the hour of supreme trial the best intelligence of the people is wiser than their rulers, better law-givers than their statesmen, and incomparably superior to their courts.

The moment that President Grant officially spoke, the reconstruction constitution of 1868 was doomed. True, the people had moved almost in mass and without leadership in 1873, and had repealed Article VIII of the constitution, disfranchising a large part of the intelligent tax-payers of the State.

The constitutional convention of 1874, with the above facts fresh before it, met and promulgated the present State constitution. G. D. Royston was president, and T. W. Newton, secretary. The session lasted from July 14 to October 31, 1874. From the hour of its adoption the clouds rolled away, and at once commenced the present unexampled prosperity of the State. Only here and there in Little Rock and other points in the State

HISTORY OF ARKANSAS.

may one see the mute but eloquent mementos of the past, in the dilapidated buildings, confiscated during the lifetime of some former owner, mayhap, some once eminent citizen, now in his grave or self-expatriated from a State which his life and genius had adorned and helped make great. Municipalities and even small remote districts are paying off the last of heavy debts of the "flush times." Long suffering and much chastened State and people, forgetting the past, and full of hope for the future, are fitly bedecking (though among the youngest) the queenliest in the sisterhood of States.

In this connection it will be of much interest to notice the names of those individuals, who, by reason of their association with various public affairs, have become well and favorably known throughout the State. The term of service of each incumbent of the respective offices has been preserved and is here given. The following table includes the acting Territorial and State governors of Arkansas, with date of inauguration, party politics, etc:

Territory and State.	Year of Election.	Date of Inauguration.	Length of Term.	By What Political Party Elected.	His Majority or Plurality.	Total Vote Cast at Election.
James Miller...	App't'd	March 3, 1819				
George Izard...	App't'd	March 4, 1825				
John Pope......	App't'd	March 9, 1829				
Wm. Fulton...	App't'd	March 9, 1835				
J. S. Conway..	1836	September 13, 1836	4 yrs.	Dem.	1,102M	7,716
Archibald Tell.	1840	November 4, 1840	4 yrs.	Dem.		
Samuel Adams.	Acting	Apr. 29 to Nov. 9, 1844				
T. S. Drew.....	1844	November 5, 1844	5 yrs.	Dem.	1,731 P	17,387
J. Williamson..	Acting	Apr. 9 to May 7, 1846				
R. C. Byrd.....	Acting	Jan. 11 to Apr. 19, 1849				
J. S. Roane.....	1849	April 19, 1849*		Dem.	163	6,809
R. C. Byrd......	Acting		1849			
J. R. Hampton	Acting		1851			
E. N. Conway..	1852	November 15, 1852	4 yrs.	Dem.	8,027	27,857
E. N. Conway..	1854	November 17, 1856	4 yrs.	Dem.	12,363	42,861
H. M. Rector...	1860	November 15, 1860	2 yrs.	I. D.	2,461	61,198
T. Fletcher.....	Acting	Nov. 4 to Nov. 15, 1862		Con.	(no record)	
H. Flannagin ..	1862	November 15, 1862	3 yrs.	Con.	10,012	26,266
I. Murphy.......	1864	April 18, 1864		Fed.	(no record)	
P. Clayton.....	1868	July 2, 1868	4 yrs.	Rep.	(no record)	
O. A. Hadley ..	Acting	January 17, 1871	2 yrs.	Rep.	(no record)	
E. Baxter.......	1872	January 6, 1873	2 yrs.	Rep.	2,948	80,721
A. H. Garland..	1874	November 12, 1874	2 yrs.	Dem.	76,453	
W. R. Miller....	1876	January 11, 1877	2 yrs.	Dem.	32,215	108,633
W. R. Miller....	1878	January 17, 1879	2 yrs.	Dem.	88,730	
T. J. Churchill	1880	January 13, 1881	2 yrs.	Dem.	52,761	115,619
J. H. Berry.....	1882	January 13, 1883	2 yrs.	Dem.	28,481	147,169
B. T. Embry...	Acting	Sep. 25 to Sep. 30, 1883				
S. P. Hughes...	1884	January 17, 1885	2 yrs.		45,236	156,310
J. W. Stayton..	Acting					
S. P. Hughes...	1886		2 yrs.	Dem.	17,411	163,889
D. E. Barker...	Acting					
J. P. Eagle.....	1888		2 yrs.	Dem.	15,006	187,397

*Special election.

The secretaries of Arkansas Territory have been: Robert Crittenden, appointed March 3, 1819; William Fulton, appointed April 8, 1829; Lewis Randolph, appointed February 23, 1835.

Secretaries of State: Robert A. Watkins, September 10, 1836, to November 12, 1840; D. B. Greer, November 12, 1840, to May 9, 1842; John Winfrey, acting, May 9, to August 9, 1842; D. B. Greer, August 19, 1840, to September 3, 1859 (died); Alexander Boileau, September 3, 1829, to January 21, 1860; S. M. Weaver, January 21, 1860, to March 20, 1860; John I. Stirman, March 24, 1860, to November 13, 1862; O. H. Oates, November 13, 1862, to April 18, 1864; Robert J. T. White, Provisional, from January 24, to January 6, 1873; J. M. Johnson, January 6, 1873, to November 12, 1874; B. B. Beavers, November 12, 1874, to January 17, 1879; Jacob Frolich, January 17, 1879, to January, 1885; E. B. Moore, January, 1885, to January, 1889; B. B. Chism (present incumbent).

Territorial auditors of Arkansas: George W. Scott, August 5, 1819, to November 20, 1829; Richard C. Byrd, November 20, 1829, to November 5, 1831; Emzy Wilson, November 5, 1831, to November 12, 1833; William Pelham, November 12, 1833, to July 25, 1835; Elias N. Conway, July 25, 1835, to October 1, 1836.

Auditors of State: Elias N. Conway, October 1, 1836, to May 17, 1841; A. Boileau, May 17, 1841, to July 5, 1841 (acting); Elias N. Conway, July 5, 1841, to January 3, 1849; C. C. Danley, January 3, 1849, to September 16, 1854 (resigned); W. R. Miller, September 16, 1854, to January 23, 1855; A. S. Huey, January 23, 1855, to January 23, 1857; W. R. Miller, January 23, 1857, to March 5, 1860; H. C. Lowe, March 5, 1860, to January 24, 1861 (acting); W. R. Miller, January 24, 1861, to April 18, 1864; J. R. Berry, April 18, 1864, to October 15, 1866; Stephen Wheeler, January 6, 1873, to November 12, 1874; W. R. Miller, October 15, 1866, to July 2, 1868; John Crawford, January 11, 1877, to January 17, 1883; A. W. Files, January, 1883, to January, 1887; William R. Miller (died in office), January, 1887, to November, 1887; W. S. Dunlop, appointed November 30, 1887, to

January, 1889; W. S. Dunlop, January, 1889 (present incumbent).

Territorial treasurers: James Scull, August 15, 1819, to November 12, 1833; S. M. Rutherford, November 12, 1833, to October 1, 1836.

State treasurers: W. E. Woodruff, October 1, 1836, to November 20, 1838; John Hutt, November 20, 1838, to February 2, 1843; John C. Martin, February 2, 1843, to January 4, 1845; Samuel Adams, January 4, 1845, to January 2, 1849; William Adams, January 2, 1849, to January 10, 1849; John H. Crease, January 10, 1849, to January 26, 1855; A. H. Rutherford, January 27, 1855, to February 2, 1857; J. H. Crease, February 2, 1857, to February 2, 1859; John Quindley, February 2, 1859, to December 13, 1860 (died); Jared C. Martin, December 13, 1860, to February 2, 1861; Oliver Basham, February 2, 1861, to April 18, 1864; E. D. Ayers, April 18, 1864, to October 15, 1866; L. B. Cunningham, October 15, 1866, to August 19, 1867 (removed by military); Henry Page, August 19, 1867 (military appointment), elected 1868 to 1874 (resigned); R. C. Newton, May 23, 1874, to November 12, 1874; T. J. Churchill, November 12, 1874, to January 12, 1881; W. E. Woodruff, Jr., January 12, 1881, to January, 1891.

Attorneys-general: Robert W. Johnson, 1843; George C. Watkins, October 1, 1848; J. J. Crittenden, February 7, 1851; Thomas Johnson, September 8, 1856; J. L. Hollowell, September 8, 1858; P. Jordon, September 7, 1861; Sam W. Williams, 1862; C. T. Jordan, 1864; R. S. Gantt, January 31, 1865; R. H. Deadman, October 15, 1866; J. R. Montgomery, July 21, 1868; T. D. W. Yonley, January 8, 1873; J. L. Witherspoon, May 22, 1874; Simon P. Hughes, November 12, 1873, to 1876; W. F. Henderson, January 11, 1877, to 1881; C. B. Moore, January 12, 1881, to 1885; D. W. Jones, January, 1885, to 1889; W. E. Atkinson, January, 1889 (present incumbent).

Commissioners of immigration and of State lands: J. M. Lewis, July 2, 1868; W. H. Grey, October 15, 1872; J. N. Smithee, June 5, 1874.

These officers were succeeded by the commissioner of State lands, the first to occupy this position being J. N. Smithee, from November 12, 1874, to November 18, 1878; D. W. Lear, October 21, 1878, to November, 1882; W. P. Campbell, October 30, 1882, to March, 1884; P. M. Cobbs, March 31, 1884, to October 30, 1890.

Superintendents of public instruction: Thomas Smith, 1868 to 1873; J. C. Corbin, July 6, 1873; G. W. Hill, December 18, 1875, to October, 1878; J. L. Denton, October 13, 1875, to October 11, 1882; Dunbar H. Pope, October 11 to 30, 1882; W. E. Thompson, October 20, 1882, to 1890.

Of the present State officers and members of boards, the executive department is first worthy of attention. This is as follows:

Governor, J. P. Eagle; secretary of State, B. B. Chism; treasurer, William E. Woodruff, Jr.; attorney-general, W. E. Atkinson; commissioner of State lands, Paul M. Cobbs; superintendent public instruction, W. E. Thompson; State geologist, John C. Brauner.

Board of election canvassers: Gov. J. P. Eagle, Sec. B. B. Chism.

Board of commissioners of the common school fund: Gov. J. P. Eagle, Sec. B. B. Chism, Supt. W. E. Thompson.

State debt board: Gov. J. P. Eagle; Aud. W. S. Dunlop, and Sec. B. B. Chism.

Penitentiary board—commissioners: The Governor; the attorney-general, W. E. Atkinson, and the secretary of State.

Lessee of penitentiary: The Arkansas Industrial Company.

Printing board: The Governor, president; W. S. Dunlop, auditor, and W. E. Woodruff, Jr., treasurer.

Board of railroad commissioners (to assess and equalize the railroad property and valuation within the State): The Governor, secretary of State and State auditor.

Board of Trustees of Arkansas Medical College: J. A. Dibrell, M. D., William Thompson, M. D., William Lawrence, M. D.

The Arkansas State University, at Fayetteville, has as its board of trustees: W. M. Fishback, Fort Smith; James Mitchell, Little Rock; W. B. Welch, Fayetteville; C. M. Taylor, South Bend; B. F. Avery, Camden; J. W. Kessee, Latour; Gov.

Eagle, *ex-officio*; E. H. Murfree, president, A. I. U.; J. L. Cravens, secretary.

Of the Pine Bluff Normal, the president is J. Corbin, Pine Bluff; the board is the same as that of the State University.

Board of dental surgery: Dr. L. Augspath, Dr. H. C. Howard, Dr. M. C. Marshall, Dr. L. G. Roberts, and Dr. N. N. Hayes.

State board of health: Drs. A. L. Breysacher, J. A. Dibrell, P. Van Patten, Lorenzo R. Gibson, W. A. Cantrell, V. Brunson.

Board of municipal corporations: *Ex-officio*—The Governor, secretary of State and State auditor.

Board of education: The Governor, secretary of State and auditor.

Board of review for donation contests: The Governor, auditor of State and attorney-general.

Board of examiners of State script: The Governor, secretary of State and auditor.

Reference to the presidential vote of Arkansas, from the year 1836 up to and including the election of 1888, will serve to show in a general way the political complexion of the State during that period. The elections have resulted as follows:*

1836—Van Buren (D), 2,400; Harrison (W), 1,162; total 3,638.

1840—Harrison (W), 5,160; Van Buren (D), 6,049; Birney (A), 889; total 11,209.

1844—Polk (D), 8,546; Clay (W), 5,504; total 15,050.

1848—Taylor (W), 7,588; Cass (D), 9,300; total 16,888.

* Scattering votes not given.

1852—Pierce (D), 12,170; Scott, 7,404; total 19,577.

1856—Buchanan (D), 21,910; Fillmore, 10,787; total 32,697.

1860—Douglas (D), 5,227; Breckenridge, 28,532; Bell, 20,297.

1864—No vote.

1868—Grant (R), 22,112; Seymour, 19,078; total 41,190.

1872—Grant (R), 41,377; Greeley, 37,927; total 79,300.

1876—Tilden (D), 58,360; Hayes (R), 38,669; total 97,029.

1880—Garfield (R), 42,435; Hancock (D), 60,475; total, 107,290.

1884—Cleveland (D), 72,927; Blaine, 50,895; total, 125,669.

1888—Harrison (R), 58,752; Cleveland (D), 88,962; Fisk, 593; total, 155,968.

In accepting the vote of Arkansas, 1876, objection was made to counting it, as follows: "First, because the official returns of the election in said State, made according to the laws of said State, show that the persons certified to the secretary of said State as elected, were not elected as electors for President of the United States at the election held November 5, 1876; and, second, because the returns as read by the tellers are not certified according to law. The objection was sustained by the Senate but not sustained by the House of Representatives."

CHAPTER V.

ADVANCEMENT OF THE STATE—MISCONCEPTIONS REMOVED—EFFECTS OF SLAVERY UPON AGRICULTURE—EXTRAORDINARY IMPROVEMENT SINCE THE WAR—IMPORTANT SUGGESTIONS—COMPARATIVE ESTIMATE OF PRODUCTS—GROWTH OF THE MANUFACTURING INTERESTS—WONDERFUL SHOWING OF ARKANSAS—ITS DESIRABILITY AS A PLACE OF RESIDENCE—STATE ELEVATIONS.

> Look forward what's to come, and back what's past;
> Thy life will be with praise and prudence graced;
> What loss or gain may follow thou may'st guess,
> Then wilt thou be secure of the success.—*Denham.*

BEFORE entering directly upon the subject of the material life and growth of Arkansas, it is necessary to clear away at the threshold some of the obstructions that have lain in its pathway. From the earliest settlement slavery existed, and the nergo slave was brought with the first agricultural communities. Slave labor was profitable in but two things —cotton and sugar. Arkansas was north of the sugar cane belt, but was a splendid field for cotton growing. Slave labor and white labor upon the farms were never congenial associates. These things fixed rigidly the one road in the agricultural progress of the State. What was therefore the very richness of heaven's bounties, became an incubus upon the general welfare. The fertile soil returned a rich reward even with the slovenly applied energies of the slaves. A man could pay perhaps $1,000 for a slave, and in the cotton field, but really nowhere else, the investment would yield an enormous profit. The loss in waste, or ill directed labor, in work carelessly done, or the want of preparation, tools or machinery, or any manner of real thrift, gave little or no concern to the average agriculturist. For personal comfort and large returns upon investments that required little or no personal attention, no section of the world ever surpassed the United States south of the 36° of north latitude. Wealth of individuals was rated therefore by the number of slaves one possessed. Twenty hands in the cotton field, under even an indifferent overseer, with no watchful care of the master, none of that saving frugality in the farming so imperative elsewhere upon farms, returned every year an income which would enable the family to spend their lives traveling and sight-seeing over the world. The rich soil required no care in its tilling from the owner. It is the first and strongest principle in human nature to seek its desires through the least exertion. To raise cotton, ship to market and dispose of it, purchasing whatever was wanted, was the inevitable result of such conditions. This was by far the easiest mode, and hence manufactures, diversity of farming or farming pursuits, were not an imperative necessity—indeed, they were not felt to be necessities at all. The evil, the blight of slavery upon the whites, was well understood by the intelligence of the South, by even those who had learned to believe that white labor could not and never would be profitable in this latitude; that—most strange! the white man who labored at manual labor, must be in the severe climate and upon the stubborn New England soil. It was simply effect following cause which made these people send off their children to school, and to buy their every want, both necessaries and luxuries—importing hay, corn, oats, bacon, mules, horses and cattle even from Northern States, when every possible natural advantage might be had in producing the same things at home. It was the easiest and cheapest way to do. In the matter of dollars and cents, the destroying of slavery was, to the farmers of the Upper Mississippi Valley, a permanent loss. Now the New South is beginning to send the products of its farms and gardens even to Illinois. The war, the abolition of slavery, the return of the Confederates to their desolated homes, and their invincible courage in rolling up their sleeves and going to work, and the results of their labors seen all over the South, form one of the grandest displays of the development of the latent forces of the great American people that can be found in history.

There is not a thing, not even ice, but that, in the new social order of Arkansas, it can produce for its own use quite as well as the most favored of Northern States. The one obstruction in the way of the completed triumph of the State is the lingering idea among farmers that for the work of raising cotton, black labor is better than white. This fallacy is a companion of the old notion that slavery was necessary to the South. Under proper auspices these two articles of Arkansas—cotton and lumber—alone may make of it the most prosperous State in the Union; and the magician's wand to transform all this to gold is in securing the intelligent laborer of the North, far more than the Northern capital prayed for by so many. The North has its homeless millions, and the recent lessons in the opening of Oklahoma should be promptly appreciated by the people of this State. For the next decade to manufacture every pound of cotton raised in the State, as well as husbanding and manufacturing all the lumber from these grand old forests, is to solve the questions in the race of State prosperity and general wealth among the people. When free labor supplanted slave labor what a wonderful advance it gave the whole section; when intelligent skilled labor supplants ignorance and unskilled labor, what a transcendent golden epoch will dawn. There is plenty of capital to-day in the State, if it was only put in proper co-operative form, to promote the establishment of manufactories that would liberally reward the stockholders, and make them and Arkansas the richest people in the world. Such will attract hundreds of thousands of intelligent and capable wage workers from the North, from all over the world, as well as the nimble-witted farm labor in the gardens, the orchards, the fields and the cotton plantations. This will bring and add to the present profits on a bale of cotton, the far richer dividend on stocks in factories, banks, railroads and all that golden stream which is so much of modern increase in wealth. The people of Arkansas may just as well have this incalculable abundance as to not have it, and at the same time pay enormous premiums to others to come and reap the golden harvests. Competent laborers—skilled wage workers, the brawn and brain of the land—are telling of their unrest in strikes, lockouts, combinations and counter combinations; in short, in the conflict of labor and capital, they are appealing strongly to be allowed to come to Arkansas—not to enter the race against ignorant, incapable labor, but simply to find employment and homes, where in comfort and plenty they can rear their families, and while enriching themselves to return profits a thousand fold. Don't fret and mope away your lives looking and longing for capital to enter and develop your boundless resources. Capital is a royal good thing, but remember it is even a better thing in your own pockets than in some other person's. Open the way for proper, useful labor to come and find employment; each department, no matter how small or humble the beginning, once started will grow rapidly, and the problem will have been solved. Only by the North taking the raw product of the South and putting it in the hands of skilled labor has their enormous capital been secured. The profits on high priced labor will always far excel that on ignorant or cheap workmen. The time is now when this kind of labor and the small farmers and gardeners are awaiting a bidding to enter Arkansas. When the forlorn hope returned from the late war, they met the stern necessity, and demonstrated the fact that here, at least, the people can create their own capital. Let them now anticipate the future by this heroic triumph of the past. The Gods help those only who help themselves.

"The fault, dear Brutus, is not in our stars,
but in ourselves."

To the Northern home-seeker the thing of first importance is to tell of the temperate climate at all seasons, and its extraordinary healthfulness, curing him of the false idea spread so wide that the topography of the State is seen from the decks of steamers, or on the lines of railroad which are built along the swamps and slashes, mostly on account of the easy grades on these lines. Then show from the records the low rate of taxation and the provisions of the law by which high taxation is forever prevented. From this preliminary may be unfolded to him some of the wonderful natural resources which are awaiting development. Here both tongue and pen will fall far short of telling all or nearly all. In climate, health, soil, timber, minerals, coal, rocks, clays, marls, sand, navigable streams, mineral and fresh waters, Arkansas may challenge any similar sized spot on the globe. It has more miles of navigable streams than any other State in the Union, and these are so placed as to give the whole territory the advantages thereof, as though the engineers had located them. It has unequaled water power—the Mammoth Spring alone furnishing enough water power to propel all the machinery west of the Mississippi River. The topography of the State is one of its most inviting features. Its variety in this respect is only equaled by the diversity of its soils. The traveler who in approaching this section concludes that it consists chiefly of swamp bottoms, and water-covered slashes, may readily learn from the records that three-quarters of the State's surface is uplands, ranging from the gentle swells of prairie and woodland to the grandly beautiful mountain scenery; and on the mountain benches, and at the base, are as rich and beautiful valleys as are kissed by the rays of the sun in his season's round. Take the whole range of agricultural products of Ohio, Indiana, Illinois and Kansas, and all can be produced quite as well in Arkansas as in any of these States. In the face of this fact, for more than a generation Arkansas raised scarcely any of the products of these Northern communities, but imported such as it had to have. It could not spare its lands from the cultivation of the more profitable crops of cotton. In a word, the truth is the State was burdened with natural wealth—this and slave labor having clogged the way and impeded its progress. With less labor, more cotton per acre and per hand, on an average, has been produced in Arkansas than in any other Southern State, and its quality has been such as to win the prize wherever it has been entered in competition. Its reputation as a fruit-growing State is not excelled. In the New Orleans Exposition, in California, Ohio and everywhere entered, it has taken the premium over all competitors. Its annual rainfall exceeds that of any Southern State, and it cannot, therefore, suffer seriously from drouths. There is not a spot upon the globe which, if isolated from all outside of its limits, could sustain in health and all the civilized comforts a population as large as might Arkansas. Fifty thousand people annually come hither and are cured, and yet a general nebulous idea prevails among many in the North that the health and climate of the State are not good. The statistics of the United States Medical Department show the mortality rate at Little Rock to be less than at any other occupied military post in the country. There is malaria in portions of the State, but considering the vast bottom stretches of timber-land, and the newness of the country's settlement, it is a remarkable fact that there is less of this disease here than in Pennsylvania; while all the severer diseases of the New England and Northern States, such as rheumatism, consumption, catarrh and blood poison, are always relieved and generally cured in Arkansas; malignant scarlet fever and diphtheria have never yet appeared. That dreadful decimator, yellow fever, has only visited the eastern portion of the State, but in every case it was brought from abroad, and has never prevailed in this locality as an epidemic. Therefore, the largest factories, schools and universities in the world should be here. The densest population, the busiest haunts of men, will inevitably come where their rewards will be greatest—the struggle for life less severe. Five hundred inhabitants to the square mile will not put to the full test the limitless resources of this wonderful commonwealth. Ten months of summer without one torrid day, with invariable cool and refreshing nights, and two months only of winter, where a man can work out of doors every day in the year in comfort, with less cost in physician's bills, expense in food, clothing and housing, are some of the inducements the State offers to the poor man. There are millions of acres of fertile lands that are offered almost without money and without price; land nearly any acre of which is worth more intrinsically than any other similar sized body of land in the world. There are 5,000,000 acres of government lands in the State, and 2,000,000 acres of State lands. The rainfall in 1886 was 46.33; average mean temperature, 58.7°; highest, 97.8°; lowest, above zero, 7.6°. Of the 33,500,000 acres in the State there are soils richer and deeper than the Nile; others that excel the alluvial corn belt of the Northern States; others that may successfully compete with the noted Cuba or James River, Virginia, tobacco red soil districts, or the most noted vineyards of France or Italy. Here is the land of wine and silk, where side by side will grow the corn and the fig—the land overhung with the soft, blue skies, and decked with flowers, the air laden with the rich perfumes of the magnolias, on the topmost pinnacle of whose branches the Southern mocking-bird by day and by night swells its throat with song—

"Where all, save the spirit of man, is divine."

The artificial and local causes which have obstructed the State's prosperity are now forever gone. There is yet the unsolved problem of the political negro, but this is in Illinois, Kansas and Ohio, exactly as it is in Arkansas. It is only the common problem to the Anglo-Saxon of the United States, which, in the future as in the past, after many mistakes and even great wrongs, he will forever settle and for the best. Throw politics to the winds; only remember to profit by the mistakes of the North in inviting immigration, and thereby avoid the ominous presence of anarchism, socialism, and those conditions of social life latent in "the conflict of labor and capital." These are some of the portentous problems now confronting the older States that are absent from Arkansas; they should be kept away, by the knowledge that such ugly conditions are the fanged whelps of the great brood of American demagogues—overdoses of politics, washed down by too much universal voting. It is of infinitely more importance to guard tax-receipts than the ballot boxes. When vice and ignorance vote their own destruction, there need be no one to compassionate their miseries, but always where taxes run high, people's liberties run low. The best government governs the least—the freest government taxes the least.

Offer premiums to the immigration of well-informed, expert labor, and small farmers, dairymen, gardeners and horticulturists and small traders. Let the 7,000,000 acres of government and State lands be given in forty-acre tracts to the heads of families, who will come and occupy them. Instead of millions of dollars in donations to great corporations and capitalists, give to that class which will create capital, develop the State, and enrich all the people. Railroads and capitalists will follow these as water runs down the hill. Arkansas needs railroads—ten thousand miles yet—it needs great factories, great cities, universities of learning and, forsooth, millionaires. But its first and greatest needs are small farmers, practical toilers, skilled mechanics, and scattered all over the State beginnings in each of the various manufactures; the beginnings, in short, of that auspicious hour when it ceases to ship any of its raw materials. It is a law of life, that, in a society where there are few millionaires, there are few paupers. Where the capital of a country is gathered in vast aggregations in the possession of a few, there the children cry for bread—the poor constantly increase, wages fall, employment too often fails, and the hoarse mutterings of parading mobs and bread riots take the places of the laughter and the songs of the laborers to and from the shops and the fields.

The following from the government official reports of the growth and value of the manufactures of the State is to be understood as reaching only to 1880, when it had but commenced to emerge from the old into the new life:

Year.	Establishments	Capital.	Males.	Females.	Children.	Wages.	Val. Materials.	Value Products
1850	261	$ 305,045	812	30	......	$150,876	$ 215,789	$ 537,908
1860	518	1,316,610	1,831	46	......	554,240	1,280,503	2,880,578
1870	1,070	1,782,913	3,077	47	82	673,963	2,506,998	4,629,234
1880	1,202	2,953,130	4,307	90	160	925,358	4,392,080	6,756,159

Ideas of values are most easily reached by comparisons. The following figures, taken from official government reports, explain themselves:

	Value of Farms.	Machinery	Live Stock.	Products.
Arkansas	$ 74,249,655	$ 4,637,497	$ 20,472,425	$43,796,261
Nebraska	105,932,541	7,820,915	33,440,265	31,708,914
Iowa	567,430,227	29,371,854	124,715,103	36,103,073
Kansas	235,178,631	9,794,634	60,907,749	52,240,561
Minnesota	193,724,260	13,089,783	31,904,821	40,468,967

The products are the profits on the capital invested. Words can add nothing to these figures in demonstrating the superiority of Arkansas as an agricultural State, except the explanation that Southern farming is yet more or less carried on under the baneful influences of the days of slavery, unintentional indifference and the absence of watchful attention by the proprietor.

Cotton grows finely in all parts of this commonwealth and heretofore in two-thirds of its territory it has been the main crop. In the fertile bottoms the product per acre has reached as high as 2,000 pounds of seed cotton, while on the uplands it runs from 600 to 1,000 pounds. The census of 1880 shows that Arkansas produces more cotton per acre, and at less expense, than any of the so-called cotton States. In 1880 the yield was 608,256 bales, grown on 1,042,970 acres. That year Georgia raised 814,441 bales, on 2,617,138 acres. The estimated cost per acre of raising cotton is $6. It will thus be seen that it cost $9,444,972 in Georgia to raise 256,185 more bales of cotton than Arkansas had grown—much more than double the land to produce less than one-fourth more cotton. Less than one-twentieth of the cotton land of the latter State has been brought under cultivation.

The superiority of cotton here is attested by the fact that the greatest cotton thread manufacturers in the world prefer the Arkansas cotton to any other in the market. The product has for years carried off the first prizes over the world's competition.

The extra census bulletin, 1880, gives the yield of corn, oats and wheat products in Arkansas for that year as follows: Corn, 24,156,517 bushels; oats, 2,219,824 bushels; wheat, 1,269,730 bushels. Remembering that this is considered almost exclusively a cotton State, these figures of the cereals will be a genuine surprise. More wheat is grown by 40,000 bushels and nearly three times as much corn as were raised in all New England, according to the official figures for that year.

From the United States agricultural reports are obtained these interesting statistics concerning the money value of farm crops per acre:

	Corn.	Rye.	Oats.	Potatoes.	Hay.
Illinois	$ 6 77	$ 6 64	$ 6 46	$30 32	$ 7 66
Indiana	8 86	7 30	5 92	30 08	7 66
Ohio	11 52	9 08	7 90	84 48	9 85
Kansas	6 44	5 98	6 12	37 40	5 89
Virginia	7 52	5 16	5 34	43 50	17 30
Tennessee	7 91	7 32	5 73	28 08	14 95
Arkansas	11 51	9 51	11 07	78 65	22 94

The following is the average cash value per acre on all crops taken together:

Maine	$13 51	North Carolina	$10 79
New Hampshire	13 56	South Carolina	10 09
Vermont	11 60	Georgia	10 35
Massachusetts	26 71	Florida	8 52
Rhode Island	29 32	Alabama	13 49
Connecticut	16 82	Mississippi	14 76
New York	14 15	Louisiana	22 40
New Jersey	18 05	Arkansas	20 40
Pennsylvania	17 68	Tennessee	12 39
Delaware	15 80	West Virginia	12 74
Maryland	17 82	Kentucky	13 58
Virginia	10 91	Ohio	15 58

Michigan	$18 96	Kansas	$ 9 11
Indiana	14 66	Nebraska	8 60
Illinois	12 47	California	17 18
Wisconsin	13 80	Oregon	17 11
Minnesota	10 29	Nevada, Colorado and the Territories	16 13
Iowa	8 88		
Missouri	10 78	Texas	14 69

The advance of horticulture in the past decade in the State has been extraordinary. Twenty years ago its orchard products amounted to very little. By the census reports of 1880, the total yield of fruit was $867,426. This was $100,000 more than the yield of Florida, with all the latter's immense orange groves. As universally as has the State been misunderstood, it is probably in reference to its fruits and berries that the greatest errors have long existed. If one visits the apple and peach regions of the North, it is found to be the general belief that Arkansas is too far south to produce either, whereas the truth is that, especially in apples, it has no equal either in the United States or in the world. This fact was first brought to public attention at the World's Fair, at New Orleans, 1884-85, where the Arkansas exhibit was by far the finest ever made, and the State was awarded the first premium, receiving the World's medal and a special notice by the awarding committee. Thus encouraged, the State was represented at the meeting of the American Pomological Society, in Boston, in September, 1887. Sixty-eight varieties of Arkansas seedling apples were in the exhibit, to contend with all the champion fruit growers of the globe. The State won the Wilder medal, which is only given by reason of extraordinary merit, and in addition to this was awarded the first premium for the largest and best collection of apples, consisting of 128 varieties.

The collection which won the Boston prizes was then shipped to Little Rock, and after being on exhibition there twenty days, was re-packed and shipped to the National Horticultural meeting in California, which met at Riverside, February 7, 1888. Arkansas again won the first prize, invading the very home of Pomona, and bearing off the first honors as it had in eastern and northern sections of the Union. The "Arkansas Shannon" is pronounced by competent judges to be the finest apple now grown anywhere.

Strawberries are another late discovery of the resources of Arkansas. The yield and quality are very superior. So rapidly has the industry grown that, during the fruit season, the Iron Mountain road runs a special daily fruit train, leaving Little Rock late in the afternoon and reaching St. Louis early the next morning. This luscious product, of remarkable size, ripens about the first of April.

Of all cultivated fruit the grape has held its place in poetry and song, in sacred and profane history, as the first. It finds in Arkansas the same conditions and climate of its native countries, between Persia and India. The fruit and its wine produced here are said by native and foreign experts to equal, if not surpass, the most famous of Italy or France. The vines are always healthy and the fruit perfect. The wild muscadine and scuppernong grow vines measuring thirty-eight and one-half inches around, many varieties fruiting here to perfection that are not on the open air lists at all further north.

The nativity of the peach is the same as that of the grape, and it, too, therefore, takes as kindly to the soil here as does the vine. Such a thing as budded peach trees are of very recent date, and as a consequence the surprises of the orchardists in respect to this fruit are many. Some of the varieties ripen in May, and so far every kind of budded peaches brought from the North, both the tree and the fruit, have improved by the transplanting. The vigor of the trees seems to baffle the borers, and no curled leaves have yet been noticed. In quality and quantity the product is most encouraging, and the next few years will see a marked advance in this industry.

For fifty years after the settlement of the State peach seedlings were grown, and from these, as in the case of the apple, new and superior varieties have been started, noted for size, flavor, abundance and never failing crops.

The Chickasaw plum is so far the most successfully grown, and is the best. It is a perfected fruit easily cultivated, and is free from the curculio, while the trees are healthy and vigorous beyond other localities.

In vegetables and fruits, except the tropical

plants, Arkansas is the banner State. In the fruit and vegetable kingdom there is found in luxuriant growth everything in the long list from corn to the fig.

The yield and quality of Arkansas tobacco is remarkable when it is remembered that this industry has received so little attention. Thirty years ago State Geologist Owen informed the people that he found here the same, if not better, tobacco soil, than the most favored districts of Cuba. The yield of tobacco, in 1880, was 970,230 pounds. Yet so little attention or experiment has been given the subject that an experimental knowledge of the State's resources in this respect cannot be claimed to have been gained.

In 1880 the State produced: Barley, 1,952 bushels; buckwheat, 548 bushels; rye, 22,387 bushels; hay, 23,295 tons; Irish potatoes, 492,627 bushels; sweet potatoes, 881,260 bushels.

From the census reports of the same year are gleaned the following: Horses, total, 146,333; mules and asses, 87,082; working oxen, 25,444; milch cows, 249,407; other cattle, 433,392; sheep, 246,757; swine, 1,565,008; wool, 557,368 pounds; milk, 316,858 gallons; butter, 7,790,013 pounds; cheese, 26,310 pounds. All parts of the State are finely adapted to stock-raising. The excellence and abundance of pure water, the heavy growth of blue grass, the cane brakes and abundant mast, sustain the animals during most of the winter in marketable condition. In respect to all domestic animals here are presented the same conditions as in nearly every line of agriculture—cheapness of growth and excellence of quality.

The improvement in cattle has been retarded by the now conceded fact that the "Texas fever" is asserted by some to be seated in the State. This affects Northern cattle when imported, while it has no effect on native animals. Except for this unfortunate reality there would be but little time lost in developing here the great dairy industry of the country. But good graded cattle are now being raised in every portion, and so rich is the locality in this regard that in stock, as in its fruits, care and attention will produce new varieties of unrivaled excellence. Arkansas is the natural home and breeding ground of animals, all growing to great perfection, with less care and the least cost.

Taxes here are not high. The total taxation in Illinois in 1880, assessed on real and personal property, as per census reports, for State, county and all civil divisions less than counties, was $24,586,018; the same year in Arkansas the total tax was $1,839,090. Farm lands are decreasing in value in Illinois nearly as fast as they are increasing in Arkansas. The total taxation in the United States in 1880 was the enormous sum of $312,750,721. Northern cities are growing, while their rural population is lessening. The reverse of this is the best for a State. The source of ruin to past nations and civilizations has all arisen from an abuse of the taxing powers. Excessive taxation can only end in general ruin. This simple but great lesson should be instilled into the minds of all youths, crystallized into the briefest maxim, and written over every threshold in the land; hung in the porches of every institution of learning; imprinted upon every plow handle and emblazoned on the trees and jutting rocks. The State that has taxed its people to build a $25,000,000 State house, has given deep shame to the intelligence of this age. Taxes are the insidious destroyer of nations and all liberty, and it is only those freemen who jealously guard against this evil who will for any length of time maintain their independence, equality or manhood.

The grade profile of the Memphis Route shows the elevations of the various cities and towns along that line to be as follows in feet, the datum plane being tide water of the Gulf of Mexico: Kansas City, 765; Rosedale, 825; Merriam, 900; Lenexa, 1,040; Olathe, 1,060; Bonita, 1,125; Ocheltree, 1,080; Spring Hill, 1,020; Hillsdale, 900; Paola, 860; Pendleton, 855; Fontana, 925; La Cygne, 840; Barnard, 810; Pleasanton, 865; Miami, 910; Prescott, 880; Fulton, 820; Hammond, 875; Fort Scott, 860; Clarksburg, 885; Garland, 865; all in Kansas; Arcadia, 820; Liberal, 875; Iantha, 990; Lamar, 1,000; Kenoma, 980; Golden City, 1,025; Lockwood, 1,065; South Greenfield, 1,040; Everton, 1,000; Ash Grove, 1,020; Bois d'Arc, 1,250; Campbells, 1,290;

Nichols Junction, 1,280; Springfield, 1,300; Turner, 1,210; Rogersville, 1,475; Fordland, 1,600; Seymour, 1,680; Cedar Gap, 1,685; Mansfield, 1,520; Norwood, 1,510; Mountain Grove, 1,525; Cabool, 1,250; Sterling, 1,560; Willow Springs, 1,400; Burnham, 1,360; Olden, 1,280; West Plains, 950; Brandsville, 1,000; Koshkonong, 970; Thayer, last point in Missouri, 575; Mammoth Spring, Ark., 485; Afton, 410; Hardy, 370; Williford, 330; Ravenden, 310; Imboden, 300; Black Rock, 290; Portia, 285; Hoxie, 295; Sedgwick, 270; Bonnerville, 320; Jonesboro, 275; Nettleton, 250; Big Bay Siding, 250; Hatchie Coon, 250; Marked Tree, 250; Tyronza, 240; Gilmore, 225; Clarketon, 240; Marion, 235; West Memphis, 200; Memphis, 280.

CHAPTER VI.

Politics—Importance of the Subject—The Two Old Schools of Politicians—Triumph of the Jacksonians—Early Prominent State Politicians—The Great Question of Secession—The State Votes to Join the Confederacy—Horror of the War Period—The Reconstruction Distress—The Baxter-Brooks Embroglio.

> In knots they stand, or in a rank they walk,
> Serious in aspect, earnest in their talk;
> Factious, and favouring this or t'other side,
> As their weak fancy or strong reason guide.—*Dryden.*

IN one sense there is no portion of the history of Arkansas more instructive than its political history, because in this is the key to the character of many of its institutions, as well as strong indications of the trend of the public mind, and the characteristics of those men who shaped public affairs and controlled very largely in the State councils.

Immediately upon the formation of the Territorial government, the President of the United States sent to Arkansas Post Gov. James Miller, Robert Crittenden, secretary, and C. Jouett, Robert P. Letcher and Andrew Scott, judges, to organize the new Territorial government. Gov. Miller, it seems, gave little attention to his office, and therefore in all the early steps of formation Crittenden was the acting governor; and from the force of character he possessed, and his superior strength of mind, it is fair to conclude that he dominated almost at will the early public affairs of Arkansas.

This was at the time of the beginning of the political rivalry between Clay and Jackson, two of the most remarkable types of great political leaders this country has produced—Henry Clay, the superb; "Old Hickory," the man of iron; the one as polished a gem as ever glittered in the political heavens—the other the great diamond in the rough, who was of the people, and who drew his followers with bands of steel. These opposites were destined to clash. It is well for the country that they did.

Robert Crittenden was a brother of John J. Crittenden, of Kentucky, and by some who knew him long and well he was deemed not only his brother's peer, but in many respects his intellectual superior. It goes without the saying, he was a born Whig, who, in Kentucky's super-loyal fashion, had Clay for his idol, and, to put it mildly, Jackson to dislike.

President Monroe had appointed the first Territorial officers, but the fact that Crittenden was secretary is evidence that politics then were not running very high. Monroe was succeeded in 1824 by John Quincy Adams. It would seem that in the early days in Arkansas, the Whigs stood upon the vantage grounds in many important respects. By the time Adams was inaugurated the war political to the death between Clay and Jackson had begun. But no man looked more carefully after his own interests than Jackson. He had large property possessions just across the line in Tennessee, besides property in Arkansas. He induced, from his ranks in his own State, some young men of promise to come to Arkansas. The prize now was whether this should be a Whig or Democratic State. President Adams turned out Democratic officials and put in Whigs, and Robert Crittenden for a long time seemed to hold the State in his hand. Jackson's superiority as a leader over Clay is manifested in the struggles between the two in Arkansas. Clay's followers here were men after his fashion, as were Jackson's men after his mold. Taking Robert Crittenden as the best type, he was but little inferior to Clay himself in his magnetic oratory and purity of principles and public life; while Jackson sent here the Seviers, Conways and Rectors, men of the people, but of matchless resolution and personal force of character. No two great commanders ever had more faithful or able lieutenants than were the respective champions of Old Hickory and Harry of the West, in the formative days of the State of Arkansas. The results were, like those throughout the Union, that Jackson triumphed in the hard strife, and Arkansas entered the Union, by virtue of a bill introduced by James Buchanan, as a Jackson State, and has never wavered in its political integrity.

As an evidence of the similarity of the contests and respective leaders of the two parties here to those throughout the country, it is only necessary to point out that Crittenden drew to his following such men as Albert Pike, a genius of the loftiest and most versatile gifts the country has so far produced, while Jackson, ever supplying reinforcements to his captains, sent among others, as secretary of the Territory, Lewis Randolph, grandson of Thomas Jefferson, and whose wife was pretty Betty Martin, of the White House, a niece of Jackson's. Randolph settled in Hempstead County when it was an unbroken wilderness, and his remains are now resting there in an unknown grave.

Clay, it seems, could dispatch but little additional force to his followers, even when he saw they were the hardest pressed by the triumphant enemy. There was not much by which one could draw comparisons between Clay and Jackson—unless it was their radical difference. As a great orator, Clay has never been excelled, and he lived in a day when the open sesame to the world's delights lay in the silver tongue; but Jackson was a hero, a great one, who inspired other born heroes to follow him even to the death.

Arkansas was thus started permanently along the road of triumphant democracy, from which it never would have varied, except for the war times that brought to the whole country such confusion and political chaos. Being a Jackson State, dominated by the blood of the first governor of Tennessee—Gen. John Sevier, a man little inferior to Jackson himself—it was only the most cruel circumstance that could force the State into secession. When the convention met on the 4th of March, 1861, "on the state of the Union," its voice was practically unanimous for the Union, and that body passed a series of as loyal resolutions as were ever penned, then adjourning to meet again in the May following. The convention met May 6, but the war was upon the country, and most of the Gulf States had seceded. Every one knew that war was inevitable; it was already going on, but very few realized its immensity. The convention did not rush hastily into secession. An ordinance of secession was introduced, and for days, and into the nights, running into the small hours, the matter was deliberated upon—no preliminary test vote was forced to an issue. Delegates were present in anxious attendance from the Carolinas, Alabama and Georgia. They knew that the fate of their action largely depended upon the attitude of Arkansas. If Arkansas voted no, then the whole secession movement would receive a severe blow. The afternoon before the final vote, which was to take place in the evening, these commissioners from other States had made up their minds that Arkansas might possibly vote down secession. When the convention adjourned for supper, they held a hurried consultation, and freely expressed their anxiety at the outlook. It was understood that the discussion was closed, and the night session was wholly for the purpose of taking a vote. All was uncertainty and intense excitement. Expressions of deepest attachment to the Union and the old flag were heard. The most fiery and vehement of the secessionists in the body were cautious and deliberative. There was but little even of vehement detestation of the abolitionists—a thing as natural then for a Southern man to despise as hatred is natural to a heated brain.

At a late hour in the evening, amid the most solemn silence of the crowded hall, an informal vote was taken. All except six members voted to secede. A suppressed applause followed the announcement of the vote. A hurried, whispered conference went on, and the effort was made to have the result unanimous. Now came the final vote. When the name of Isaac Murphy, afterward the military governor, was reached, it was passed and the roll call continued. It was so far unanimous, with Mr. Murphy's name still to call. The clerk called it. Mr. Murphy arose and in an earnest and impressive manner in a few words explained the dilemma he was in, but said, "I cannot violate my honest convictions of duty. I vote 'No.'"

When the day of reconstruction began, at first it was under the supervision of the military, and it is yet the greatest pity that Congress did not let the military alone to rehabilitate the States they had conquered. Isaac Murphy was made governor.

No truer Union man lived than he. He knew the people, and his two years of government were fast curing the wounds of war. But he was turned out of office.

The right to vote compels, if it is to be other than an evil, some correct and intelligent understanding of the form of government prevailing in the United States, and of the elementary principles of political economy. The ability to read and write, own property, go to Congress or edit a political paper, has nothing to do with it, no more than the color of the skin, eyes or hair of the voter. The act of voting itself is the sovereign act in the economic affairs of the State; but if the government under its existing form is to endure, the average voter must understand and appreciate the fundamental principles which, in the providence of God, have made the United States the admiration of the world.

Arkansas, the Democratic State, was in political disquiet from 1861 to 1874—the beginning of the war and the end of reconstruction. When in the hands of Congress it was returned at every regular election as a Republican party State. The brief story of the political Moses who led it out of the wilderness is of itself a strange and interesting commentary on self-government.

When the war came there lived in Batesville Elisha Baxter, a young lawyer who had been breasting only financial misfortunes all his life. Utterly failing as a farmer and merchant, he had been driven to study law and enter the practice to make a living. An honest, kind-hearted, good man, loving his neighbor as himself, but a patriot every inch of him, and loving the Union above all else, his heart was deeply grieved when he saw his adopted State had declared for secession. He could not be a disunionist, no more than he could turn upon his neighbors, friends and fellow-citizens of Arkansas. He determined to wash his hands of it all and remain quietly at home. Like all others he knew nothing of civil war. His neighbors soon drove him from his home and family, and, to save his life, he went to the Northern army, then in Southern Missouri. He was welcomed and offered a commission in the Federal army and an opportunity to return to his State. He declined the offer; he could not turn and shed the blood of his old neighbors and former friends. In the vicissitudes of war this non-combatant was captured by an Arkansas command, paroled and ordered to report to the military authorities at Little Rock. He made his way thither, and was thrown into a military prison and promptly indicted for high treason. Then only he began to understand the temper of the times, for the chances of his being hanged were probably as a thousand to one to acquittal. In this extremity he broke jail and fled. He again reached the Northern army in which he accepted a commission, and returned to his old home in Batesville, remaining in military command of the place. He was actively engaged in recruiting the Union men of Northern Arkansas and forming them into regiments. It goes without saying that Baxter never raised a hand to strike back at those who had so deeply wronged him, when their positions were reversed and he had the power in his hands.

At the fall election, 1871, Baxter was the regular Republican candidate for governor, and Joseph Brooks was the Independent Republican nominee. The Republican party was divided and each bid for the Democratic vote by promises to the ex-Confederates. Brooks may have been elected, but was counted out. Baxter was duly inaugurated. When he had served a year the politicians, it is supposed, who controlled Arkansas, finding they could not use Baxter, or in other words that they had counted in the wrong man, boldly proceeded to undo their own acts, dethrone Baxter and put Brooks in the chair of State. An account of the Baxter-Brooks war is given in another chapter.

Thus was this man the victim of political circumstances; a patriot, loving his country and his neighbors, he was driven from home and State; a non-combatant, he was arrested by his own friends as a traitor and the hangman's halter dangled in his face; breaking prison and stealing away like a skulking convict, to return as ruler and master by the omnipotent power of the bayonet; a non-party man, compelled to be a Republican in politics, and finally, as a Republican, fated to lead the Democratic party to success and power.

The invincible Jacksonian dynasty, built up in Arkansas, with all else of public institutions went down in the sweep of civil war. It has not been revived as a political institution. But the Democratic party dominates the State as of old.

CHAPTER VII.

SOCIETIES, STATE INSTITUTIONS, ETC.—THE KU KLUX KLAN—INDEPENDENT ORDER OF ODD FELLOWS—ANCIENT, FREE AND ACCEPTED MASONS—GRAND ARMY OF THE REPUBLIC—BUREAU OF MINES—ARKANSAS AGRICULTURAL ASSOCIATIONS—STATE HORTICULTURAL SOCIETY—THE WHEEL—THE STATE CAPITAL—THE CAPITOL BUILDING—STATE LIBRARIES—STATE MEDICAL SOCIETY—STATE BOARD OF HEALTH—DEAF MUTE INSTITUTE—SCHOOL FOR THE BLIND—ARKANSAS LUNATIC ASYLUM—ARKANSAS INDUSTRIAL UNIVERSITY—THE STATE DEBT.

> Heaven forming each on other to depend,
> A master, or a servant, or a friend,
> Bids each on other for assistance call,
> Till one man's weakness grows the strength of all.—*Pope.*

SECRET societies are a form of social life and expression which, in some mode of existence, antedate even authentic history. Originally a manner of securing defense from the common enemies of tribes and peoples, they have developed into social and eleemosynary institutions as advances in civilization have been made. At first they were but a severe necessity, and as that time slowly passed away, they became a luxury and a pleasure, having peculiar and strong attraction to nearly all men. That part of one's nature which loves to lean upon others for aid, even in the social scale, finds its expression in some of the many forms of societies, clubs, organizations or institutions that now pervade nearly all the walks of life. In every day existence, in business, church, state, politics and pleasure, are societies and organizations everywhere—for the purposes of gain, charity and comfort—indeed, for the sole purpose of finding something to do, would be the acknowledgment of many a society motto. The causes are as diversified as the bodies, secret and otherwise, are numerous.

The South furnishes a most remarkable instance of the charm there is in mystery to all men, in the rise and spread of the Ku Klux Klan, a few years ago. Three or four young men, in Columbia, Tenn., spending a social evening together, concluded to organize a winter's literary society. All had just returned from the war, in which they had fought for the "lost cause," and found time hanging dull upon them. Each eagerly caught at the idea of a society, and soon they were in the intricacies of the details. Together, from their sparse recollections of their schoolbooks, they evolved the curious name for the society. The name suggested to them that the sport to be derived from it might be increased by making it a secret society. The thing was launched upon this basic idea. In everything connected with it each one was fertile it seems in adding mystery to mystery in their meetings and personal movements.

The initiation of a new member was made a grand and rollicking affair. So complete had the members occasioned their little innocent society to be a mystery, that it became in an astonishingly brief time a greater enigma to themselves than even to outsiders. It swiftly spread from the village to the county, from the county to the State, and over-ran the Southern States like a racing prairie fire, changing in its aims and objects as rapidly as it had grown. From simply frightening the poor night-prowling darkeys, it became a vast and uncontrollable semi-military organization; inflicting punishment here, and there taking life, until the State of Tennessee was thrown into utter confusion, and the military forces were called out; large rewards were offered for the arrest even of women found making any of the paraphernalia of the order. Government detectives sent to pry into their secrets were slain, and a general reign of terror ensued. No rewards could induce a member to betray his fellows; and the efforts of the organizers to control the storm they had raised, were as idle as the buzzing of a summer fly. Thousands and thousands of men belonged to it, who knew really little or nothing about it, and who to this day are oblivious of the true history of one of the most remarkable movements of large bodies of men that has ever occurred in this or perhaps any country. It was said by leading members of the order that they could, in twenty-four hours, put tens of thousands of men in line of battle, all fully armed and equipped. It was indeed the "Invisible Empire." By its founders it was as innocent and harmless in its purposes as a Sunday-school picnic, yet in a few weeks it spread and grew until it overshadowed the land—but little else than a bloody, headless riot. The imaginations of men on the outside conjured up the most blood-curdling falsehoods as to its doings; while those inside were, it seems, equally fertile in schemes and devices to further mystify people, alarm some and terrify others, and apparently the wilder the story told about them, the more they would enjoy it. Its true history will long give it rank of first importance to the philosophic and careful, painstaking historian.

Among societies of the present day, that organization known as the Independent Order of Odd Fellows is recognized as a prominent one. The Grand Lodge of the order in Arkansas was organized June 11, 1849. Its first past grand master was John J. Horner, elected in 1854. His successors to date have been as follows: James A. Henry, 1858; P. O. Hooper, 1859–1866; Richard Bragg, Sr., 1862; Peter Brugman, 1867, 1868, 1871; Isaac Eolsom, 1873; Albert Cohen, 1874; John B. Bond, 1876; E. B. Moore, 1878; James S. Holmes, 1880; Adam Clark, 1881; W. A. Jett, 1882; James A. Gibson, 1884; George W. Hurley, 1885; H. S. Coleman, 1886, and A. S. Jett, 1887. The present able officers are R. P. Holt, grand master; J. P. Woolsey, deputy grand master; Louis C. Lincoln, grand warden; Peter Brugman, grand secretary; H. Ehrenbers, grand treasurer; H. S. Coleman, grand representative; A. S. Jett, grand representative; Rev. L. B. Hawley, grand chaplain; John R. Richardson, grand marshal; J. G. Parker, grand conductor; William Mosby, grand guardian; W. J. Glenn, grand herald. In the State there are eighty-two lodges and a total membership, reported by the secretary at the October meeting, 1888, of 2,023. The revenue from subordinate lodges amounts to $13,832, while the relief granted aggregates $2,840. There were sixteen Rebekah lodges organized in 1887–88.

The Masonic fraternity is no less influential in the affairs of every part of the country, than the society just mentioned. There is a tradition—too vague for reliance—that Masonry was introduced into Arkansas by the Spaniards more than 100 years ago, and that therefore the first lodge was established at Arkansas Post. Relying, however, upon the records the earliest formation of a lodge of the order was in 1819, when the Grand Lodge of Kentucky granted a dispensation for a lodge at Arkansas Post. Robert Johnson was the first master. Judge Andrew Scott, a Federal judge in the Territory, was one of its members. But before this lodge received its charter, the seat of government was removed to Little Rock, and the Arkansas Post lodge became extinct. No other lodge was attempted to be established until 1836, when a dispensation was granted Washington Lodge No. 82, at Fayetteville, October 3, 1837. Onesimus Evans, was master; James McKissick, senior warden; Mathew Leeper, junior warden.

In 1838 the Grand Lodge of Louisiana granted the second dispensation for a lodge at Arkansas Post— Morning Star Lodge No. 42; the same year granting a charter to Western Star Lodge No. 43, at Little Rock. Of this Edward Cross was master; Charles L. Jeffries, senior warden; Nicholas Peay, junior warden. About this time the Grand Lodge of Alabama granted a charter to Mount Horeb Lodge, of Washington, Hempstead County.

November 21, 1838, these four lodges held a convention at Little Rock and formed the Grand Lodge of Arkansas.

The representatives at this convention were: From Washington Lodge No. 82, of Fayetteville, Onesimus Evans, past master; Washington L. Wilson, Robert Bedford, Abraham Whinnery, Richard C. S. Brown, Samuel Adams and Williamson S. Oldham.

From Western Star Lodge No. 43, of Little Rock, William Gilchrist, past master; Charles L. Jeffries, past master; Nicholas Peay, past master; Edward Cross, past master; Thomas Parsel, Alden Sprague and John Morris.

From Morning Star Lodge No 42, of the Post of Arkansas, John W. Pullen.

From Mount Horeb Lodge, of Washington, James H. Walker, Allen M. Oakley, Joseph W. McKean and James Trigg.

Of this convention John Morris, of Western Star Lodge No. 43, was made secretary. Mr. Morris is still living (1889), a resident of Auburn, Sebastian County, and is now quite an old man. Mr. John P. Karns, of Little Rock, was in attendance at the convention, although not a delegate. These two are the only ones surviving who were present on that occasion.

The Grand Lodge organized by the election of William Gilchrist, grand master; Onesimus Evans, deputy grand master; James H. Walker, grand senior warden; Washington L. Wilson, grand junior warden; Alden Sprague, grand treasurer, and George C. Watkins, grand secretary.

The constituent lodges, their former charters being extinct by their becoming members of a new jurisdiction, took new numbers. Washington Lodge, at Fayetteville, became No. 1; Western Star, of Little Rock, became No. 2; Morning Star, of the Post of Arkansas, became No. 3, and Mount Horeb, of Washington, became No. 4. Of these Washington No. 1, and Western Star No. 2, are in vigorous life, but Morning Star No. 3, and Mount Horeb No. 4, have become defunct.

From this beginning of the four lodges, with a membership of probably 100, the Grand Lodge now consists of over 400 lodges, and a membership of about 12,000.

The following are the officers for the present year: R. H. Taylor, grand master, Hot Springs; J. W. Sorrels, deputy grand master, Farmer, Scott County; D. B. Warren, grand lecturer, Gainesville; W. A. Clement, grand orator, Rover, Yell County; W. K. Ramsey, grand senior warden, Camden; C. A. Bridewell, grand junior warden, Hope; George H. Meade, grand treasurer, Little Rock; Fay Hempstead, grand secretary, Little Rock; D. D. Leach, grand senior deacon, Augusta; Samuel Peete, grand junior deacon, Batesville; H. W. Brooks, grand chaplain, Hope; John B. Baxter, grand marshal, Brinkley; C. C. Hamby, grand sword bearer, Prescott; S. Solmson, senior grand steward, Pine Bluff; A. T. Wilson, junior grand steward, Eureka Springs; J. C. Churchill, grand pursuivant, Charlotte, Independence County; Ed. Metcalf, grand tyler, Little Rock.

The first post of the Grand Army of the Republic, Department of Arkansas, was organized under authority from the Illinois Commandery, and called McPherson Post No. 1, of Little Rock. The district then passed under command of the Department of Missouri, and by that authority was organized Post No. 2, at Fort Smith.

The Provisional Department of Arkansas was organized June 18, 1883, Stephen Wheeler being department commander, and C. M. Vaughan, adjutant-general. A State encampment was called to meet at Fort Smith, July 11, 1888. Six posts were represented in this meeting, when the following State officers were elected: S. Wheeler, commander; M. Mitchell, senior vice; R. E. Jackson, junior vice; H. Stone, quartermaster, and the following council: John F. Owen, A. S. Fowler, W. W. Bailey, A. Walrath, Benton Turner.

There are now seventy-four posts, with a membership of 2,500, in the State. The present officers are: Department commander, A. S. Fowler; senior vice commander, John Vaughan; junior vice commander, E. A. Ellis; medical director, T. G. Miller; chaplain, T. R. Early.

The council of administration includes A. A. Whissen, Thomas Boles, W. S. Bartholomew, R. E. Renner and I. B. Lawton. The following were the appointments on the staff of the department commander: Assistant adjutant-general, N. W. Cox; assistant quartermaster-general, Stephen Wheeler; judge advocate, S. J. Evans; chief mustering officer, S. K. Robinson; department inspector, R. S. Curry. Headquarters were established at Little Rock, Ark.

There are other bodies in the State whose aims and purposes differ materially from those previously mentioned. Among these is the Arkansas Bureau of Mines, Manufactures and Agriculture, which was organized as a State institution at the session of the legislature in 1889. The governor appointed M. F. Locke commissioner, the latter making M. W. Manville assistant. They at once proceeded to organize the department and open an office in the State-house. The legislature appropriated for the next two years for the bureau the sum of $18,000.

This action of the legislature was in response to a demand from all parts of the State, which, growing in volume for some time, culminated in the meeting in Little Rock of numerous prominent men, and the organization of the Arkansas State Bureau of Immigration, January 31, 1888. A demand from almost every county prompted Gov. Senior P. Hughes to issue a call for a State meeting. The meeting was composed only of the best representative citizens. Gov. Hughes, in his address, stated that "the State should have an agricultural, mining and manufacturing bureau, which should be a bureau of statistics and immigration, also." Hon. Logan H. Roots was elected president of the convention. He voiced the purposes of the meeting still further when he said, "We want to educate others on the wealth-making properties of our State." A permanent State organization was effected, one delegate from each county to constitute a State Board of Immigration, and the following permanent officers were chosen: Logan H. Roots, of Little Rock, president; Dandridge McRae, of Searcy, vice-president; H. L. Remmel, of Newport, secretary; George R. Brown, of Little Rock, treasurer; J. H. Clendening, of Fort Smith, A. M. Crow, of Arkadelphia, W. P. Fletcher, of Lonoke, additional executive committee. The executive committee issued a strong address and published it extensively, giving some of the many inducements the State had to offer immigrants. The legislature could not fail to properly recognize such a movement of the people, and so provided for the long needed bureau.

Arkansas Agricultural Association was organized in 1885. It has moved slowly so far, but is now reaching the condition of becoming a great and prosperous institution. The entire State is soon to be made into sub-districts, with minor organizations, at least one in each Congressional district, with a local control in each, and all will become stockholders and a part of the parent concern. A permanent State fair and suitable grounds and fixtures are to be provided in the near future, when Arkansas will successfully vie with any State in the Union in an annual display of its products.

The officers of the Agricultural Association for 1889, are as follows: Zeb. Ward, president, Little Rock; B. D. Williams, first vice-president, Little Rock; T. D. Culberhouse, vice-president First Congressional district; D. McRae, vice-president Second Congressional district; W. L. Tate, vice-president Third Congressional district; J. J. Sumpter, vice-president Fourth Congressional district; J. H. Vanhoose, vice-president Fifth Congressional district; M. W. Manville, secretary; D. W. Bizzell, treasurer.

Arkansas State Horticultural Society was organized May 24, 1879, and incorporated January 31, 1889. Under its completed organization the first fair was held in Little Rock, commencing Wednesday, May 15, 1889. President, E. F. Babcock; secretary, M. W. Manville; executive committee, S. H. Nowlin, chairman, Little Rock; George P. C. Rumbough, Little Rock; Rev. S. H. Buchanan, Little Rock; E. C. Kinney, Judsonia, and Fred Dengler, Hot Springs, constitute the official board.

In 1881 three farmers of Prairie County met and talked over farm matters, and concluded to organize a society for the welfare of the farming community. The movement grew with astonishing rapidity. It was organized as a secret, non-political society, and in matters of trade and commerce proposed to give its members the benefit of combination. In this respect it advocated action in concert with all labor unions or organizations of laborers. A State and National organization was effected, and the sub-organizations, extending to the smallest school districts, were required to obtain authority and report to the State branch and it in return to the National head. Thus far its originators sought what they believed to be the true co-operative method in their business affairs.

The next object was to secure beneficial legislation to farmers—each one to retain his political party affiliations, and at the ballot-box to vote for either farmers or those most closely identified with their interests as might be found on the respective party tickets.

The officers of the National society are: Isaac McCracken, president, Ozone, Ark., and A. E. Gardner, secretary and treasurer, Dresden, Tenn. The Arkansas State Wheel officers are: L. P. Featherstone, president, Forrest City; R. H. Morehead, secretary, White Chapel, and W. H. Quayle, treasurer, Ozan.

The scheme was inviting to honest farmers and the humble beginning soon grew to be a most prosperous society—not only extending over the State, but reaching boldly across the line into other States. When at the zenith of its prosperity, it is estimated there were 60,000 members of the order in Arkansas. This was too tempting a prospect for the busy political demagogues, and to the amazement of the better men in the society, they soon awoke to the fact that they were in the hands of the wily politicians. It is now estimated that the ranks in Arkansas are reduced to 20,000 or less—all for political causes. The movement now is to purge the society of politics and in the near future to meet the Farmer's Alliance in St. Louis, and form a combination of the two societies. It is hoped by this arrangement to avoid the demagogues hereafter, and at the same time form a strong and permanent society, which will answer the best interests of the farming community.

As stated elsewhere, the location of a capital for Arkansas early occupied the attention of its citizens. On November 20, 1821, William Russell and others laid off and platted Little Rock as the future capital of the Territory and State. They made a plat and a bill of assurances thereto, subdividing the same into lots and blocks. They granted to Pulaski County Lots 3 and 4 in trust and on the conditions following, viz.: "That the said county of Pulaski within two years" should erect a common jail upon said Lots 3 and 4. Out of this transaction grew a great deal of litigation. The first jail was built of pine logs in 1823. It stood until 1837, when it was burned, and a brick building was erected in its stead. This stood for many years, but through the growth of the city, it in time became a public nuisance and was condemned, and the location moved to the present site of the stone jail.

The Territory was organized by Congress in 1819, and the seat of government located at the Post of Arkansas. In the early part of 1820 arose the question of a new site for the seat of government, and all eyes turned to Pulaski County. A capital syndicate was formed and Little Rock Bluff fixed upon as the future capital. The one trouble was that the land at this point was not yet in market, and so the company secured "sunk land scrip" and located this upon the selected town site. The west line of the Quapaw Indian reservation struck the Arkansas River at "the Little Rock" and therefore the east line of the contemplated capital had to be west of this Quapaw line. This town survey "west of the point of rocks, immediately south of the Arkansas River, and west of the Quapaw line," was surveyed and returned to the recorder at St. Louis as the new town site and Territorial capital—called Little Rock. The dedication of the streets, etc., and the plat as laid off, was dated November 10, 1821. Grounds were given for a State house, and other public buildings and purposes, and for "the permanent seat of justice of said county (Pulaski)" was dedicated an entire half square, "bounded on the north by Markham Street and on the west by Spring Street and on the south by Cherry (now Second) Street" for court house purposes. In return the county was to erect a court house and jail on the lots specified for these purposes, "within ten years from the date hereof." A market house was to be erected by the city on Lots 4 and 5, Block 99. The latter in time was built on these lots, the upper story containing a council chamber, which was in public use until 1864, when the present city hall was erected.

By an act of the legislature, October 24, 1821, James Billingsly, Crawford County, Samuel C. Roane, Clark County, and Robert Bean, Independence County, were appointed commissioners, "to fix on a proper place for the seat of justice of the County of Pulaski;" the act further specifying "they shall take into consideration donations and future divisions." The latter part of the sentence is made still more important by the fact that at that time the western boundary of Pulaski County was 100 miles west, at the mouth of Petit Jean, and the eastern boundary was a few miles below Pine Bluff.

October 18, 1820, the Territorial seat of government was removed from the Post of Arkansas to the Little Rock, the act to take effect June 1, 1821. It provided "that there shall be a bond * * * for the faithful performance of the promise and good faith by which the seat of government is moved."

In November, 1821, about the last of the belongings of the Territorial capital at the Post were removed to Little Rock. It was a crossing point on the river of the government road leading to Missouri, and the place had often been designated as the "Missouri Crossing," but the French had generally called it Arkapolis.

During the short time the Territorial capital was at Arkansas Post, no effort was made to erect public buildings, as from the first it was understood this was but a temporary location. When the capital came to Little Rock a one-story double log house was built, near the spot where is now the Presbyterian Church, or near the corner of Scott and Fifth Streets. This building was in the old style of two rooms, with an open space between, but all under the same roof. In 1826 the log building was superseded by a one-story frame. March 2, 1831, Congress authorized the Territory to select ten sections of land and appropriate the same toward erecting capitol buildings; and in 1832 it empowered the governor to lease the salt springs. With these different funds was erected the central building of the present capitol, the old representative hall being where is now the senate chamber. In 1836, when Arkansas became a State, there was yet no plastering in any part of the brick building, and in the assembly halls were plain pine board tables and old fashioned split bottomed chairs, made in Little Rock.

In 1886, at the remarkably small cost of $35,000, were added the additions and improvements and changes in the capitol building, completing it in its present form. And if the same wisdom controls the State in the future that has marked the past, especially in the matter of economy in its public buildings, there will be only a trifling additional expenditure on public buildings during the next half century. The State buildings are sufficient for all public needs; their plainness and cheapness are a pride and glory, fitting monuments to the past and present generation of rulers and law makers, testifying to their intelligence and integrity.

The State library was started March 3, 1838, at first solely as a reference and exchange medium. It now has an annual allowance of $100, for purchasing books and contains 25,000 volumes, really more than can suitably be accommodated.

The Supreme Court library was established in January, 1851. It has 8,000 volumes, including all the reports and the leading law works. The fees of attorneys' license upon admission to the bar, of ten dollars, and a dollar docket fee in each case in court, constitute the fund provided for the library.

The State Medical Society, as now constituted, was formed in May, 1875. It held its fourteenth annual session in 1889, at Pine Bluff. Edward Bentley is the acting president, and L. P. Gibson, secretary. Subordinate societies are formed in all parts of the State and are represented by regular delegates in the general assemblies. In addition to the officers for the current year above given are Z. Orts, assistant secretary, A. J. Vance, C. S. Gray, B. Hatchett and W. H. Hill, vice presidents in the order named.

The State Board of Health was established by act of the legislature, March 23, 1881. It is composed of six commissioners, appointed by the governor, "a majority of whom are to be medical graduates and of seven years' practice in the profession." The board is required to meet once in every three months. The secretary is allowed a salary of $1,000 per annum, but the others receive no compensation except traveling expenses in the discharge of official duties.

The present board is composed of Dr. A. L. Breysacher, president; Dr. Lorenzo R. Gibson, secretary; Doctors J. A. Dibrell, P. Van Patton, W. A. Cantrell and V. Brunson.

The beginning which resulted in the present elegant State institution for deaf mutes was a school established near the close of the late war, in Little Rock, by Joseph Mount, an educated mute, who gathered a few of these unfortunate ones together and taught a private school. The State legislature incorporated the school and made a small provision for it, July 17, 1868, the attendance that year being four pupils. The buildings are on the beautiful hill just west of the Union Depot, the improvement of the grounds being made in 1869. The attendance in 1870 was 43 pupils, which in the last session's report, 1888, reached the number of 109; and the superintendent, anticipating an attendance for the current two years of 150, has solicited appropriations accordingly.

The board of trustees of the Deaf Mute Institute includes: Hon. George E. Dodge, president; Col. S. L. Griffith, vice-president; Maj. R. H. Parham, Jr., secretary; Hon. W. E. Woodruff, treasurer; Maj. George H. Meade and Col. A. R. Witt. The officers are: Principal, Francis D. Clarke; instructors: John W. Michaels, Mrs. I. H. Carroll, Miss Susan B. Harwood, Miss Kate P. Brown, Miss Emma Wells, S. C. Bright; teacher of articulation, Miss Lottie Kirkland. Mrs. M. M. Beattie is matron; Miss Lucinda Nations, assistant; Miss Clara Abbott, supervises the sewing, and Mrs. Amanda Harley is housekeeper. The visiting physician is J. A. Dibrell, Jr., M. D.; foreman of the printing office, T. P. Clarke; foreman of the shoe shop, U. G. Dunn. Of the total appropriations asked for the current two years, $80,970, $16,570 is for improvements in buildings, grounds, school apparatus, or working departments.

The Arkansas School for the Blind was incorporated by act of the legislature, February 4, 1859, and opened to pupils the same year in Arkadelphia. In the year of 1868 it was removed to Little Rock, and suitable grounds purchased at the foot of Center Street, on Eighteenth Street.

This is not an asylum for the aged and infirm, nor a hospital for the treatment of disease, but a school for the young of both sexes, in which are taught literature, music and handcraft Pupils between six and twenty-six years old are received, and an oculist for the purpose of treating pupils is a part of its benefits; no charge is made for board or tuition, but friends are expected to furnish clothing and traveling expenses.

It is estimated there are 300 blind of school age in the State. The legislature has appropriated $140 a year for each pupil. On this allowance in two years the steward reported a balance unexpended of $1,686.84. In 1886 was appropriated $6,000 to build a workshop, store-room, laundry and bake-oven. In 1860 the attendance was ten—five males and five females; in 1862, seven males and six females. The year 1888 brought the attendance up to fifty males and fifty-two females, or a total of 102. During the last two years six have graduated here—three in the industrial department, and three in the industrial and literary department. Four have been dismissed on account of recovered eyesight.

The trustees of the school are: J. R. Rightsell, S. M. Marshall, W. C. Ratcliffe, J. W. House, and D. G. Fones; the superintendent being John H. Dye.

Another commendable institution, carefully providing for the welfare of those dethroned of reason, is the Arkansas State Lunatic Asylum, which was authorized by act of the legislature of 1873, when suitable grounds were purchased, and highly improved, and buildings erected. The institution is three miles west of the capitol and one-half mile north of the Mount Ida road. Eighty acres of ground were originally purchased and enclosed and are now reaching a high state of improvement. The resident population of the asylum at present is 500 souls, and owing to the crowded conditions an additional eighty acres were purchased in 1887, making in all 160 acres. A careful inquiry shows there are in the State (and not in the asylum, for want of room) 198 insane persons, entitled under the law to the benefits of the institution. Of the 411 patients in the asylum in 1888, only four were pay patients.

John G. Fletcher, R. K. Walker, A. L. Breysacher, John D. Adams and William J. Little are trustees of the institution, while Dr. P. O. Hooper is superintendent.

In 1885 the legislature made an appropriation of $92,500 for the erection of additional buildings and other needed improvements. This fund was not all used, but the remainder was returned into the State treasury. The total current expenses for the year 1887 aggregated $45,212.60. The current expenses on patients the same year were $29,344.80. The comfort of the unfortunates—the excellence of the service, the wholesome food given them, and at the same time the minimum cost to the tax payers, prove the highest possible commendation to those in charge.

The Arkansas Industrial University is the promise, if not the present fulfillment, of one of the most important of State institutions. It certainly deserves the utmost attention from the best people of the State, as it is destined to become in time one of the great universities of the world. It should be placed in position to be self-supporting, because education is not a public pauper and never can be permanently successful on charity. Any education to be had must be earned. This law of nature can no more be set aside than can the law of gravitation, and the ignorance of such a simple fact in statesmen and educators has cost our civilization its severest pains and penalties.

The industrial department of the institution was organized in June, 1885. The act of incorporation provided that all males should work at manual labor three hours each day and be paid therefor ten cents an hour. Seven thousand dollars was appropriated to equip the shops. Practical labor was defined to be not only farm and shop work, but also surveying, drawing and laboratory practice. Mechanical arts and engineering became a part of the curriculum. The large majority of any people must engage in industrial pursuits, and to these industrial development and enlightenment and comfort go hand-in-hand. Hence the real people's school is one of manual training. Schools of philosophy and literature will take care of themselves; think of a school (classical) endeavoring to train a Shakespeare or Burns! To have compelled either one of these to graduate at Oxford would have been like clipping the wings of the eagle to aid his upward flight. In the education at least of children nature is omnipotent and pitiless, and it is the establishment of such training schools as the Arkansas Industrial University that gives the cheering evidence of the world's progress. In its continued prosperity is hope for the near future; its failure through ignorance or bigotry in the old and worn out ideas of the dead past, will go far toward the confirmation of the cruel cynicism that the most to be pitied animal pell-melled into the world is the new-born babe.

The University is situated at Fayetteville, Washington County. It was organized by act of the legislature, based on the "Land Grant Act" of Congress of 1862, and supplemented by liberal donations from the State, the County of Washington, and the city of Fayetteville. The school was opened in 1872. March 30, 1877, the legislature passed the act known as the "Barker Bill," which made nearly a complete change in the purview of the school and brought prominently forward the agricultural and mechanical departments. "To gratify our ambitious" [but mistaken] "youth," says the prospectus, "we have, under Section 7 of the act, provided for instruction in the classics."

Under the act of Congress known as the "Hatch Bill," an Agricultural Experimental Station has been organized. Substantial buildings are now provided, and the cost of board in the institution is reduced to $8 per month. The attendance at the present time is ninety-six students, and steps are being taken to form a model stock-farm. The trustees, in the last report, say: "We recommend that girls be restored to the privileges of the institution." The law only excludes females from being beneficiaries, and females may still attend as pay students.

A part of the University is a branch Normal School, established at Pine Bluff, for the purpose of educating colored youth to be school teachers. These Normal Schools have for some years been a favorite and expensive hobby in most of the Northern States. There is probably no question that, for the promotion of the cause of education among the negroes, they offer unusual attractions.

The following will give the reader a clear comprehension of the school and its purposes. Its departments are:

Mechanic arts and engineering, agriculture, experiment station, practical work, English and modern languages, biology and geology, military science and tactics, mathematics and logic, preparatory department, drawing and industrial art, and music.

To all these departments is now added the medical department, located at Little Rock. This branch was founded in 1871, and has a suitable building on Second Street. The tenth annual course of lectures in this institution commenced October 3, 1888; the tenth annual commencement being held March 8, 1889. The institution is self-supporting, and already it ranks among the foremost medical schools in the country. The graduating class of 1888 numbered twenty.

The State Board of Visitors to the medical school are Doctors W. W. Hipolite, W. P. Hart, W. B. Lawrence, J. M. Keller, I. Folsom.

The debt of Arkansas is not as large as a cursory glance at the figures might indicate. The United States government recently issued a statistical abstract concerning the public debt of this State that is very misleading, and does it a great wrong. In enumerating the debts of the States it puts Arkansas at $12,029,100. This error comes of including the bonds issued for railroad and levee purposes, that have been decided by the Supreme Court null and void, to the amount of nearly $10,000,000. They are therefore no part of the State indebtedness.

The real debt of the State is $2,111,000, including principal and accumulated interest. There is an amount in excess of this, if there is included the debt due the general government, but for all such the State has counter claims, and it is not therefore estimated in giving the real indebtedness.

CHAPTER VIII.

The Bench and Bar—An Analytic View of the Profession of Law—Spanish and French Laws—English Common Law—The Legal Circuit Riders—Territorial Law and Lawyers—The Court Circuits—Early Court Officers—The Supreme Court—Prominent Members of the State Bench and Bar—The Standard of the Execution of Law in the State.

> Laws do not put the least restraint
> Upon our freedom, but maintain 't;
> Or if they do, 'tis for our good,
> To give us freer latitude;
> For wholesome laws preserve us free
> By stinting of our liberty.—*Butler.*

THE Territory when under Spanish or French rule was governed by much the same laws and customs. The home government appointed its viceroys, who were little more than nominally under the control of the king, except in the general laws of the mother country. The necessary local provisions in the laws were not strictly required to be submitted for approval to the master powers before being enforced in the colony. Both governments were equally liberal in bestowing the lands upon subjects, and as a rule, without cost. But the shadow of feudal times still lingered over each of them, and they had no conception that the real people would want to be small landholders, supposing that in the new as in the old world they would drift into villanage, and in some sense be a part of the possession of the landed aristocracy. Hence, these governments are seen taking personal charge as it were of the colonies; providing them masters and protectors, who, with government aid, would transport and in a certain sense own them and their labor after their arrival. The grantee of certain royal rights and privileges in the new world was responsible to the viceroy for his colony, and the viceroy to the king. The whole was anti-democratic of course, and was but the continued and old, old idea of "the divine rights of rulers."

The commentaries of even the favorite lawwriters to-day in this democratic country are blurred on nearly every page with that monstrous heresy, "the king can do no wrong"—the governing power is infallible, it needs no watching, no jealous eye that will see its errors or its crimes; a fetich to be blindly worshiped, indiscriminately, whether it is an angel of mercy or a monster of evil. When Cannibal was king he was a god, with no soul to dictate to him the course he pursued. "The curiosities of patriotism under adversity" just here suggests itself as a natural title-page to one of the most remarkable books yet to be written.

The bench and bar form a very peculiar result

of modern civilization—to-day fighting the most heroic battles for the poor and the oppressed; tomorrow, perhaps, expending equal zeal and eloquence in the train of the bloody usurper and tyrant. As full of inconsistencies as insincerity itself, it is also as noted for as wise, conservative and noble efforts in behalf of our race as ever distinguished patriot or sage.

The dangers which beset the path of the lawyer are a blind adherence to precedent, and a love of the abstruse technicalities of the law practice. When both or either of these infirmities enter the soul of the otherwise young and rising practitioner, his usefulness to his fellow man is apt to be permanently impaired. He may be the "learned judge," but will not be the great and good one.

The history of the bench and bar should be an instructive one. The inquirer, commencing in the natural order of all real history, investigating the cause or the fountain source, and then following up the effects flowing from causes, is met at the threshold with the question, Why? What natural necessity created this vast and expensive supernumerary of civilization? The institution in its entirety is so wide and involved, so comprehensive and expensive, with its array of court officials, great temples, its robes, ermine and wool-sacks; its halls, professors, schools and libraries, that the average mind is oppressed with the attempt to grasp its outlines. In a purely economic sense it produces not one blade of grass. After having elucidated this much of the investigation as best he can, he comes to a minor one, or the details of the subject. For illustration's sake, let it be assumed that he will then take up the consideration of grand juries, their origin, history and present necessity for existence. These are mere hints, but such as will arrest the attention of the student of law of philosophical turn of mind. They are nothing more than the same problems that come in every department of history. The school of the lawyer is to accept precedent, the same as it is a common human instinct to accept what comes to him from the fathers—assuming everything in its favor and combating everything that would dispute "the old order." It is the exceptional mind which looks ancient precedent in the face and asks questions, Whence? Why? Whither? These are generally inconvenient queries to indolent content, but they are the drive-wheels of moving civilization.

One most extraordinary fact forever remains, namely, that lawyers and statesmen never unfolded the science of political economy. This seems a strange contradiction, but nevertheless it is so. The story of human and divine laws is much alike. The truths have not been found, as a rule, by the custodians of the temples. The Rev. Jaspers are still proclaiming "the world do move." Great statesmen are still seriously regulating the nation's "balance of trade," the price of interest on money, and through processes of taxation enriching peoples, while the dear old precedents have for 100 years been demonstrated to be myths. They are theoretically dead with all intelligent men, but are very much alive in fact. Thus the social life of every people is full of most amusing curiosities, many of them harmless, many that are not.

The early bench and bar of Arkansas produced a strong and virile race of men. The pioneers of this important class of community possessed vigorous minds and bodies, with lofty ideals of personal honor, and an energy of integrity admirably fitted to the tasks set before them.

The law of the land, the moment the Louisiana purchase was effected, was the English common law, that vast and marvelous structure, the growth of hundreds of years of bloody English history, and so often the apparent throes of civilization.

The circuit riders composed the first bench and bar here, as in all the western States. In this State especially the accounts of the law practice—the long trips over the wide judicial circuits; the hardships endured, the dangers encountered from swollen streams ere safe bridges spanned them; the rough accommodations, indeed, sometimes the absence of shelter from the raging elements, and amid all this their jolly happy-go-lucky life, their wit and fun, their eternal electioneering, for every lawyer then was a politician; their quickened wits and schemes and devices to advantage each other, both in and out of the courts, if all could be told in detail, would read like a fascinating romance. These riders often traveled in companies of from three to fifteen, and among them would be found the college and law-school graduates, and the brush graduates, associated in some cases and opposed in others. And here, as in all the walks of life, it was often found that the rough, self educated men overmatched the graduates in their fiercest contests. While one might understand more of the books and of the learned technicalities of law, the other would know the jury best, and overthrow his antagonist. In the little old log cabin court rooms of those days, when the court was in session, the contest of the legal gladiators went on from the opening to the closing of the term. Generally the test was before a jury, and the people gathered from all the surrounding country, deeply interested in every movement of the actors. This was an additional stimulus to the lawyer politicians, who well understood that their ability was gauged by the crowd, as were their successes before the jury. Thus was it a combination of the forum and "stump." Here, sometimes in the conduct of a noted case, a seat in Congress would be won or lost. A seat in Congress, or on the "wool sack," was the ambition of nearly every circuit rider. Their legal encounters were fought out to the end. Each one was dreadfully in earnest—he practiced no assumed virtues in the struggle; battling as much at least for himself as his client, he would yield only under compulsion, even in the minor points, and, unfortunately, sometimes in the heat of ardor, the contest would descend from a legal to a personal one, and then the handy duello code was a ready resort. It seems it was this unhappy mixture of law and politics that caused many of these bloody personal encounters. In the pure practice of the law, stripped of political bearings, there seldom, if ever, came misunderstandings.

They must have been a fearless and earnest class of men to brave the hardships of professional life, as well as mastering the endless and involved intricacies of the legal practice of that day. The law then was but little less than a mass of unmeaning technicalities. A successful practitioner required to have at his fingers' ends at least Blackstone's Commentaries and Chitty's Pleadings, and much of the wonders contained in the Rules of Evidence. Libraries were then scarce and their privations here were nearly as great as in the common comforts for "man and beast." There have been vast improvements in the simplifying of the practice, the abolition of technical pleadings especially, since that time, and the young attorney of to-day can hardly realize what it was the pioneers of his profession had to undergo.

A judicial circuit at that early day was an immense domain, over which the bench and bar regularly made semi-annual trips. Sometimes they would not more than get around to their starting point before it would be necessary to go all over the ground again. Thus the court was almost literally "in the saddle." The saddle-bags were their law offices, and some of them, upon reaching their respective county-seats, would signalize their brief stays with hard work all day in the court-room and late roystering at the tavern bar at night, regardless of the demurrers, pleas, replications, rejoinders and sur-rejoinders, declarations and bills that they knew must be confronted on the morrow. Among these jolly sojourners, "during court week" in the villages, dignity and circumspection were often given over exclusively to the keeping of the judge and prosecutor. Circumstances thus made the bench and bar as social a set as ever came together. To see them returning after their long journeyings, sunburned and weatherbeaten, having had but few advantages of the laundry or bathtub, they might have passed for a returning squad of cavalry in the late war. One eccentric character made it a point never to start with any relays to his wardrobe. When he reached home after his long pilgrimage it would be noticed that his clothes had a stuffed appearance. The truth was that when clean linen was needed he bought new goods and slipped them on over the soiled ones. He would often tell how he dreaded the return to his home, as he knew that after his wife attended to his change of wardrobe he was "most sure to catch cold."

On one occasion two members of the bar met at a county seat where court was in session a week. They had come from opposite directions, one of them riding a borrowed horse seventy miles, while the other on his own horse had traveled over 100 miles. Upon starting home they unwittingly exchanged horses, and neither discovered the mistake until informed by friends after reaching their destination. The horses could hardly have been more dissimilar, but the owners detected no change. It was nearly the value of the animals to make the return exchange, yet each set out, and finally returned with the proper horse. No little ingenuity must have been manifested in finally unraveling the great mystery of the affair.

Surrounded as they were with all these ill conditions, as a body of men they were nevertheless learned in the law, great in the forum, able and upright on the bench. Comparisons are odious, but it is nothing in disparagement to the present generation of courts and lawyers, to say that to be equally great and worthy with these men of the early bench and bar of Arkansas, is to exalt and ennoble the profession in the highest degree.

Sixty years have now passed since the first coming of the members of this calling to the State of Arkansas. In 1819 President Monroe appointed James Miller, governor, Robert Crittenden, secretary, and Charles Jouitt, Andrew Scott and Robert P. Letcher, judges of the Superior Court, for the new Territory of Arkansas. All these, it seems, except Gov. Miller, were promptly at the post of duty and in the discharge of their respective offices. In the absence of Mr. Miller, Mr. Crittenden was acting governor. These men not only constituted the first bench and bar, but the first Territorial officials and the first legislature. They were all located in the old French town of Arkansas Post. The lawyers and judges were the legislative body, which enacted the laws to be enforced in their respective districts. At their first legislative session they established but five statute laws, and from this it might be inferred that there were few and simple laws in force at that time, but the reader will remember that from the moment of the Louisiana purchase all the new territory passed under the regulation and control of the English common law—substantially the same system of laws then governing England.

It is a singular comment on American jurisprudence that this country is still boasting the possession of the English habeas corpus act, wrung by those sturdy old barons from King John,—a government by the people, universal suffrage, where the meanest voter is by his vote also a sovereign, and therefore he protects himself against —whom?—why, against himself by the English habeas corpus act, which was but the great act of a great people that first proclaimed a higher right than was the "divine right of kings." When these old Englishmen presented the alternative to King John, the writ or the headsman's ax, he very sensibly chose the lesser of the two great inconveniences. And from that moment the vital meaning of the phrase "the divine right of kings" was dead in England.

In America, where all vote, the writ of habeas corpus has been time and time again suspended, and there are foolish men now who would gladly resort to this untoward measure, for the sake of party success in elections. There is no language of tongue or pen that can carry a more biting sarcasm on our boasted freemen or free institutions than this almost unnoticed fact in our history.

One of the acts of the first legislative session held in August, 1819, was to divide the Territory into two judicial circuits. As elsewhere stated, the counties of Arkansas and Lawrence constituted the First circuit; Pulaski, Clark and Hempstead Counties forming the Second.

The judges of the Superior Courts were assigned to the duties of the different circuits. At the first real Territorial legislature, composed of representatives elected by the people, the Territory was divided into three judicial circuits. The courts, however, for the different circuits, were all held at the Territorial capital. There was no circuit riding, therefore, at this time.

Judicial circuits and judges residing therein were not a part of judiciary affairs until 1823. The judges of the First circuit from that date, with time of appointment and service, were: T. P. Eskridge,

December 10, 1823; Andrew Scott, April 11, 1827; Sam C. Roane, April 17, 1829-36. The list of prosecuting attorneys includes: W. B. R. Horner, November 1, 1823; Thomas Hubbard, November 5, 1828, to February 15, 1832; G. D. Royston, September 7, 1833; Shelton Watson, October 4, 1835; A. G. Stephenson, January 23, 1836.

Of the Second circuit the judges were: Richard Searcy, December 10, 1823, and J. W. Bates, November, 1825, to 1836; while the prosecuting attorneys were R. C. Oden, November 1, 1823; A. H. Sevier, January 19, 1824 (resigned); Sam C. Roane, September 26, 1826; Bennett H. Martin, January 30, 1831; Absalom Fowler, ———; D. L. F. Royston, July 25, 1835; Townsend Dickinson, November 1, 1823; A. F. May, March 29, 1825 (died in office); W. H. Parrott, April 21, 1827; S. S. Hall, August 31, 1831; J. W. Robertson, September 17, 1833; E. B. Ball, July 19, 1836.

Samuel S. Hall was judge of the Third circuit, serving from December, 1823, to 1836. As prosecuting attorneys, are found the names of T. Dickinson, January 10, 1823; A. D. G. Davis, June 21, 1829; S. G. Sneed, November 11, 1831; David Walker, September 13, 1833; Thomas Johnson, October 4, 1835; W. F. Denton, January 23, 1836.

The appointment of Charles Caldwell as judge of the Fourth circuit dates from December 27, 1828; while E. T. Clark, February 13, 1830; J. C. P. Tolleson, February 1, 1831; and W. K. Sebastian, from January 25, 1833, served as prosecuting attorneys.

The Supreme Court of Arkansas has ever comprised among its members men of dignity, wisdom and keen legal insight. The directory of these officials contains the names of many of those whose reputation and influence are far more than local. It is as follows:

Chief justices: Daniel Ringo, 1836; Thomas Johnson, 1844; George C. Watkins, 1852 (resigned); E. H. English, 1854 (also Confederate); T. D. W. Yonley, 1864 (Murphy constitution); E. Baxter, 1864 (under Murphy regimè); David Walker, 1866 (ousted by military); W. W. Wilshire, 1868 (removed); John McClure, 1871, (removed); E. H. English, 1874. Sterling R. Cockrill is present chief justice

Associate justices: Thomas J. Lacey, 1836; Townsend Dickinson, 1836; George W. Paschal, 1842; W. K. Sebastian, 1843; W. S. Oldham, 1845; Edward Cross, 1845; William Conway, 1846; C. C. Scott, 1848; David Walker, 1847 and 1874; Thomas B. Hanley, 1858 (resigned); F. I. Batson, 1858 (resigned); H. F. Fairchild, 1860 (died); Albert Pike, 1861 (also Confederate); J. J. Clendenin, 1866 (ousted); T. M. Bowen, 1868; L. Gregg, 1868; J. E. Bennett, 1871; M. L. Stephenson, 1872; E. J. Searle, 1872; W. M. Harrison, 1874; J. T. Bearden, 1874 (appointed); Jesse Turner, 1878; J. R. Eakin, 1878; W. W. Smith, 1882; B. B. Battle, 1885, re-elected. By law three additional judges were elected April 2, 1889: Simon B. Hughes, W. E. Hemingway and Mont. H. Sandels.

Reporters: Albert Pike, N. W. Cox, E. H. English, J. M. Moore, L. E. Barber, B. D. Turner and W. W. Mansfield (present incumbent).

Clerks: H. Haralson, L. E. Barber, N. W. Cox, and W. P. Campbell (in office).

Special chief justices: William Story, F. W. Compton, J. L. Witherspoon, S. H. Hempstead, C. B. Moore, Thomas Johnson, R. A. Howard, George A. Gallagher, B. B. Battle, Sam W. Williams, A. B. Williams, G. N Cousin, Isaac Strain, N. Haggard, Edward Cross, R. C. S. Brown, L. A. Pindall, Sam C. Roane, George Conway, Sackfield Macklinin, John Whytock, C. C. Farrelley, W. W. Smith, W. I. Warwick, B. B. Morse, B. D. Turner, George W. Caruth, S. H. Harrington.

In this list are the names of nearly all early members of the Arkansas bar. Commencing here as young attorneys in their profession, many of them have left illustrious names—names that adorn the history of the State and Nation, and time will not dim nor change the exalted esteem now given them. Not one of them but that was an example of that wonderful versatility of American genius—the young lawyer becoming great in the practice of his profession in the wild wood; or celebrated on the bench for decisions that came to the world like beacon lights from the unknown land; or as senators holding civilized people spell-bound by their wisdom and eloquence; and all, at all times, listening for their country's call to play as conspicuous a part in camp and field as they had in the walks of civil life. To undertake all these things is not wonderful with a people so cosmopolitan as those of the west, but to be pre-eminent in each or all alike is most remarkable.

Of this brilliant galaxy of pioneer legal lights —giants indeed—there now remain as a connecting link with the present generation only the venerable Gen. Albert Pike, of Washington City, and Judge Jesse Turner, of Van Buren.

Writing in a reminiscent way of the bench and bar, Albert Pike says: "When I came to the bar there were William Cummins, Absalom Fowler, Daniel Ringo, Chester Ashley, and Samuel Hall, at Little Rock. I served on a jury in 1834 where Robert Crittenden was an attorney in the case; the judge was Benjamin Johnson, who died in December, 1834, at Vicksburg. Parrott and Oden died before I went to Little Rock. Judge William Trimble was an old member of the bar when I entered it, as was Col. Horner, of Helena. Thomas B. Hanley had recently come to Helena from Louisiana. I think Maj. Thomas Hubbard and George Conway were practicing at Washington in 1835. Judge Andrew Scott had been Territorial judge, but retired and lived in Pope County. Frederick W. Trapnall and John W. Cocke came from Kentucky to Little Rock in 1836, and also William C. Scott and his partner, Blanchard. I think Samuel H. Hempstead and John J. Clendenin came in 1836. John B. Floyd lived and practiced law in Chicot County." Gen. Pike further mentions Judge David Walker, John Linton, Judges Hoge and Sneed, John M. Wilson, Alfred W. Wilson, Archibald Yell, Judge Fowler, Judge Richard C. S. Brown, Bennett H. Martin, Philander Little, Jesse Turner and Sam W. Williams as among the eminent lawyers of the early courts of Arkansas.

The list of those who have occupied positions as circuit judges and prosecuting attorneys in the various circuits, will be found of equal interest with the names mentioned in connection with a higher tribunal. It is as below, the date affixed indicating the beginning of the term of service:

Judges of the First circuit: W. K. Sebastian, November 19, 1840; J. C. P. Tolleson, February 8, 1843; John T. Jones, December 2, 1842; Mark W. Alexander, ———; George W. Beasley, September 6, 1855; C. W. Adams, November 2, 1852; Thomas B. Hanley, ———; E. C. Bronough, August 25, 1858; O. H. Oates, March 3, 1859; E. C. Bronough, August 23, 1860; Jesse M. Houks, September 17, 1865; John E. Bennett, July 23, 1868; C. C. Waters, February 23, 1871; M. L. Stephenson, March 24, 1871; W. H. H. Clayton, March 10, 1873; J. N. Cypert, October 31, 1874; M. T. Saunders, October 30, 1882. Prosecuting attorneys: W. S. Mosley, November 14, 1840; A. J. Greer, November 9, 1841; S. S. Tucker, January 20, 1840; Alonzo Thomas, August 5, 1842; W. N. Stanton, December 2, 1842; N. M. Foster, December 4, 1843; A. H. Ringo, March 2, 1849; H. A. Badham, March 12, 1851; L. L. Mack, September 6, 1855; S. W. Childress, August 30, 1856; Lincoln Featherstone, August 23, 1860; Z. P. H. Farr, December 1, 1862; B. C. Brown, January 7, 1865; P. O. Thweat, October 15, 1866; C. B. Fitzpatrick, March 16, 1871; W. H. H. Clayton, March 23, 1871; Eugene Stephenson, April 23, 1873; C. A. Otey, October 31, 1874; D. D. Leach, October 13, 1876; P. D. McCulloch (three terms); Greenfield Quarles, October 30, 1884; S. Brundridge, October 30, 1886.

Judges of the Second circuit: Isaac Baker, November 23, 1840; John C. Murray, August 18, 1851; W. H. Sutton, January 11, 1845; John C. Murray, August 22, 1858; Josiah Gould, February 26, 1849; W. M. Harrison, May 17, 1865; T. F. Sorrells, August 22, 1853; W. C. Hazeldine, April 14, 1871; J. F. Lowery, December 12, 1863; L. L. Mack, October 31, 1874; William Story, July 23, 1868; W. F. Henderson, April 26, 1874; J. G. Frierson, October 31, 1882; W. A. Case, vice Frierson, deceased, March 17, 1884, elected September 1, 1884; J. E. Riddick, October 30, 1886. Prosecuting attorneys: John S. Roane, November 15, 1840; Samuel Wooly, September 19, 1842; J. W. Bocage, November 20,

1843; S. B. Jones, April 20, 1846; T. F. Sorrells, February 26, 1849; W. P. Grace, August 22, 1853; S. F. Arnett, August 23, 1856; D. W. Carroll, August 30, 1860; C. C. Godden, May 17, 1865; W. F. Slemmons, October 15, 1866; D. D. Leach, December 16, 1868; R. H. Black, May 6, 1873; J. E. Riddick, October 13, 1876; W. A. Cate, October 14, 1878; E. F. Brown, May 5, 1870; W. B. Edrington (four terms), October 30, 1880; J. D. Block, October, 1888.

Judges of the Third circuit: Thomas Johnson, November 13, 1840; William Conway, November 15, 1844; W. C. Scott, December 11, 1846; R. H. Nealy, February 28, 1851; W. C. Bevins, August 23, 1856; W. R. Cain, August 23, 1860; L. L. Mack, March 15, 1866; Elisha Baxter, July 23, 1868; James W. Butler, March 10, 1873; William Byers, October 30, 1874; R. H. Powell (three terms), October 30, 1882; J. W. Butler, May, 1887. Prosecuting attorneys: N. Haggard, November 30, 1840; S. S. Tucker, January 20, 1842; S. H. Hempstead, February, 1842; A. R. Porter, December 2, 1842; S. C. Walker, December 2, 1846; J. H. Byers, March 5, 1849; W. K. Patterson, August 30, 1856; F. W. Desha, August 30, 1860; L. L. Mack, July 8, 1861; T. J. Ratcliff, July 9, 1865; M. D. Baber, October 15, 1866; W. A. Inman, December 8, 1868; J. L. Abernathy, October 31, 1874; Charles Coffin, October 14, 1878; M. N. Dyer (two terms), October 30, 1882; W. B. Padgett, October 30, 1886; J. L. Abernathy, October, 1888.

Judges of the Fourth circuit: J. M. Hoge, November 13, 1840; S. G. Sneed, November 18, 1844; A. B. Greenwood, March 3, 1851; F. I. Batson, August 20, 1853; J. M. Wilson, February 21, 1859; J. J. Green, August 23, 1860; Y. B. Sheppard, May 9, 1863; Thomas Boles, August 3, 1865; W. N. May, April 24, 1868; M. L. Stephenson, July 23, 1868; C. B. Fitzpatrick, March 23, 1871; J. Huckleberry, April 10, 1872; J. M. Pittman, October 31, 1874; J. H. Berry, October 21, 1878; J. M. Pittman (three terms), October 31, 1882. Prosecuting attorneys: Alfred M. Wilson, November 13, 1840; A. B. Greenwood, January 4, 1845; H. F. Thomasson, September 6, 1853; Lafayette Gregg, August 23, 1856; B. J. Brown, December 1, 1862; J. E. Cravens, January 7, 1865; Squire Boon, October 15, 1866; Elias Harrell, August 11, 1868; S. W. Peel, April 26, 1873; E. I. Stirman, October 13, 1876; H. A. Dinsmore (three terms), October 14, 1878; J. Frank Wilson, October 30, 1884; J. W. Walker, October 30, 1866; S. M. Johnson, October 30, 1888.

Judges of the Fifth circuit: J. J. Clendenin, December 28, 1840; W. H. Field, December 24, 1846; J. J. Clendenin, September 6, 1854; Liberty Bartlett, November 12, 1854; E. D. Ham, July 23, 1868; Benton J. Brown, September 30, 1874; W. W. Mansfield, October 31, 1874; Thomas W. Pound, September 9, 1878; W. D. Jacoway, October 31, 1878; G. S. Cunningham (three terms), October 31, 1882. Prosecuting attorneys: R. W. Johnson, December 29, 1840; George C. Watkins, January 11, 1845; J. J. Clendenin, February 17, 1849, to 1854; J. L. Hollowell, September 8, 1858, to 1860; Sam W. Williams, May 10, 1860; Pleasant Jordan, September 7, 1861; Sam W. Williams, July 6, 1863; John Whytock, December 19, 1865; R. H. Dedman, October 15, 1866; N. J. Temple, August 15, 1868; Arch Young, August 24, 1872; Thomas Barnes, April 23, 1873; J. P. Byers, October 31, 1873; A. S. McKennon, October 14, 1878; J. G. Wallace (two terms), October 31, 1882; H. S. Carter, October 30, 1886.

Sixth circuit—judges: William Conway, December 19, 1840; John Field, February 3, 1843; George Conway, August 1, 1844; John Quillin, March 2, 1849; Thomas Hubbard, August 22, 1854; A. B. Smith, February 7, 1856; Shelton Watson, September 26, 1858; Len B. Green, April 5, 1858; A. B. Williams, January 28, 1865; J. T. Elliott, October 2, 1865; J. J. Clendenin, October 31, 1874; J. W. Martin, October 31, 1878; F. T. Vaughan, October 31, 1882; J. W. Martin, October 30, 1886. Prosecuting attorneys: G. D. Royston, November 11, 1840; O. F. Rainy, June 12, 1843; Isaac T. Tupper, January 18, 1844; A. W. Blevins, January 11, 1847; E. A. Warner, March 3, 1851; Orville Jennings, August 23, 1853; E. W. Gantt, August 22, 1854; James K. Young, August 30, 1860; Robert Carrigan, September 13,

1865; J. F. Ritchie, October 15, 1866; T. B. Gibson, January 11, 1868; Charles C. Reid, Jr., April 30, 1871; F. T. Vaughan, September 18, 1876; T. C. Trimble, September 30, 1878; F. T. Vaughan, September 30, 1880; T. C. Trimble, October 31, 1882; R. J. Lea, October 30, 1884; Gray Carroll, October 30, 1886; R. J. Lea, October 30, 1888.

Seventh circuit—judges: R. C. S. Brown, 1840; W. W. Floyd, November 30, 1846. (December 20, 1849, the State was re-districted into six circuits. Hence this was abolished for the time.) William Byers, July 8, 1861; R. H. Powell, May 11, 1866; John Whytock, July 23, 1868; J. J. Clendenin, May 29, 1874; Jabez M. Smith, October 31, 1874; J. P. Henderson (three terms), October 31, 1882. Prosecuting attorneys: John M. Wilson, November 20, 1840; J. M. Tebbetts, December 5, 1844; Elisha Baxter, December 7, 1861; W. B. Padgett, August 29, 1865; W. R. Coody, October 15, 1866; E. W. Gantt, July 31, 1868; J. M. Harrell, May 5, 1873; M. J. Henderson, October 31, 1874; James B. Wood, October 14, 1878; J. P. Henderson (three terms), October 31, 1882; W. H. Martin, October 30, 1888.

Eighth circuit—judges: C. C. Scott, December 2, 1846; William Davis, July 3, 1848 (abolished December 20, 1849); James D. Walker, July 25, 1861; Elias Harrell, May 8, 1865; William Story. March 27, 1867; E. J. Earle, July 23, 1868; T. G. T. Steele, February 23, 1873; L. J. Joyner, October 31, 1874; H. B. Stuart, October 31, 1878; R. D. Hearn, October 30, 1886. Prosecuting attorneys: Richard Lyons, February 5, 1847; N. W. Patterson, October 25, 1865; C. G. Reagan, January 7, 1865; J. C. Pratt, July 23, 1868; T. M. Gunter, October 15, 1866; Duane Thompson, January 4, 1874; George A. Kingston, July 26, 1871; J. D. McCabe, October 31, 1874; J. H. Howard, April 26, 1873; Rufus D. Hearn (three terms), July 6, 1874; Lafayette Gregg, November 13, 1862; W. M. Green (three terms), October 30, 1884.

Ninth circuit—judges: H. B. Stuart, November 28, 1862; W. N. Hargrave, ——, 1865; E. J. Searle, February 25, 1867; G. W. McCowan, July 23, 1868; J. T. Elliott, April 26, 1873; J. K. Young, October 31, 1874; C. F. Mitchell, October 31, 1882; L. A. Byrne, November 4, 1884; A. B. Williams, vice Mitchell, resigned, September 10, 1884; C. E. Mitchell, October 30, 1886. Prosecuting attorneys: A. J. Temple, July 8, 1861; A. T Craycraft, January 7, 1865; E. J. Searle, February 19, 1866; R. C. Parker, October 15, 1866; N. J. Temple, January 20, 1867; J. R. Page, January 9, 1869; J. M. Bradley, April 26, 1873; Dan W. Jones, October 31, 1874; B. W. Johnson, October 13, 1876; John Cook, October 14, 1880; T. F. Webber (four terms), October 31, 1882.

Judges of the Tenth circuit: H. P. Morse, July 23, 1868; D. W Carroll, October 28, 1874; T. F. Sorrells, October 31, 1874; J. M. Bradley, October 30, 1882; C. D. Wood, October 30, 1886. Prosecuting attorneys: J. McL. Barton, March 29, 1869; H. King White, April 20, 1871; M. McGehee, April 29, 1873; J. C. Barrow, October 31, 1874; C. D. Woods, October 30, 1882; M. L. Hawkins, vice Woods, October 10, 1886; R. C. Fuller, October 30, 1888.

Eleventh circuit—judges: J. W. Fox, April 30, 1873; H. N. Hutton, July 24, 1874; John A. Williams, October 31, 1874; X. J. Pindall, October 31, 1878; J. A. Williams (two terms), October 30, 1882. Prosecuting attorneys: H. M. McVeigh, April 26, 1873; Z. L. Wise, October 31, 1874; T. B. Martin, October 10, 1878; J. M. Elliott (five terms), October 10, 1880.

Twelfth circuit—judges: P. C. Dooley, April 26, 1873; J. H. Rogers, April 20, 1877; R. B. Rutherford, October 2, 1882; John S. Little, October 20, 1886. Prosecuting attorneys: D. D. Leach, April 26, 1873; John S. Little (three terms), April 2, 1877; A. C. Lewers (two terms), September 20, 1884; J. B. McDonough, October 30, 1888.

Thirteenth circuit—judges: M. D. Kent, April 26, 1873; B. F. Askew, October 30, 1882; C. W. Smith, October 30, 1886. Prosecuting attorneys: W. C. Langford, April 26, 1873; W. F. Wallace, June 5, 1883; H. P. Snead (three terms), October 30, 1884.

Fourteenth circuit—judges: George A. Kingston, April 26, 1873; R. H. Powell, May, 1887. Prosecuting attorneys: Duane Thompson, April 26, 1873; De Ross Bailey, May, 1887.

L. D. Belden was appointed judge of the Fifteenth circuit April 26, 1873, the prosecuting attorney being G. G. Lotta, elected April 23, 1873.

Sixteenth circuit—judge: Elisha Mears, April 26, 1873. Prosecuting attorneys: H. N. Withers, September 27, 1873; V. B. Shepard, April 30, 1874.

By an act of April 16, 1873, the State was divided into sixteen judicial circuits, but two years later a reduction to eleven in number was made.

CHAPTER IX.

THE LATE CIVIL WAR—ANALYTICAL VIEW OF THE TROUBLOUS TIMES—PASSAGE OF THE ORDINANCE OF SECESSION—THE CALL TO ARMS—THE FIRST TROOPS TO TAKE THE FIELD—INVASION OF THE STATE BY THE FEDERAL ARMY—SKETCHES OF THE REGIMENTS—NAMES OF OFFICERS—OUTLINE OF FIELD OPERATIONS—CLAIBOURNE AND YELL—EXTRACTS FROM PRIVATE MEMORANDA—EVACUATION OF THE STATE—RE-OCCUPATION—THE WAR OF 1812—THE MEXICAN WAR—STANDARD OF AMERICAN GENERALSHIP.

> The cannon's hush'd! nor drum nor clarion sound;
> Helmet and hauberk gleam upon the ground;
> Horsemen and horse lie weltering in their gore;
> Patriots are dead, and heroes dare no more;
> While solemnly the moonlight shrouds the plain,
> And lights the lurid features of the slain.—*Montgomery.*

ARKANSAS was not among the States that may be called leaders in inaugurating the late war. It only passed a secession ordinance May 6, 1861, nearly a month after hostilities had commenced, and Lincoln had issued his call for 75,000 ninety-day troops "to put down the rebellion." The reluctance with which the State finally joined its sister States is manifested by the almost unanimous refusal of the State convention, which met in March, 1861—the day Lincoln was inaugurated—and nearly unanimously voted down secession and passed a series of conservative resolutions, looking to a national convention to settle in some way the vexed question of slavery, and then voting a recess of the convention. When this re-assembled war was upon the country, and the ordinance of secession was passed, only, however, after full discussion, pro and con. There was but one vote against secession finally, and that was given by Isaac Murphy—afterward the military governor of Arkansas.

Local authorities received instructions to arm and equip forty regiments of State troops. The ruling minds of the State were averse to war, and resisted it until they were forced into the position of siding with their neighbors or with the Union cause. In the South, as in the North, there were inconsiderate hot-heads, who simply wanted war for war's sake—full of false pretexts, but eager for war with or without a pretext. These extremists of each party were, unconsciously, perhaps, but in fact, the two blades of the pair of scissors, to cut asunder the ties of the Union of States. Slavery, possibly not directly the cause of the war, was the handiest pretext seized upon at the time, with such disastrous results. In the dispensations of heaven, had the fanatics of the North and the fire-eaters of the South been hung across the clothes-line, as a boy sometimes hangs cats, and left in holy peace to fight it out, what a blessing for mankind it would have been!

The history of the late war cannot yet be written. Its most profound effects are not yet evolved. The actual fighting ceased nearly a generation ago, and the cruel strife is spoken of as over. It is the effects that true history observes. The chronicler records the dates and statistics, and files these away for the future historian. It is highly probable that there is no similar period in history where the truth will be so distorted as by him who tells "the story of the war."

Anyone can begin to see that there are many things now that were unknown before the war. Great changes are still being worked out, and whether or not yet greater ones are to come, no one knows. The abolitionists thirty years ago hated the slave owners,—the slave holders loved slavery. The former thought to forever end slavery on this continent by liberating the slaves, and now the once alarmed slave owner has discovered that the great benefits of the abolition of slavery have been to the whites far more than to the blacks.

There is little idea of what the real historian one hundred years from now will be compelled to say of these "blessed times." He will most probably smile in pity upon all this self-laudation and wild boast. If men could have known the effects to follow in all the important movements of peoples, it is highly probable there would have been no civil war. Those who "sectionally hated" may sleep quietly in their graves, because they died unconscious as to whether their supposed bloody revenge, driven hurtling at the enemy, was a bullet or a boomerang.

The Southern individual may look with envy to the pension fund now being poured out in Northern States, while, instead of this, he should only remember that the Southern soldier is making his way unaided in the world. It should not be forgotten that the rapid development of the South is sadly in want of the constant labor of thousands of immigrants, and that the New South is just entering upon a period of surprising and unexampled prosperity, which certainly must continue.

In Arkansas, as in Illinois, when Fort Sumter was fired on, instantly there was a storm of excitement to "let slip the dogs of war." Action took the place of argument. The best men in the community, those who had so long talked and pleaded against war, closed their mouths, and with sore hearts turned their eyes away from the sad outlook. The young and the inconsiderate seized the power to rule, and (though they knew it not) to ruin. Bells were rung, drums were beaten, and fifes made strident martial music, and people rushed into the streets. Open air meetings for the Confederate cause gathered, and songs and speeches inflamed the wildest passions of men. Poor men! they little recked the cruel fate into which they were plunging their country—not only themselves, but generations to come. A fifer and drummer marching along the streets, making harsh and discordant noises, were soon followed by crowds of men, women and children. Volunteers were called for by embryo captains, and from these crowds were soon recruited squads to be crystallized into armies with heavy tramp and flying banners—the noisy prologue to one of the bloodiest tragedies on which time has ever rung up the curtain.

The first official action of the State was that authorizing the raising and equipping of seven regiments. These were soon ready to report with full ranks. Seven regiments! Even after the war was well on foot, men were forming companies in hot haste, in fear that before they could reach the field of action the war would be over. And after they were mustered in and at their respective rendezvous, without uniforms and with sticks for guns, learning the rudiments of drill, they were restless, troubled seriously with the fear that they would never see or feel the glory of battle. The youths of the State had rushed to the recruiting stations with the eager thoughtlessness with which they would have put down their names for picnic, hunting or fishing expeditions, and the wild delights of a season of camp life. Perhaps to some came indistinct ideas of winning glory on the field and a triumphant return home, to be met by the happy smiles of a people saved—when the bells would ring and flowers be strewn in the highway.

The seven regiments first authorized by the military board (the board consisting of the governor, Col. Sam W. Williams and Col. B. C. Totten) had hardly been formed when more soldiers were wanted. Ten additional regiments were authorized, and of the ten seven were recruited and organized. Fourteen infantry regiments besides the cavalry and artillery had been a strong demand on the people, but the calls for men were increased. By voluntary enlistments twenty-one infantry regiments were finally in the field. Including cavalry and artillery, Arkansas had about 25,000 volunteer soldiery.

Then came the remorseless conscription. The glamour of soldiering was now all gone. Ragged, hungry, wounded and worn with hard marches, men had suffered the touch of the hand of the angel of destruction. The relentless conscripting went on. The number of years before old age exempted was lengthened, and the age of youth exempting was shortened, until as said by Gen. Grant, they were "robbing the cradle and the grave" to recruit their decimated ranks in the army.

There are no records now by which can be told the number of men Arkansas had in the Confederate army, but it is supposed by those best informed to have had nearly 40,000. In addition to this the State furnished soldiers to the Union army. In the history of wars it is doubtful if there is anything to exceed this in the heroic sacrifices of any people.

The original seven regiments were authorized as the first exuberant war expression of the State. They were State troops, armed and equipped by the State; but the fact is that the poorest men went into the army at their individual expense and armed and equipped themselves. This was the rule—not by men only who were fighting for their slave property, but largely by men who had never owned or expected to own a slave. When the Union army under Gen. Curtis was bearing down to invade Arkansas, ten more regiments were authorized and responded to this call, and seven additional regiments were raised and mustered into the State's service.

A military board had been provided for, consisting of three men, the governor and two advisors, who had a general supervision in organizing and equipping the army.

The first regiment raised in the State is known as the Pat Cleburne regiment. Patrick A. Cleburne, colonel, was soon made a general, and took his brigade east of the Mississippi River. The gallant and dashing leader was killed in the battle of Franklin, November 30, 1864. At the first call to arms he raised a company and named it the Yell Rifles, of which he was first captain, and on the formation of the first regiment he became colonel, rising up and up by rapid promotions to a major-generalship.

The names of Yell and Pat Cleburne are entwined closely in the hearts of the people of Arkansas. Yell was killed at the bloody battle of Buena Vista, Mexico, at the head of his charging column. The military lives and deaths of the two men were much alike. Their names and fames are secure in history. There is a touch of romance about Pat Cleburne's life in Arkansas. A Tipperary boy, of an excellent family, born in 1828, he had, when not more than sixteen years of age, joined the English army, where he was for more than a year before his whereabouts became known. His friends secured his release from the army, when he at once bade adieu to his native land and sailed for America. Stopping in 1849, a short time in Cincinnati, he was for a while a drug clerk. In 1859 he came to Helena, Ark., and engaged here also as a prescription clerk, in the meantime reading law; he was made a licensed attorney in 1856. In the bloody street affray soon after, between Hindman and Dorsey Rice, he was drawn into the fracas and was shot through the body by a brother of Rice's, who came upon the ground during the melée. The latter noticed the encounter, and seeing that Cleburne stood at one side, pistol in hand, fired. On turning to see who had shot him, Cleburne saw James Marriott, a brother-in-law of Dorsey Rice, with pistol in hand, and under the mistake that he was the assailant, shot him dead. Cleburne lingered a long time from his wound but finally recovered.

In the yellow fever scourge in Helena, in 1855, he was at one time about the only well person remaining to care for the sick and dying. He was a strict member of the church and for some years a vestryman in St. John's Episcopal Church, Helena. He was engaged to wed Miss Tarleton, of Mobile, when he fell upon the battle field, and the dead soldier lay upon the ground, with his arms folded over his breast, as if even in death he would protect the sacred tokens of love that he wore next his heart.

The military board elected two brigadier-generals—James Yell and N. B. Pierce. The latter was sent to Northwestern Arkansas, where was fought the first battle on Arkansas soil—Pea Ridge, or as it is better known in the South, Elkhorn. This was a severe engagement, and a decisive one.

There is yet some confusion in referring to the respective numbers of the Arkansas regiments. Gen. Pierce, supposing he had full power, gave numbers Third, Fourth and Fifth to what the board, the proper and only authority, designated as numbers Second, Third and Fourth. The following shows the board's numbering and names of the colonels:

First, Col. P. H. Cleburne; Second, Col. Gratiot; Third, Col. Dockery; Fourth, Col. Davis Walker; Fifth, Col. D. C. Cross; Sixth, Col. Lyon; Seventh, Col. Shaver; Eighth, Col. W. K. Patterson; Ninth, Col. John Roane; Tenth, Col. T. D. Merrick; Eleventh, Col. Jabez M. Smith; Twelfth, Col. E. W. Gantt; Thirteenth, Col. J. C. Tappan; Fourteenth, Col. W. C. Mitchell, (never completed); Fifteenth, Col. Dawson; Seventeenth, Col. G. W. Lamar, Lieut.-Col. Sam W. Williams.

In the scraps of records now to be found there are mentioned as the different arms in the Confederate service of Arkansas men, in addition to those above given, the following: Light artillery, Hill's; batteries, Blocher's, Brown's, Etter's, Hughey's, Marshall's and West's; cavalry battalions, Chrisman's, Crawford's, Hill's, Witherspoon's; detached companies, Brown's, Coarser's, Desha's, Ranger's, Fitzwilliam's, Miller's and Palmer's; regiments, Carroll's, Dobbins', Newton's; infantry, regiments from one to thirty-nine, inclusive.

Four regiments of infantry of Federal recruits were raised in Arkansas, the First commanded by Col. M. La Rue Harrison; the Fourth by Elisha Baxter. The First Arkansas Light Artillery was 150 strong. The Arkansas Infantry Brigade was under command of Col. James M. True. August 5, 1863, Adj't Gen. Thomas made a trip to the Southwest for the purpose of gathering in all the negroes possible by scouting bands, and to enlist the able bodied men. The First Arkansas Battery was commanded by Capt. Dent D. Stark, and the First Arkansas Cavalry by Maj. J. J. Johnson. The Second Arkansas Cavalry is mentioned. Lieut.-Col. E. J. Searle, authorized to raise the Third Arkansas Cavalry, reported 400 strong. The Fourth Arkansas Cavalry comprised nine companies, commanded by Capt. W. A. Martin.

The Second and Third Arkansas colored infantry regiments are mentioned, in addition to the Second and Third white regiments.

In the spring of 1861, the Richmond government authorized Col. T. B. Flournoy to raise a regiment. It was collected in and about Little Rock and Col. Fagan was elected commander. This command went to Virginia. Gen. Churchill organized the first regiment of cavalry, with rendezvous at Little Rock. Gen. T. C. Hindman organized Hindman's Legion. It consisted of infantry and cavalry and had fifteen companies. He took his command east of the river. Under the direction of the military board Col. Rosey Carroll's regiment of cavalry was raised. The Second Arkansas Regiment of Mounted Infantry was mustered at Osage Springs, by Col. Dandridge McRea. James McIntosh became colonel and Capt. H. H. Brown, major, J. P. Eagle was first lieutenant-colonel and afterward colonel. Col. McIntosh was killed at Pea Ridge, but had been promoted a brigadier-general a few days before his death.

The absence of war archives from the State,

the most of them that were preserved until after the war being now in Washington, and the passing away of so many of the prominent participants, and a common fault of human memory, make it well-nigh impossible to gather for permanent form any satisfactory roster of the different Confederate commands or the order of their organization. No Arkansan so far, which is much to be regretted, has attempted to write a history of the State in the civil struggle.

Gov. J. P. Eagle happened to keep duplicates of certain reports he made while in the service, and discovered them recently where they had been laid away and forgotten among old papers. Fortunately when he made the reports the idea occurred to him to keep a copy for himself, that some day he might look over them and be interested.

"This is a list of the killed and wounded in my regiment," he remarked, "the Second Arkansas, from May 8 to August 31, 1864, and the other is a report of the same from November 26, 1864, to March 21, 1865."

The Second Arkansas at the beginning of the war was a mounted regiment, commanded by Col. James McIntosh. It was dismounted early in the conflict. Col. McIntosh was promoted to the rank of brigadier-general in the spring of 1862. He led his brigade bravely into the heaviest fighting at the battle of Elkhorn (Pea Ridge), where he was killed. He was succeeded by Col. Embry, who was soon after succeeded by Col. Flannagin, afterwards the "War Governor" of Arkansas. Flannagin was succeeded by Col. James Williamson, who lost a leg at the battle of Resaca, Ga., May 14, 1864. Col. J. T. Smith then became colonel. He was killed July 28 following, in the fight at Lick Skillet Road, and J. P. Eagle, now governor of Arkansas, became colonel. Col. Eagle had been wounded at Moore's Mills, and at the time of his promotion was not with the famous regiment. He remained in command until the regiment was consolidated with other regiments and the whole formed into one regiment, with Col. H. G. Bunn commanding. Gov. Eagle became lieutenant-colonel and George Wells, major.

The battle of Elkhorn checked the advance of Curtis' army into Arkansas, and the Federals remained hovering in the southwest of Missouri and northwest of Arkansas for some time. Immediately after the fight Van Dorn's forces were withdrawn and taken east of the Mississippi to resist the Federal advance down the river to Vicksburg. Gen. T. C. Hindman returned and took command of the Confederates in Arkansas and established headquarters at Little Rock and slightly fortified the place.

Gen. Curtis then moved with the Federal army down the valley of White River, acting in conjunction with the river fleet, and when he reached Cotton Plant a flank attack was made on his army and the battle of Cotton Plant was fought. The Confederates were repulsed, and Curtis moved on and took possession of Helena, the Confederates retiring. Northern and Northeastern Arkansas were then in the possession of the Union army. The Federals were in the possession of the Mississippi down to a point just above Vicksburg. The Confederates made a futile effort to re-capture Helena, July 4, 1863, but heavy rains, swollen streams and impassable roads thwarted every move.

June 2, 1862, Gov. Rector issued the following:

"It being essential that but one military organization shall exist within the Trans-Mississippi department, all Arkansas troops are hereby transferred to the Confederate service." (Signed) H. M. RECTOR, Gov. & Prest. Mil. Board.

The authorities at Richmond, as well as in the Trans-Mississippi district, were anxiously awaiting news of the war steamer, "Arkansas," then building up the mouth of Red River. June 2, 1862, she steamed out of that river and passed the fleet guarding the river for the purpose of capturing the rebel steamer. The attempt and success in running the fiery gauntlet was one of the most exciting scenes ever witnessed on western rivers. Proudly the vessel kept on her course, sending volleys into every vessel to the right and left, and at nearly every turn of her wheels encountering new enemies. A Federal surgeon of the Union fleet said that wonderful trip of the "Arkansas" reminded him of the Irishman's advice on going into the "free fight"—"wherever you see a head hit it." The Confederate reports say two Federal gun-boats were captured and others disabled.

August 7, following, the "Arkansas," when five miles above Baton Rouge on her way down the river, again encountered Federal gun-boats. Her machinery being disabled, after she had fought long and well, her crew "blew her up, and all escaped."

January 3, 1863 Gen. J. M. Schofield wrote to Gen. Curtis, from Fayetteville, Ark.: "The operations of the army since I left it have been a series of blunders, from which it narrowly escaped disaster * * * At Prairie Grove (fought in December, 1862) Blunt and Herron were badly beaten in detail and owed their escape to a false report of my arrival with re-enforcements." It now is revealed that Hindman did not know the extent of his victory, but supposed he was about to be overwhelmed by the enemy. Thus the two armies were as secretly as possible running away from each other.

July 13, 1863, Gen. E. Kirby Smith wrote from Shreveport, headquarters of the Trans-Mississippi district, to Govs. Thomas C. Reynolds, F. R. Lubbock, H. Flannagin and Thomas O. Moore, calling on these, as the heads of their respective States, to meet him at Marshall, Tex., August 15, following: "I have attempted to impartially survey the field of my labor. * * I found on my arrival the headquarters of Arkansas district at Little Rock. * * Vicksburg has fallen. The enemy possesses the key to this department. * * The possession of the Mississippi River by the enemy cuts off this department from all communication with Richmond, consequently we must be self-sustaining, and self-reliant in every respect. * * With God's help and yours I will cheerfully grapple with the difficulties that surround us," etc.

This was a gloomy but a correct view of the situation west of the Mississippi River after the fall of Vicksburg.

On January 11, 1863, from Helena, Gen. Fiske reported to Washington: "Found Gorman actively organizing expedition to go up White River to co-operate with Gen. McClernand on Arkansas River. Twenty-five transports are waiting the signal to start."

From "Prairie Landing, twenty-five miles up Arkansas, January 13, 1863," Amos F. Eno, secretary *pro tem* of Arkansas and adjutant-general, telegraphed Staunton: "Left Helena on 11th, and took with me books and papers of office of military government of Arkansas."

January 14, 1863, the Federals captured St. Charles, the Confederates evacuating the day before.

January 18, Gen. W. A. Gorman occupied Devall's Bluff, which the Confederates had also evacuated.

These captures and evacuations were the preliminary movements looking toward Little Rock, the Federals clearing out the small outposts, and the Confederates gathering in their forces.

On August 5, 1863, Gen. Frederick Steele "assumed the command of the army to take the field from Helena, and advance upon Little Rock."

In his order for movement mention is made of the following: First division—cavalry under command of Gen. J. W. Davidson; Second division—Eighteenth, Forty-third, Fifty-fourth, Sixty-first, One Hundred and Sixth, and One Hundred and Twenty-sixth regiments, Illinois Infantry; Twelfth Michigan, Twenty-second Ohio, Twenty-seventh Wisconsin, Third Minnesota, Fortieth Iowa and Forty-third Indiana Infantry regiments; Third division—Twenty-ninth, Thirty-third and Thirty sixth Iowa, Forty-third Indiana, Twenty-eighth Wisconsin, and Seventy-first Ohio Infantry regiments; and the Fifth Kansas, First Indiana Cavalry, and a brigade under Col. Powell Clayton. Four batteries of field pieces—five wagons to each regiment; 160 rounds of ammunition, 40 rounds to each cartridge-box; 400 rounds to each piece of artillery, and sixty days' rations for the whole army, were the supplies granted these forces.

Gen. Steele was occupied in the expedition from Helena to Little Rock, from August 5 to September 10. The cavalry under Gen. Davidson had to scour the country to the right and left as they made their slow advance. Twelve miles east of Little Rock, at Bayou Meta bridge, was a heavy

HISTORY OF ARKANSAS. 79

skirmish, indeed, a regular battle, being the first serious effort to check the Federal advance upon the capital. Again there was heavy fighting six miles east of Little Rock, at what is now the Brugman place. Here Confederate Col. Coffee, of Texas, was killed. This was the last stand made in defense of the city, and in a short time Davidson's cavalry appeared in Argenta, and trained their field pieces on the city, and fired a few shots, when the place was surrendered by the civil authorities, September 10, 1863. The Confederates had evacuated but a few hours before the Federal cavalry were galloping through the streets, and posting sentinels here and there.

There was no confusion, no disorder, and none of the usual crimes of war under similar circumstances. In an hour after Gen. Steele was in possession of the city he had it under strict control, and order prevailed. Gen. Reynolds was put in command of Little Rock.*

The Confederates wisely retreated to Arkadelphia. They were pursued by the Federals as far as Malvern, but no captures were made and no heavy skirmishing occurred.

It is said that Price evacuated Little Rock under the impression that his force was far inferior to that of Gen. Steele. Those who were Confederate officers and in Little Rock now believe that his force was equal at least in numbers to Steele's.

They think that Price had based his idea of the enemy's numbers by allowing the usual proportion of armies of infantry and artillery to cavalry. They believe also that the Confederates at Little Rock at the evacuation had between 11,000 and 12,000 men present—not the number for duty—basing this upon the number of rations issued that day.

After the occupation of Little Rock the Federals dominated all that portion of the State north and east of the Arkansas River, and yet their actual occupied posts were the only grounds over which Confederate rangers were not frequently roving with impunity.

The Confederates exercised ruling power all south and west of the Ouachita River, and for quite a while the territory between the Arkansas and Ouachita Rivers was a kind of "No Man's Land" so far as the armies were concerned.

Steele early in 1864, having been re-enforced, began to move on Arkadelphia. Price retreated to Camden, where the Confederates had several factories for the manufacture of war materials.

Price made a stand against Steele and fought the battle of Prairie D'Ann, but there was nothing decisive in this engagement, although it was a severe one. Price withdrew and fell back on Rondo, in the southwest corner of the State.

In the meantime Banks' expedition was ascending Red River, the plan being to catch Price between Banks and Steele, and destroy the Confederate army. Price and Gen. Dick Taylor did not wait for Banks, but met and overwhelmingly defeated him. Having defeated Banks, they turned and gave Steele battle at Jenkins' Ferry, and defeated him. This was the great and decisive battle of the Trans-Mississippi district.

Steele retreated and fell back on Little Rock, his superior generalship being shown in extricating his badly crippled army and saving it on the withdrawal.

The Federal expeditions were well planned for "bagging" the whole Confederate Trans-Mississippi army, but the vicissitudes of war ordained otherwise. Banks' expedition and its overwhelming misfortunes ruined him as a military man throughout

*Abstract from consolidated tri-monthly report of the Army of Arkansas, Maj.-Gen. Frederick Steele commanding, for September 10, 1863; headquarters, Little Rock:

Command.	Present for duty.		Aggregate pres't.	Aggregate pres'nt and absent.	Pieces of artillery.
	Officers.	Men.			
First Division (Davidson)	200	3,828	5,372	7,735	18
Second Division (Englemann)	140	2,047	2,990	6,885	
Third Division (Rice)	123	1,683	2,316	4,007	
Infantry Brigade (True)	89	1,796	2,250	2,825	6
Cavalry Brigade (Clayton)	30	445	736	1,200	5
Artillery (Hayden)	15	495	607	844	28
Cavalry escort (McLean)	4	64	91	12	
Total	619	9,854	14,362	23,620	57

Gen. Price had not made a mistake of the comparative strength of the two armies. The commissary informs me that on the morning of the evacuation he issued 8,000 rations—full number.

the North, while the brilliant successes of Price raised the hopes of the Confederacy. Some, however, still criticise.

Price failed to follow up his advantage and either destroy or capture Steele's entire army. Had he fully known the condition of affairs at Richmond possibly he might have adopted that course. The Federals were confined within their fortified posts and Confederate bands were again scouring over the State.

Price, losing no time, then started on his raid back into Missouri to carry out his long cherished hope of re-possessing that State. The history of that raid and the dissolution and end of the Confederacy are a familiar part of the country's history.

Other wars than that mentioned have occupied the attention of people of this section, though perhaps not to such an extent as the great civil strife. There were not people in Arkansas to go to the War of 1812, and the State becomes connected with that struggle chiefly because Archibald Yell, the brave young hero, was at the battle of New Orleans, and afterward became one of the most prominent citizens of Arkansas. He was born in North Carolina, in August, 1797, and consequently was but fifteen years of age when the second war with England began. But the lad then and there won the inalienable friendship of Gen. Jackson.

Arkansas acquired no little fame in the Mexican War, chiefly, however, through the gallantry and death of Gov. Yell, the leader of the Arkansas forces. When troops were called for in the year 1846, in the war with Mexico, Yell was a member of Congress. A regiment of cavalry was raised and he was asked to take the command, and obedient to this request he promptly resigned his seat to assume leadership. Albert Pike was a captain in the regiment.

At the battle of Buena Vista, on February 22, 1847, Yell led his cavalry command in one of the most desperate charges in the annals of war. In his enthusiasm he spurred on his horse far in advance of his men. He was charging the enemy, which outnumbered his force more than five to one. He reached the ranks of the enemy almost alone, and raising himself in the saddle commenced to slash right and left, totally unmindful that it was one against thousands. Just as the foremost of his men came up he was run through the body and killed. William A. L. Throckmorton, of Fayetteville, it is agreed, was the first to reach the side and catch the falling form of his loved leader. Mr. Throckmorton says he saw the man who gave the fatal thrust and quickly killed him, thus avenging so far as the wretched greaser's life could go the life of as gallant and noble a knight as ever responded to bugle call. He was the dashing cavalier, great in peace, superb in war. Leading his trusty followers in any of the walks of life, death alone could check him, nothing could conquer him.

After the war was over the government brought his remains and delivered them to his friends in Fayetteville, his home, who lovingly deposited them beneath the cold white marble shaft which speaks his fame. The burial ceremony occurred August 3, 1847, and a vast concourse of people, the humblest and highest in the State, were the sincere and deep mourners on the occasion.

Arkansas won everlasting laurels through its gallant soldiers in the Mexican War.

Omitting all reference to the Revolutionary War, there are conclusions to be drawn from the wars our countrymen have been engaged in since the days when Gen. Jackson was the national hero. None of these were significant enough to be used by the philosophic historian from which to draw conclusions as to the character of modern or contemporary Americans as warriors, or their distinguishing characteristics as a warlike nation. The late Civil War, however, furnishes a wide and ample field for such investigation. An impartial view of the late struggle presents first of all this remarkable fact. In by far the longest and greatest war of modern times, neither side has given the age a great captain, as some call greatness, though one furnished Grant, the other, Lee, both men without a superior; whilst in the ranks and among the sub-commands, no battles in history are at all comparable for excellence and superior soldiership to those of the great Civil War. On both sides there were any number of great field commanders, as great as ever drew a sword. But they received orders, did not give them, and in the execution of orders never were excelled. Lee, Grant, Jackson, Sherman, Hancock, Johnston, Sheridan and hundreds of others on both sides, to the humblest in the ranks, were immortal types of the soldier in the field. These men were like Napoleon's marshals—given a command or order they would risk life itself to execute it. But on neither side was there the least exhibition of the qualities of a Napoleon or Von Moltke.

Napoleon was his own secretary of war, government, cabinet, and commander in the field, and for this very reason, he was Von Moltke's inferior as a great commander, whose genius saw the weak point, the point of victory on the map of the enemy's country, and struck it with a quick and decisive blow.

Our Civil War and the Franco-German War were closely together in time. War was hardly over in America when it commenced in Europe. Any student of German history who has studied the German-Prussian war, can not but know that Von Moltke was the pre-eminent captain in all the histories of wars. Had Washington or Richmond had his peer at the commencement of our struggle, the high probabilities are that the war would have been over before the first twelve months had expired.

In war, it is a fact, that it is the strategy before the armies meet in battle array which decides the struggle. It is only thus that one man can become more powerful than a million with guns in their hands. It is in this sense—this application of the science of modern warfare, that a commander wins battles and decides victories. He conquers enemies, not by drawing his sword, but, studying his maps in his quiet den when others sleep, he directs the movements of his armies and leaves the details of the actual fight to others. He is indifferent to the actual fighting part of it, because he has settled all that long beforehand by his orders.

In all actual battles, as was testified by the Federal commanders before Congress about the battle of Gettysburg, if victory is not organized beforehand, all is chance, uncertainty, and both armies are little else than headless mobs—ignorant of whether they are whipping or being whipped. The field commander may save the day and turn the tide and gain a victory, but what is it after all, —so many men killed and captured on either side, and then recruited up, and rested a little, only to repeat the bloody carnage again and again.

Let it be assumed that the absence of great military genius on both sides is the highest compliment that can be paid to American civilization. War is barbarism. The higher civilization will eradicate all practical knowledge of the brutality of warfare from men's minds. Then there will be no wars, save that of truth upon the false—intelligence upon ignorance How grandly divine will be, not only the great leaders in this holy struggle for victory, but the humblest of all privates!

CHAPTER X.

PUBLIC ENTERPRISES—THE REAL ESTATE BANK OF ARKANSAS—STATE ROADS AND OTHER HIGHWAYS—THE MILITARY ROADS—NAVIGATION WITHIN THE STATE FROM THE EARLIEST TIMES TO THE PRESENT—DECADENCE OF STATE NAVIGATION—STEAMBOAT RACING—ACCIDENTS TO BOATS—THE RISE AND GROWTH OF THE RAILROAD SYSTEMS—A SKETCH OF THE DIFFERENT LINES—OTHER IMPORTANT CONSIDERATIONS.

> From the blessings they bestow
> Our times are dated, and our eras move.—*Prior.*

THE first session of the new State legislature, among other acts, incorporated the State Bank, and as if further determined to show that the legislature was at least in the front in those days of wild-cat bank enterprises, proceeded to make money cheap and all rich by incorporating the celebrated Real Estate Bank of Arkansas. Already John Law's Mississippi bubble had been forgotten—the old continental money and the many other distressing instances of those cruel but fascinating fictions of attempts to make credits wealth. No statesman in the world's history has ever yet made an approach to the accomplishment of such an impossibility, and still nearly all financial legislation is founded upon this basic idea. State and national banks have been the alluring will-o'-the-wisps in this persistent folly. All experience teaches that the government that becomes a money-changer soon becomes the powerful robber, and the places of just rulers are filled with tax bandits—there the lordly rulers are banditti, and the people the most wretched of slaves.

The State Bank was, as were all such institutions of that day in any of the States, demoralizing in the financial affairs of the people, encouraging extravagance and debt, and deceiving men with the appearances of wealth to their ultimate ruin.

The Real Estate Bank, as its name indicates, was for the purpose of loaning money on real estate security. Up to that time the American farmer had not learned to base his efforts upon anything except his labor. To produce something and sell it was the whole horizon of his financial education. If, while his crop was maturing, he needed subsistence he went to his merchant and bought the fewest possible necessities on credit. It was an evil hour when he was tempted to become a speculator. Yet there were some instances in which the loans on real estate resulted in enabling men to make finely improved cotton plantations. But the rule was to get people in debt and at the same time exhaust the cash in the bank. The bank could collect no money, and the real estate owner was struggling under mortgages he could not pay. Both lender and borrower were sufferers, and the double infliction was upon them of a public and individual indebtedness. The Real Estate

Bank made an assignment in 1842, and for years was the source of much litigation. It practically ceased to do business years before it had its doors closed and was wound up, and the titles to such lands as it had become the possessor of passed to the State.

The old State Bank building, in front of the State house, is the only reminder of the institution which promised so much and did so little for the public. The old building is after the style of all such buildings—a low, two-story brick or stone, with huge Corinthian columns in front, having stone steps to ascend to the first floor. Similar structures can be found in Illinois, Missouri and all the Western and Southern States. The one in Little Rock is unsightly and gloomy and does little else but cumber the ground. It is in the way, owing to a difficulty in the title, of such a modern and elegant building as would be in keeping with the rapidly advancing and beautiful "City of Roses."

Roads and highways have always occupied public consideration. Being so crossed with rivers passing from the west toward the Mississippi River, the early settlers all over the confines of this State passed up the streams and for some time used these as the only needed highways. In the course of time they began to have bridle-paths crossing from settlement to settlement.

The United States military road from Western Missouri passed through Arkansas and led on to Shreveport, La. This extended through Eastern Arkansas, and Arkansas Post was an important point on the route. It was surveyed and partially cut out early in the nineteenth century. A monthly mail proceeded over the route on horseback, the mail rider generally being able to carry the mail in his pocket.

A trail at first was the road from the mouth of the White River to Arkansas Post. This portage soon became a highway, as much of the business and travel for the Post was landed at the mouth of White River and transported across to the Red River.

In 1821 Congress authorized the survey and opening of a public highway from Memphis, via Little Rock, to Fort Smith. The work was completed in 1823. This was the first highway of any importance in the Territory. The other routes mentioned above were nothing more than trails, or bridle-paths. A weekly mail between Little Rock and Memphis was established in 1829.

In 1832 a government road leading on a direct line from Little Rock to Batesville was cut out, and the Indians removed from Georgia were brought by water to the capital and taken over this road. At that time it was the best public course as well as the longest in the State, and became in time the main traveled road from the northern part of the State to its center.

Arkansas was settled sparsely along the Mississippi River some years before Fulton invented the steamboat. The first steamboat ever upon western waters passed down that river in the latter part of 1811—the "Orleans," Capt. Roosevelt.

The Indians had their light cedar bark canoes, and were remarkably expert in handling them. These were so light that the squaws could carry them on their backs, and in their expeditions in ascending the streams frequently saved much time by traveling across the great bends of the river and carrying their conveyances. Of course in going with the current, they kept the stream, skimming over the waters with great speed. At one time the migratory Indians at stated seasons followed the buffalo from the Dakotas to the Gulf, the buffalo remaining near, and the Indians on the streams. The latter could thus out-travel the immense herds and at certain points make forays upon them and so keep an abundant supply of meat. The buffalo had the curious habit of indulging in long stops when they came to a large river in their course, as if dreading to take to the water and swim across. They would gather on the bank of the river at the selected crossing-place, and after having devoured everything near at hand and hunger began to pinch, would collect into a close circle and begin to move, circling round and round, the inside ones ever crowding the outside ones closer and closer to the water. This continued until some one, crowded into the deep water, had to make the plunge, when all followed.

These animals when attacked by other animals, or when danger threatened, formed in a compact circle, with the cows and calves on the inside and the bulls on the outer ring. In this battle array there was nothing in the line of beasts that dared molest them.

The white man came and to the canoe he added the skiff, the pirogue, the raft, the keel boat and the flat boat. The raft never made but one trip and that was down stream always, and when its destination was reached it was sold to be converted into lumber. Other water crafts could be hauled back by long tow lines, men walking on the banks and pulling them up stream. There are those now living who can remember when this was the only mode of river navigation. The younger people of this generation can form no adequate idea of the severity of the toil and the suffering necessarily involved in the long trips then made by these hardy pioneers. If the people of to-day were compelled to procure the simple commodities of life at such hard sacrifices, by such endurance, they would do without them, and go back to fig leaves and nuts and roots for subsistence.

When Fulton and Livingston had successfully navigated their boat from Pittsburg to New Orleans, they made the claim of a sort of royal patent to the exclusive navigation of the Mississippi River and its tributaries. This claim was put forth in perfect good faith and it was a new question as well as a serious one for the courts, when these claimants arrested Captain Shreve upon his arrival in New Orleans with his boat, and carried him before the court to answer in damages for navigating by steam the river that belonged to them as the first steam navigators. This curious incident indicates how little even the inventor of the steamboat appreciated of what vast importance to civilization his noble invention really was. To him and his friend it was but a small personal right or perquisite—a licensed monopoly, out of which they could make a few dollars, and when they passed away probably the invention too would die and be forgotten. How infinitely greater had the noble, immortal originator builded than he knew! The revolving paddles of the steamboat were but the wheels now whirling so rapidly beneath the flying railroad trains over the civilized world. From this strange, rude craft, the "Orleans," have evolved the great steamships, iron-clad war vessels, and the palatial steamboats plying the inland waters wherever man's wants or luxuries are to be supplied. The genius and glory of such men as Fulton belong to no age, much less to themselves—they and theirs are a part of the world, for all time.

In 1812 Jacob Barkman opened up a river trade between Arkadelphia and New Orleans, carrying his first freights in a pirogue. It took six months to make a round trip. He conveyed to New Orleans bear skins and oil, pelts, and tallow secured from wild cattle, of which there were a great many; these animals had originally been brought to the country by the Spaniards and French, and had strayed away, and increased into great herds, being as wild and nearly as fleet as the deer. He brought back sugar, coffee, powder, lead, flints, copperas, camphor, cotton and wool cards, etc., and soon after embarking was able to own his negro crews. He purchased the steamboat "Dime" and became one of the most extensive and enterprising men in the State. With his boat he ascended rivers, and purchased the cotton, owning his cargo, for a return trip.

In 1819, James Miller, the first governor of the Territory, and a military suite of twenty persons, embarked at Pittsburg in the United States keel-boat, "Arkansas," for Arkansas Post. The trip occupied seventy days, reaching the point of destination January 1, 1820. It was difficult to tell which excited the greatest curiosity among the natives—the new governor or the keel-boat.

The flood-tide of western river navigation reached its highest wave soon after the close of the late war. The Mississippi River and tributaries were crowded with craft, and the wharves of cities and towns along the banks were lined with some of the finest boats ever built, all freighted to the water's edge and crowded with passengers. Builders vied with each other in turning out the most magnificent floaters, fitted with every elegance and luxury money could procure. The main point after elegance, in which they rivaled most, was the speed of their respective craft. From the close of the war to 1870, steamboating was the overshadowing business on western waters. Of the boats of this era, some will go into history, noted for their fleetness, but unlike the fleet horses of history, they could not leave their strain in immortal descendants, rivaling their celebrated feats. Racing between boats that happened to come together on the river was common, and sometimes reckless and dangerous, as well as exciting. Occasionally a couple of "tubs," as the boys called a slow boat, engaged in a race and away they would go, running for hours side by side, the stokers all the time piling in the most inflammable material they could lay hands on, especially pine knots and fat bacon, until the eager flames poured out of the long chimney tops; and it was often told that the captain, rather than fall behind in the race, would seat a darkey on the end of the lever of the safety valve, and at the same time scream at the stokers to pile on the bacon, pine knots, oil, anything to make steam. Roustabouts, officers, crew and passengers were all as wildly excited as the captain, and as utterly regardless of dangers. From such recklessness accidents of course did happen, but it is wonderful there were so few.

Not infrequently commanders would regularly engage beforehand for a race of their boats; fixing the day and time and as regularly preparing their vessels as a jockey trains and grooms his race-horse. The two most noted contests of this kind on the Mississippi River were, first, in the early times, between the "Shotwell" and "Eclipse," from Louisville to New Orleans. The next and greatest of all was just at the time of the commencement of the decline in steamboating, between the steamers "Robert E. Lee" and "Natchez," from New Orleans to St. Louis. The speed, the handling of these boats, the record they made, have never been equaled and probably never will be, unless steamboating is revived by some new invention. The race last mentioned took place in 1868.

Fearful steamboat calamities, from explosions and from fires, like the awful railroad accidents, have marked the era of steam navigation.

The most disastrous in history occurred in 1865, in the loss of the "Sultana," on the Mississippi, a few miles above Memphis, a part of the navigable waters of Arkansas. The boat was on her way up stream from New Orleans laden principally with soldiers, some of them with their families, and several citizens as passengers. There were 2,350 passengers and crew on the vessel. A little after midnight the sudden and awful explosion of the boilers came, literally tearing the boat to pieces, after which the wreck took fire. Over 2,000 people perished.

The early decline of the steamboat industry kept even pace with the building of railroads over the country. Main lines of railroads were soon built, the streams being used as natural road beds through the rock hills and mountains. In passing over the country in trains one will now often see the flowing river close to the railroad track on one hand, when from the opposite window the high rock mountain wall may almost be touched. Then, too, the large towns were along the navigable rivers, lakes and ocean. The sage conclusion of the philosopher when he went out to look at the world, and was impressed with the curious coincidence that the rivers ran so close by the big towns, is a trite one: A great convenience to those who used water.

The first railroad built in Arkansas was the Memphis & Little Rock Railroad. Work was commenced with the intention of first constructing it from Little Rock to Devall's Bluff, on White River, whence passengers might proceed by boat to Memphis. It was started at both ends of the line and finished in 1859, the next year being extended to St. Francis River, and then in 1860 completed to the river opposite Memphis. When the Federal army took possession of the Mississippi River, and their forces began to possess the northeastern portion of the State, the Confederates as they retired toward Little Rock destroyed the road and burned the bridges. Indeed, when the war ended in 1865, Arkansas was without a mile of railroad. Soon after the war closed the road was rebuilt and put in operation, and for some time was the only one in the State.

The next was the old Cairo & Fulton Railroad, now the St. Louis, Iron Mountain & Southern Road. It was organized in 1853, and in 1854-55 obtained a large Congressional land grant in aid of the enterprise, and built first from Fulton to Beebe, in 1872; it was completed to Texarkana in 1873, and soon came to be the most important line in the State. The Camden branch, from Gurdon to Camden, was completed in 1882. The Memphis branch, from Bald Knob to Memphis, ninety-three miles, was finished and the first passenger train passed over the line May 10, 1888. The branch from Newport to Cushman, a distance of forty-six miles, was built in 1882. The Helena branch, from Noble to Helena, 140 miles, was completed in 1882.

The main line of the St. Louis & Iron Mountain Railroad enters the State on the north, at Moark (combination for Missouri and Arkansas), and passes out at Texarkana (combination for Arkansas and Texas). The distance between these two points is 305 miles.

The first section of the St. Louis, Arkansas & Texas Railroad, from Clarendon to Jonesboro, was built in 1882, and the next year completed to Texarkana. It was built as a narrow gauge and made a standard gauge in 1886. Its northern terminus for some time was Cairo, where it made its St. Louis connection over the St. Louis & Cairo Narrow Gauge Road, now a standard, and a part of the Mobile & Ohio system. The Magnolia branch of this road runs from McNeal to Magnolia, about twenty miles, and was built in 1885. The Altheimer branch, from Altheimer to Little Rock, was constructed and commenced operation in 1888. The main line of this road enters the State from the north in Clay County, on the St. Francis River, penetrating into Texas at Texarkana.

The Little Rock, Mississippi River & Texas Railroad, now in course of construction, is a much needed road from Little Rock to Pine Bluff, on to Warren and Mississippi, and will form an important outlet for Arkansas toward the Gulf. This was built from Arkansas City to Pine Bluff, and then completed to Little Rock in 1880.

The Pine Bluff & Swan Lake Railroad was built in 1885. It is twenty-six miles long, and runs between the points indicated by its name.

The Arkansas Midland Railroad, from Helena to Clarendon, was built as a narrow gauge and changed to a standard road in 1886.

The Batesville & Brinkley Railroad is laid as far as Jacksonport. It was changed in 1888 to a standard gauge, and is now in course of construction on to Batesville.

The Kansas City, Fort Scott & Memphis Railroad enters the State at Mammoth Spring, and runs to West Memphis. Its original name was Kansas City, Springfield & Memphis Railroad. It now is a main road from Kansas City to Birmingham, Ala.

Work was commenced on the Little Rock & Fort Smith Railroad in 1871 at Little Rock, and built to Ozark; later it was finished to Van Buren, there using a transfer, and was completed to Fort Smith.

The Hot Springs Railroad, from Malvern, on the main line of the Iron Mountain Railroad, to Hot Springs, was built and is owned by "Diamond Joe" Reynolds. Operations were commenced in 1874.

The line of the St. Louis & San Francisco Railroad passes near the west line of Arkansas adjacent to Fort Smith. There is a branch road of this line from Jensen to Mansfield, sixteen miles long.

It looks a little as though the sponsor for the name of the Ultima Thule, Arkadelphia & Mississippi Railroad intended to use the name for a main track through the State. It was built in 1887 for the use of the Arkadelphia Lumber Company. Eureka Springs branch runs from Seligman to Eureka Springs. Another branch goes from Rogers to Bentonville. Still another, extending from Fayetteville to St. Paul, is thirty-five miles in length. The branch from Fayetteville is now in course of building.

The Russellville & Dardanelle Railroad is four miles long, extending from the south bank of the Arkansas River to Russellville.

The Southwestern, Arkansas & Indian Territory Railroad indicates that there is nothing in a name, as this road is but twenty-seven miles long, running from Southland to Okolona on the west, and also extending east from the main line.

A line is being surveyed and steps actively taken to build a road from Kansas City to Little Rock, which is to cross the Boston Mountains near the head waters of White River.

Several other important lines are at this time making preparations to build in the near future. Charters for nearly 100 routes in the State have been secured since 1885. There is not only plenty of room, but a great necessity for yet hundreds of miles of new roads here. They will greatly facilitate the development of the immense resources of this favored locality.

CHAPTER XI.

THE COUNTIES OF THE STATE—THEIR FORMATION AND CHANGES OF BOUNDARY LINES, ETC.—THEIR COUNTY SEATS AND OTHER ITEMS OF INTEREST CONCERNING THEM—DEFUNCT COUNTIES—NEW COUNTIES—POPULATION OF ALL THE COUNTIES OF THE STATE AT EVERY GENERAL CENSUS.

> Not chaos-like, together crush'd and bruised;
> But as the world, harmoniously confused;
> Where order in variety we see,
> And where, though all things differ, they agree.—*Pope.*

PERHAPS to many, no more interesting subject in the history of the State can be presented than that referring to the name, organization, etc., of each county within its limits. Careful research has brought forth the following facts presented in a concise, but accurate manner:

Arkansas County was formed December 13, 1813. As the first municipal formation within the boundary of the State, in Lower Missouri Territory, it was first a parish under Spanish rule and then under French. October 23, 1821, a part of Phillips County was added to it; the line between Pulaski and Arkansas was changed October 30, 1823; Quapaw Purchase divided between Arkansas and Pulaski October 13, 1827; line between Arkansas and Phillips defined November 21, 1829; boundaries defined November 7, 1836. County seat, De Witt; first county seat, Arkansas—opposite Arkansas Post.

Ashley, formed November 30, 1848, named for Hon. Chester Ashley, who died a United States Senator; line between Chicot changed January 19, 1861. County seat, Hamburg.

Baxter, March 24, 1873; line between Izard and Fulton defined October 16, 1875; line between Marion changed March 9, 1881. County seat, Mountain Home.

Benton, September 30, 1836, named in honor of Hon. Thomas H. Benton. County seat, Bentonville.

Boone, April 9, 1869; named for Daniel Boone; line between Marion defined December 9, 1875. Harrison, county seat.

Bradley, December 18, 1840; part of Calhoun

attached October 19, 1862; part restored to Ashley County January 1, 1859. Warren, county seat.

Calhoun, December 6, 1850; named for John C. Calhoun; part added to Union and Bradley November 19, 1862. County seat, Hampton.

Carroll, November 1, 1833; named in honor of the signer of the declaration; boundary defined December 14, 1838; line between Madison defined January, 11, 1843, and again January 20, 1843; line between Marion defined December 18, 1846; line between Madison defined December 29, 1854, and again January 16, 1857; part of Madison attached April 8, 1869. Berryville, county seat.

Chicot, October 25, 1823; boundary defined November 2, 1835; part attached to Drew December 21, 1846; line between Ashley changed January 19, 1861; line between Drew changed November 30, 1875; line changed between Desha February 10, 1879. Lake Village, county seat.

Clark, December 15, 1818, while Lower Missouri Territory; named in honor of Gov. Clark, of Missouri; the line between Pulaski and Clark, changed October 30, 1823; divided November 2, 1829; line between Hot Springs and Dallas changed April 3, 1868; line between Pike defined April 22, 1873; line between Montgomery changed April 24, 1873; line between Pike changed March 8, 1887. Arkadelphia, county seat.

Clay, March 24, 1873; named for Henry Clay. This county, formed as Clayton County, was changed to Clay on December 6, 1875. The act of March 24, 1873, changed the boundaries of a large number of counties. Boydsville and Corning, county seats.

Cleburne, formed February 20, 1883; named in honor of Gen. Patrick A. Cleburne. Heber is the county seat.

Cleveland, formed in 1885; named for President Cleveland; was formed as Dorsey County. Toledo, county seat.

Columbia, December 17, 1852; part of Union County added December 21, 1858; line between Nevada defined April 19, 1873. Magnolia, county seat.

Conway, December 7, 1825; named after the noted Conways; the northeast boundary defined October 27, 1827; line between Pulaski and Conway defined October 20, 1828; part of Indian purchase added October 22, 1828; line between Conway, Pulaski and Independence defined November 5, 1831; part added to Pope January 6, 1853; part added to White January 11, 1853; act of March, 1873; line between Pope defined May 28, 1874. County seat, Morrillton.

Craighead, formed February 19, 1850. Jonesboro, county seat.

Crawford, October 18, 1820; boundary was changed October 30, 1823; divided and county of Lovely established October 13, 1827; part of the Cherokee Country attached to, October 22, 1828; boundary defined December 18, 1837; line between Scott defined; line between Washington defined November 24, 1846; line between Franklin defined March 4, 1875; line changed between Washington March 9, 1881. Van Buren, county seat.

Crittenden, October 22, 1825; named for Robert Crittenden; St. Francis River declared to be the line between St. Francis and Crittenden Counties November, 1831; portion attached to Mississippi County January, 1861; act, March, 1873. Marion, county seat.

Cross, November 15, 1862, 1866, 1873. Wittsburg, the county seat.

Dallas, January 1, 1845; line between Hot Springs and Clark changed April 3, 1869. Princeton the county seat.

Desha, December 12, 1838; named for Hon. Ben Desha; portion attached to Drew January 21, 1861; part of Chicot attached February 10, 1879; also of Lincoln, March 10, 1879. Arkansas City, county seat.

Drew, November 26, 1846; part Chicot attached December 21, 1846; part of Desha attached January 21, 1861; March, 1873; line between Chicot changed November 30, 1875. Monticello, county seat.

Faulkner, April 12, 1873; line defined December 7, 1875. Conway, county seat.

Franklin, December 19, 1837; line between Johnson defined December 14, 1833; line between Crawford defined March 4, 1875. Ozark, county seat.

Fulton, December 21, 1842; part attached to Marion County January 18, 1855; part of Lawrence attached January 18, 1855, March, 1873; line between Baxter and Izard defined February 16, 1875. County seat, Salem.

Garland, April 5, 1873; named after Gov. A. H. Garland. Hot Springs, county seat.

Grant, February 4, 1869. Sheridan, county seat.

Greene, November 5, 1833; act March, 1873. Paragould, county seat.

Hempstead, December 15, 1818, when this was Lower Missouri Territory; Lafayette County carved out of this territory October 15, 1827; line between Pike defined December 14, 1838. Washington, county seat.

Hot Spring, November 2, 1829; certain lands attached to March 2, 1838; Montgomery taken out of December 9, 1842; line between Saline defined December 23, 1846; line between Montgomery changed December 27, 1848; line between Saline changed February 19, 1859, and changed again January 10, 1861; line between Clark and Dallas changed April 3, 1869; March, 1873. Malvern, county seat.

Howard, April 17, 1873. County seat, Centre Point.

Independence, October 20, 1820; part of eastern boundary defined October 30, 1823; Izard County formed of October 27, 1825; part of Independence added October 22, 1828; line between Independence and Izard defined November 5, 1831; line between Independence and Conway, November 5, 1831; between Independence and Jackson, November 8, 1836; between Izard February 21, 1838; December 14, 1840; Lawrence changed December 26, 1840; March, 1873; Sharp County defined February 11, 1875. Batesville, county seat.

Izard, October 27, 1825; western boundary line extended October 13, 1827; part of the Indian purchase added October 22, 1828; between Independence and Izard defined November 5, 1831; between Conway and Izard, November 5, 1831; southern boundary established November 11, 1833; line between Independence defined February 21, 1838, and December 14, 1838, and December 21, 1840; western boundary line defined December 24, 1840, March, 1873; between Baxter and Fulton defined February 16, 1875; between Sharp changed March 9, 1877. Melbourne, county seat.

Jackson, November 5, 1829; line between Independence defined November 8, 1836; part of St. Francis attached January 10, 1851. Jacksonport, county seat.

Jefferson, November 2, 1829; boundaries defined November 3, 1831, and again October 29, 1836; line changed between Lincoln and Desha March 20, 1879. Pine Bluff, county seat.

Johnson, November 16, 1833; southern line defined November 3, 1835; east line defined October 5, 1836; line between Franklin defined December 14, 1838, 1848; between Pope February 19, 1859, again March 27, 1871; line between Pope re-established on March 6, 1875; between Pope changed March 9, 1877. Clarksville, county seat.

Lafayette, October 15, 1827; the line between Union defined November 26, 1846. Lewisville, county seat.

Lawrence, on January 15, 1815, while Lower Missouri Territory; east line defined October 30, 1823; between Independence changed December 20, 1840; part attached to Fulton January 18, 1855; part attached to Randolph January 18, 1861; nearly half the county cut off the west side to form Sharp County, 1868. Powhatan, county seat.

Lee, April 17, 1873. Marianna, county seat.

Lincoln, March 28, 1871; part transferred to Desha County, March 10, 1879. Star City, county seat.

Little River, March 5, 1867. Richmond is the county seat.

Logan, originally Sarber County, March 22, 1871; amended, February 27, 1873; changed to Logan, December 14, 1875; line between Scott changed, March 21, 1881. Paris, county seat.

Lonoke, April 16, 1873; named for the lone oak tree, by simply spelling phonetically—the suggestion of the chief engineer of the Cairo & Fulton Railroad. Line between Prairie defined November 30, 1875, and again, December 7, 1875. Lonoke, county seat.

Lovely, October 13, 1827; abolished October 17, 1828.

Madison, September 30, 1836; west boundary changed on November 26, 1838; between Carroll defined January 11, 1843, and again January 20, 1843, 1846; between Newton, December 21, 1848; between Carroll, April 8, 1869. Huntsville, county seat.

Marion, September 25, 1836; originally Searcy County; changed to Marion, September 29, 1836 (Searcy County created out of December 13, 1838); west boundary defined November 18, 1837; between Carroll defined December 18, 1846; part of Fulton attached January 18, 1855; between Van Buren and Searcy defined January 20, 1855, and March, 1873; line between Boone defined December 9, 1875; line between Baxter changed March 9, 1881. Yellville, county seat.

Miller, April 1, 1820; the greater portions fell within the limits of Texas; county abolished therefore, 1836; re-established, December 22, 1874, and eastern boundary extended. Texarkana, county seat.

Mississippi, November 1, 1833, 1859; portion of Crittenden attached, January 18, 1861. Osceola, county seat.

Monroe, November 2, 1829; boundaries defined December 25, 1840; line between Prairie changed December 7, 1850; line changed April 12, 1869, March, 1873, April, 1873, and May 27, 1874. Clarendon, county seat.

Montgomery, December 9, 1842; line between Yell defined January 2, 1845; between Perry, December 23, 1846; between Perry re-established December 21, 1848; between Hot Spring changed December 27, 1848; between Polk changed February 7, 1859, March, 1873; between Clark changed April 24, 1873; line between Pike defined December 16, 1874. Mount Ida, county seat.

Nevada, March 20, 1871; line between Columbia defined April 10, 1873. Prescott, county seat.

Newton, December 14, 1842; line between Madison defined December 21, 1848; between Pope January 10, 1853. Jasper, county seat.

Ouachita, November 29, 1842; line between Union changed January 6, 1853. Camden, county seat.

Perry, December 18, 1840; line between Pulaski, Saline and Montgomery defined December 23, 1846; old line between Montgomery re-established December 21, 1848. Perryville, county seat.

Phillips, May 1, 1820; part attached to Arkansas County October 23, 1821; west boundary defined October 30, 1823; act to divide and create Crittenden County October 22, 1825; divided and St. Francis County created October 13, 1827; line between Arkansas County defined November 21, 1828, 1840, March, 1873. Helena, county seat.

Pike, November 1, 1833; line between Sevier defined November 15, 1833; between Hempstead, December 14, 1838; between Clark, April 22, 1873; between Montgomery, December 16, 1874; between Clark defined March 8, 1877. Murfreesboro, county seat.

Poinsett, February 28, 1838, 1859. Harrisburg, county seat.

Polk, November 30, 1844; line between Montgomery changed February 7, 1859; part of Sebastian County added by ordinance of convention, June 1, 1861. Dallas, county seat.

Pope, November 2, 1829; part added to Yell January 5, 1853; part of Conway attached January 6, 1853; line between Newton, January 10, 1853; part of Van Buren attached January 12, 1853; between Van Buren defined February 17, 1859; between Johnson, October 19, 1859, March, 27, 1871; between Conway, May 28, 1874; between Johnson re-established March 6, 1875; between Johnson changed March 9, 1877. Dover, county seat.

Prairie, October 25, 1846; between Pulaski changed December 30, 1848; between Monroe changed December 7, 1850; line changed April 12, 1869; between White defined April 17, 1873; line changed April 26, 1873, May 27, 1874; between Lonoke changed November 30, 1875; separated into two districts, 1885. Devall's Bluff, county seat.

Pulaski, December 15, 1818, while a part of Lower Missouri Territory; line between Arkansas and Pulaski October 30, 1823; between Clark changed October 30, 1823; divided October 20, 1825; Quapaw Purchase divided—Arkansas and

Pulaski, October 13, 1827; northwest boundary defined October 23, 1827; between Pulaski and Conway, October 20, 1828; line between Saline defined February 25, 1838, December 14, 1838; between White changed February 3, 1843; between Saline defined December 21, 1846; between Perry defined December 23, 1846; between Prairie changed December 30, 1848; between Saline defined April 12, 1873; again, December 7, 1875. Little Rock, county seat.

Randolph, October 29, 1835; part of Lawrence attached January 18, 1864, March, 1873. Pocahontas, county seat.

Saline, November 2, 1835; boundaries defined November 5, 1836; between Pulaski, February 25, 1838, December 14, 1838, December 21, 1846; between Hot Spring, December 23, 1846, February 19, 1859, January 19, 1861; between Pulaski, April 12, 1873, December 17, 1875. Benton, county seat.

Scott, November 5, 1833; boundaries defined October 24, 1835; between Crawford, December 16, 1838; part of Sebastian attached by convention June 1, 1861; line between Logan changed March 21, 1873. Waldron, county seat.

Searcy, November 5, 1835; boundaries defined September 26, 1836; name changed to Marion September 29, 1836; county created out of Marion December 13, 1838; between Van Buren defined October 2, 1853; between Van Buren and Marion defined October 20, 1855, March, 1873. Marshall, county seat.

Sebastian, January 6, 1851; part attached to Scott and Polk by the convention June 1, 1861. Fort Smith and Greenwood, county seats.

Sevier, October 17, 1828; boundaries defined November 8, 1833; between Pike, November 15, 1833; southeast boundary defined October 29, 1836. Lockesburg, county seat.

Sharp, July 18, 1868; act March 3, 1873; between Independence defined February 11, 1875; line between Izard changed March 9, 1877, 1883. Evening Shade, county seat.

St. Francis, October 13,. 1827; St. Francis River declared boundary line between Crittenden November 3, 1831; part attached to Jackson January 1, 1851, March, 1873. Forrest City, county seat.

Stone, April 21, 1873. Mountain View, county seat.

Union, November 2, 1829; boundaries defined November 5, 1836; line between Lafayette, November 26, 1846; line between Ouachita changed January 6, 1853; part added to Columbia, December 21, 1851; part of Calhoun attached October 19, 1862. El Dorado, county seat.

Van Buren, November 11, 1833; boundaries defined November 4, 1836; part attached to Pope January 12, 1853; between Searcy and Marion defined January 20, 1855; between Pope defined February 17, 1859. Clinton, county seat.

Washington, October 17, 1828; certain lands declared to be in Washington County October 26, 1831; line between Crawford defined November 24, 1846; line changed between Crawford March 8, 1883. Fayetteville, county seat.

White, October 23, 1835; line between Pulaski changed February 3, 1843; part of Conway attached January 11, 1853; line between Prairie defined April 17, 1873. Searcy, county seat.

Woodruff, November 26, 1862; but vote, in pursuance to ordinance of conventions 1861, 1866, 1869; line changed April 26, 1873. Augusta, county seat.

Yell, December 5, 1840; northern boundary, December 21, 1840; line between Montgomery, January 2, 1845; part Pope attached January 6, 1853. Danville and Dardanelle, county seats.

The following table will prove valuable for comparison in noting the growth in population of the counties throughout the State in the various decades from their organization:

HISTORY OF ARKANSAS.

AGGREGATE POPULATION BY COUNTIES.

Counties in the State.	1880	1870	1860	1850	1840	1830	1820	1810
	802,525	484,471	435,450	209,897	97,574	30,388	14,235	1,062
Arkansas	8,038	8,288	8,884	3,245	1,346	1,426	1,260	1,062
Ashley	10,156	8,042	8,590	2,058				
Baxter	6,004							
Benton	20,327	13,831	9,306	3,710	2,228			
Boone	12,146	7,032						
Bradley	6,285	8,646	8,388	3,829				
Calhoun	5,671	3,853	4,103					
Carroll	13,337	5,780	9,383	4,617	2,844			
Chicot	10,117	7,214	9,234	5,115	3,806	1,165		
Clark	15,771	11,953	9,735	4,070	2,300	1,369	1,040	
Clay	7,213							
Columbia	14,090	11,397	12,459					
Conway	12,755	8,112	6,697	3,583	2,892	982		
Craighead	7,037	4,577	3,066					
Crawford	14,740	8,957	7,850	7,960	4,266	2,440		
Crittenden	9,415	3,831	4,920	2,648	1,561	1,272		
Cross	5,050	3,915						
Dallas	6,505	5,707	8,283	6,877				
Desha	8,873	6,125	6,459	2,911	1,598			
Dorsey	8,370							
Drew	12,231	9,960	9,087	3,276				
Faulkner	12,786							
Franklin	14,951	9,627	7,298	3,972	2,665			
Fulton	6,720	4,843	4,024	1,819				
Garland	9,023							
Grant	6,185	3,943						
Greene	7,480	7,573	5,843	2,593	1,586			
Hempstead	19,015	13,768	13,989	7,672	4,921	2,512	2,246	
Hot Spring	7,775	5,877	5,635	3,609	1,907	458		
Howard	9,917							
Independence	18,086	14,566	14,307	7,767	3,669	2,031		
Izard	10,857	6,806	7,215	3,212	2,240	1,266		
Jackson	10,877	7,268	10,493	3,086	1,540	333		
Jefferson	22,386	15,733	14,971	5,834	2,566	772		
Johnson	11,565	9,152	7,612	5,227	3,433			
Lafayette	5,730	9,139	8,464	5,220	2,280	748		
Lawrence	8,782	5,981	9,372	5,274	2,835	2,806	5,592	

AGGREGATE POPULATION BY COUNTIES.

Counties in the State.	1880	1870	1860	1850	1840	1830	1820	1810
	802,525	484,471	435,450	209,897	97,574	30,388	14,255	1,062
Lee	13,288							
Lincoln	9,255							
Little River	6,405	3,246						
Logan	14,865							
Lonoke	12,146							
Madison	11,455	8,231	7,740	4,823	2,775			
Marion	7,907	3,979	6,192	2,308	1,325			
Miller	9,919							
Mississippi	7,142	3,633	3,895	2,368	1,410			
Monroe	9,574	8,336	5,657	2,049	936	461		
Montgomery	5,729	2,984	3,633	1,958				
Nevada	12,959							
Newton	6,120	4,374	3,393	1,758				
Ouachita	11,758	12,975	12,936	9,591				
Perry	3,872	2,685	2,465	978				
Phillips	21,262	15,372	14,877	6,935	3,547	1,152	1,197	
Pike	6,345	3,788	4,026	1,861	969			
Poinsett	2,192	1,720	3,621	2,308	1,320			
Polk	5,857	3,376	4,262	1,263				
Pope	14,322	8,386	7,883	4,710	2,850	1,483		
Prairie	8,435	5,604	8,854	2,097				
Pulaski	32,616	32,066	11,699	5,657	5,350	2,395	1,921	
Randolph	11,724	7,466	6,261	3,275	2,196			
St. Francis	8,389	6,714	8,672	4,457	2,499	1,505		
Saline	8,953	3,911	6,540	3,903	2,061			
Scott	9,174	7,483	5,142	3,083	1,694			
Searcy	7,278	5,613	5,271	1,979	936			
Sebastian	19,560	12,940						
Sevier	6,192	4,492	10,516	4,240	2,810	634		
Sharp	9,047	5,400						
Stone	5,089							
Union	13,419	10,571	12,288	10,298	2,889	640		
Van Buren	9,565	5,107	5,357	2,864	1,518			
Washington	28,884	17,266	14,673	9,970	7,148	5,182		
White	17,794	10,347	8,316	2,619	920			
Woodruff	8,646	6,891						
Yell	13,852	8,048	6,333	3,341				

CHAPTER XII.

EDUCATION—THE MENTAL TYPE CONSIDERED—TERRITORIAL SCHOOLS, LAWS AND FUNDS—CONSTITUTIONAL PROVISIONS FOR EDUCATION—LEGISLATIVE PROVISIONS—PROGRESS SINCE THE WAR—THE STATE SUPERINTENDENTS—STATISTICS—ARKANSAS LITERATURE—THE ARKANSAW TRAVELER.

> Delightful task! to rear the tender thought,
> To teach the young idea how to shoot;
> To pour the fresh instructions o'er the mind,
> To breathe th' enlivening spirit, and to fix
> The generous purpose in the glowing breast.—*Thomson.*

HERE is one subject at least in the economic institutions of our country where men do not divide on political lines. To the historian it is a restful and refreshing oasis in the arid desert. From the Canadas to the Gulf communities and States earnestly vie with each other in the establishment of the best public schools. The present generation has nearly supplanted the former great universities with the free public high schools. A generation ago the South sent its boys to the North to school; the North sent its boys to the old universities of Europe. Oxford and Heidelburg received the sons of ambitious, wealthy Americans of the North, while Yale, Harvard and Jefferson Colleges were each the *alma mater* of many of the youths of the South. The rivalry in the schools between the two sections at that time was not intense, but the educated young men of the South met in sharpest rivalry in the halls of Congress the typical Northern man. As the highest types of the North and the South in active political life may be placed Thomas Jefferson and Daniel Webster. In peace or in war the differences in the intellectual advancement of the two sections were more imaginary than real. The disadvantage the South met was the natural tendency to produce an aristocratic class in the community. Cotton and the negro were impediments in the Southern States that clogged the way to the advancement of the masses. They retarded the building of great institutions of learning as well as the erection of large manufactories. This applied far more to collegiate education than to the common or public school system. The Southern man who was able to send his children away from his State to school realized that he gave them two advantages over keeping them at home; he aided them in avoiding negro contact and association, and provided the advantage of a better knowledge of different peoples in different sections.

Arkansas may have lagged somewhat in the cause of education in the past, but to-day, though young as a State, it is far in advance of many older communities who are disposed to boast greatly of their achievements in this direction.

When still a Territory the subject of education received wise and considerate attention. March 2, 1827, Congress gave the State seventy-two sections of land for the purpose of establishing "a seminary of learning." A supplemental act was passed by Congress, June 23, 1836, one week after it became a State, offering certain propositions for acceptance or rejection: 1. The sixteenth section of every township for school purposes. 2. The seventy-two sections known as the saline lands. By article 9, section 4, State constitution of 1869, these lands were given to the free schools. 3. The seventy-two sections, known as the seminary lands, given to the Territory in 1827, were vested and confirmed in the State of Arkansas for the use of said seminary. October 18, 1836, the State accepted the propositions entire; and the legislature passed the act known as "the ordinance of acceptance and compact." December 18, 1844, the general assembly asked Congress for a modification of the seminary grant, so as to authorize the legislature to appropriate these seventy-two sections of land for common school purposes. Congress assented to this on July 29, 1846, and the lands were added to the free school fund. These congressional land grants formed the basis of the State's free school system.

The first State constitution of 1836 recognized the importance of popular education, and made it the duty of the general assembly to provide by law for the improvement of such lands as are, or may be, granted by the United States for the use of schools, and to pass such laws as "shall be calculated to encourage intellectual, scientific and agricultural improvement."

The general assembly of 1842 established a system of common schools in the State, which was approved and became a law February 3, 1853, providing for the sale of the sixteenth section, and election of school trustees in each township, to expend the money from the sale of land in the cause of education. The act required schools to be maintained in each township "for at least four months in each year, and orthography, reading, writing, English grammar, arithmetic and good morals should be taught." The trustees were required to visit the schools once in each month, and the school age was fixed at from five to twenty-one years. The act also provided for the establishment of manual labor schools. It went to the extent of appropriating a sum of money for the purchase of text-books. This was a long step in advance of any other portion of the country at that time. To the fund arising from lands the act added "all fines for false imprisonment, assault and battery, breach of the peace, etc." This act of the assembly placed the young State in the vanguard of States in the cause of free schools. It is an enduring monument to the men of that legislature. Under this law the reports of the county commissioners of education were ordered to be made to the State auditor, but if so made none can be found in the State archives.

A State board of education was provided for by the act of 1843, and the board was required to make a complete report of educational matters, and also to recommend the passage of such laws as were deemed advisable for the advancement of the cause of education. By an act of January 11, 1853, the secretary of State was made *ex-officio* State commissioner of common schools, and required to report to the governor the true condition of the schools in each county; which report the governor presented to the general assembly at each regular session. The provisions of an act of January, 1855, relate to the sale of the sixteenth section, and defined the duties of the school trustees and commissioners. Article 8, in the constitution of 1867, is substantially the same as the provisions of the law of 1836.

From 1836 to 1867, as is shown by the above, the provisions of the law were most excellent and liberal toward the public schools; legislative enactments occur at frequent intervals, indicating that the State was well abreast of the most liberal school ideas of the time, and large funds were raised sacred to the cause.

Investigation shows that from the date of the State's admission into the Union, until 1867, there were many and admirable stipulations and statutes, by which large revenues were collected from the sale of lands, but the records of the State department give no account of the progress of free schools during this period, leaving the inference that but little practical benefit accrued to the cause from these wise and liberal measures put forth by Congress and the State.

By act approved May 18, 1867, the legislature made a marked forward movement in the cause of education. Considering the chaotic conditions of society, and the universal public and private bankruptcy, the movement is only the more surprising. The act stipulated that a tax of 20 cents on every $100 worth of taxable property should be levied for the purpose of establishing and maintaining a system of public schools. The second section made this fund sacred—to be used for no other purpose whatever. The fourth section provided for a superintendent of public instruction and defined his duties. The eighth section provided for a school commissioner, to be chosen by the electors of each county, who should examine any one applying for a position as school teacher; granting to those qualified to teach a certificate, without which no one could be legally employed to teach. Prior to this a license as teacher was not considered essential, and there was no one authorized to examine applicants or grant certificates. The Congressional township was made the unit of the school district, the act also setting forth that in the event of the trustees failing to have a school taught in the district at least three months in the year, the same thereby forfeited its portion of the school revenue. These wise and liberal arrangements were made, it must be remembered, by a people bankrupt by war and suffering the hard trials of reconstruction.

No regular reports were made—at least none can be found—prior to 1867, the date of the appointment of a superintendent. Though reports were regularly received from the year mentioned, the most of them were unsatisfactory and not reliable.

The constitution of 1868 created some wise amendments to the previous laws. It caused the schools to become free to every child in the State; school revenues were increased, districts could have no part of the school fund unless a free school had been taught for at least three months. The legislature following this convention, July 23, 1868, amended the school laws to conform to this constitutional provision. In addition to State superintendent, the office of circuit superintendent was created, and also the State board of education.

The constitutional convention of 1874 made changes in the school law and provided for the school system now in force in the State. The act of the legislature, December 7, 1876, was passed in conformity with the last preceding State convention. This law with amendments is the present school law of Arkansas.

Hon. Thomas Smith was the first State superintendent, in office from 1868 to 1873. The present incumbent of that position, Hon. Woodville E. Thompson, estimates that the commencement of public free schools in Arkansas may properly date from the time Mr. Smith took possession of the office—schools free to all; every child entitled to the same rights and privileges, none excluded; separate schools provided for white and black; a great number of schools organized, school houses built, and efficient teachers secured. Previous to this time people looked upon free schools as largely pauper schools, and the wealthier classes regarded them unfavorably.

Hon. J. C. Corbin, the successor of Mr. Smith, continued in office until December 13, 1875.

Hon. B. W. Hill was appointed December 18, 1875, and remained in office until 1878. It was during his term that there came the most marked change in public sentiment in favor of public schools. He was a zealous and able worker in the cause, and from his report for 1876 is learned the following: State apportionment, $213,000; district tax, $88,000; school population, 189,000. Through the directors' failure to report the enrollment only shows 16,000. The total revenue of 1877 was $270,000; of 1878, $276,000.

Mr. Hill was succeeded in 1878 by Hon. J. L. Denton, whose integrity, earnestness and great ability resulted in completing the valuable work so well commenced by his predecessor—removing the Southern prejudices against public schools. He deserves a lasting place in the history of Arkansas as the advocate and champion of free schools.

The present able and efficient State superintendent of public instruction, as previously mentioned, is Hon. Woodville E. Thompson. To his eminent qualifications and tireless energy the schools of Arkansas are largely indebted for the rapid advance now going on, and which has marked his past term of office. From his biennial report are gleaned most of the facts and statistics given below.

The growth of the institution as a whole may be defined by the following statistics: In 1879 the revenue raised by the State and county tax was $271,000; in 1880, $285,000; in 1881, $710,000; in 1882, $722,000; in 1883, $740,000; in 1884, $931,000; in 1885, $1,199,000; in 1886, $1,327,000. The district tax in 1884 was $346,521; in 1885, $343,850, and in 1886, $445,563. The district tax is that voted by the people.

Arkansas to-day gives the most liberal support to her free schools, all else considered, of any State in the Union. It provides a two mill tax, a poll tax, and authorizes the districts to vote a five mill tax. This is the rule or rate voted in nearly all the districts, thus making a total on all taxable property of seven mills, besides the poll tax.

The persistent neglect of school officers to report accurate returns of their school attendance is to be regretted. The number of pupils of school age (six to twenty-one years) is given, but no account of attendance or enrollment. This leaves counties in the unfavorable light of a large school population, with apparently the most meager attendance. The following summaries exhibit the progress of the public schools: Number of school children, 1869, 176,910; 1870, 180,274; 1871, 196,237; 1872, 194,314; 1873, 148,128; 1874, 168,929; 1875, 168,929; 1876, 189,130; 1877, 203,567; 1878, 216,475; 1879, 236,600; 1880, 247,547; 1881, 272,841; 1882, 289,617; 1883, white, 227,538; black, 76,429; total, 304,962; 1884, white, 247,173; black, 76,770; total, 323,943; 1885, white, 252,290; black, 86,213; total, 338,506; 1886, white, 266,188; black, 91,818; total, 358,006; 1887, white, 279,224; black, 98,512; total, 377,736; 1888, white, 288,381; black, 99,747; total, 388,129. The number of pupils enrolled in 1869 was 67,412; 1888, 202,754, divided as follows: White, 152,184; black, 50,570. Number of teachers employed 1869, 1,335; number employed 1888, males, 3,431, females, 1,233. Total number of school houses, 1884, 1,453; erected that year, 263. Total number school houses, 1888, 2,452; erected in that year, 269. Total value of school houses, 1884, $384,827.73. Total value, 1888, $705,276.92. Total amount of revenues received, 1868, $300,669.63. For the year, 1888: Amount on hand June 30, 1887, $370,942.25; received common school fund, $315,403.28; district tax, $505,069.92; poll tax, $146,604.22; other sources, $45,890.32; total, $1,683,909.32.

While there were in early Territorial days great intellectual giants in Arkansas, the tendency was not toward the tamer and more gentle walks of literature, but rather in the direction of the fiercer battles of the political arena and the rostrum. Oratory was cultivated to the extreme, and often to the neglect apparently of all else of intellectual pursuits. The ambitious youths had listened to the splendid eloquence of their elders—heard their praises on every lip, and were fired to struggle for such triumphs. Where there are great orators one expects to find poets and artists. The great statesman is mentally cast in molds of stalwart proportions. The poet, orator, painter, and eminent literary character are of a finer texture, but usually not so virile.

Gen. Albert Pike gave a literary immortality to Arkansas when it was yet a Territorial wilderness. The most interesting incident in the history of literature would be a true picture of that Nestor of the press, Kit North, when he opened the mail package from that dim and unknown savage world of Arkansas, and turned his eyes on the pages of Pike's manuscript, which had been offered the great editor for publication, in his poem entitled "Hymn to the Gods." This great but merciless critic had written Byron to death, and one can readily believe that he must have turned pale when his eye ran over the lines—lines from an unknown world of untamed aborigines, penned in the wilderness by this unknown boy. North read the products of new poets to find, not merit, but weak points, where he could impale on his sharp and pitiless pen the daring singer. What a play must have swept over his features as his eye followed line after line, eager and more eager from the first word to the last. To him could this be possible—real—and not the day dream of a disturbed imagination. This historical incident in the literature of the wild west—the pioneer boy not only on the outer confines of civilization, but to the average Englishman, in the impenetrable depths of a dark continent, where dwelt only cannibals, selecting the great and severe arbiter of English literature to whom he would transmit direct his fate as a poet; the youth's unexpected triumph in not only securing a place in the columns of the leading review of the world, but extorting in the editorial columns the highest meed of praise, is unparalleled in the feats of tyros in literature. The supremacy of Pike's genius was dulled in its brilliancy because of the versatility of his mental occupations. A poet, master of *belles lettres*, a lawyer and a politician, as well as a soldier, and eminent in all the varied walks he trod, yet he was never a bookmaker—had no ambition, it seems, to be an author. The books that he will leave, those especially by which he will be remembered, will be his gathered and bound writings thrown off at odd intervals and cast aside. His literary culture could produce only the very highest type of effort. Hence, it is probable that Lord North was the only editor living to whom Pike might have submitted his "Hymn to the Gods" with other than a chance whim to decide its fate.

There was no Boswell among the early great men of Arkansas, otherwise there would exist biographies laden with instruction and full of interest. There were men and women whose genius compelled them to talk and write, but they wrote disconnected, uncertain sketches, and doubtless often published them in the columns of some local newspaper, where they sank into oblivion.

The erratic preacher-lawyer, A. W. Arrington, wrote many and widely published sketches of the bench and bar of Arkansas, but his imagination so out-ran the facts that they became mere fictions—very interesting and entertaining, it is said, but entirely useless to the historian. Arrington was a man of superior natural genius, but was so near a moral wreck as to cloud his memory.

Years ago was published Nutall's History of Arkansas, but the most diligent inquiry among the oldest inhabitants fails to find one who ever heard of the book, much less the author.

Recently John Hallum published his History of Arkansas. The design of the author was to make three volumes, the first to treat of the bench and bar, but the work was dropped after this volume was published. It contains a great amount of valuable matter, and the author has done the State an important service in making his collections and putting them in durable form.

A people with so many men and women competent to write, and who have written so little of Arkansas, its people or its great historical events, presents a curious phase of society.

A wide and inviting field has been neglected and opportunities have been lost; facts have now gone out of men's memories, and important historical incidents passed into oblivion beyond recall.

Opie P. Read, now of Chicago, will be known in the future as the young and ambitious literary worker of Arkansas. He came to Little Rock from his native State, Tennessee, and engaged in work on the papers at that city. He soon had a wide local reputation and again this soon grew to a national one. His fugitive pieces in the newspapers gained extensive circulation, and in quiet humor and unaffected pathos were of a high order. He has written several works of fiction and is now running through his paper, The Arkansaw Traveler, Chicago, a novel entitled "The Kentucky Colonel," already pronounced by able critics one among the best of American works of fiction. Mr. Read is still a comparatively young man, and his pen gives most brilliant promise for the future. His success as an editor is well remembered.

CHAPTER XIII.

THE CHURCHES OF ARKANSAS—APPEARANCE OF THE MISSIONARIES—CHURCH MISSIONS ESTABLISHED IN THE WILDERNESS—THE LEADING PROTESTANT DENOMINATIONS—ECCLESIASTICAL STATISTICS—GENERAL OUTLOOK FROM A RELIGIOUS STANDPOINT.

> No silver saints by dying misers giv'n
> Here bribed the rage of ill-requited Heav'n;
> But such plain roofs as piety could raise,
> And only vocal with the Maker's praise.—*Pope.*

IN all histories of the early settlers the pioneer preachers and missionaries of the Church are of first interest. True missionaries, regardless of all creeds, are a most interesting study, and, in the broad principles of Christianity, they may well be considered as a class, with only incidental references to their different creeds. The essence of their remarkable lives is the heroic work and suffering they so cheerfully undertook and carried on so patiently and bravely. Among the first of pioneers to the homes of the red savages were these earnest churchmen, carrying the news of Mount Calvary to the benighted peoples. It is difficult for us of this age to understand the sacrifices they made, the privations they endured, the moral and physical courage required to sustain them in their work. The churches, through their missionaries, carried the cross of Christ, extending the spiritual empire in advance, nearly always, of the temporal empire. They bravely led the way for the hardy explorers, and ever and anon a martyr's body was given to the flames, or left in the trackless forests, food for ravenous wild beasts.

The first white men to make a lodgment in what is now Arkansas having been Marquette and Joliet, France and the Church thus came here hand in hand. The Spånish and French settlers at Arkansas Post were the representatives of Catholic nations, as were the French-Canadians who came down from the lakes and settled along the banks of the lower Mississippi River.

After 1803 there was another class of pioneers that came in—Protestant English by descent if not direct, and these soon dominated in the Arkansas country. The Methodists, Baptists and Cumberland Presbyterians, after the building of the latter by Rev. Finis Ewing, were the prevailing pioneer preachers. Beneath God's first temples these missionaries held meetings, traveled over the Territory, going wherever the little column of blue smoke from the cabin directed them, as well as visiting the Indian tribes, proclaiming Christ and His cause. Disregarding the elements, swollen streams, the dim trails, and often no other guide on their dreary travels than the projecting ridges, hills and streams, the sun or the polar star; facing hunger, heat and cold, the wild beast and the far fiercer savage, without hope of money compensation, regardless of sickness and even death, these men took their lives in their hands and went forth. Could anything be more graphic or pathetic of the conditions of these men than the extract from a letter of one of them who had thus served his God and fellow-man more than fifty years: "In my long ministry I often suffered for food and I spent no money for clothing. * * The largest yearly salary I received was $100." Were ever men inspired with more zeal in the cause of their Master? They had small polish and were as rugged as the gnarled old oaks beneath whose branches they so often bivouacked. They never tasted the refinements of polite life, no doubt despising them as heartily as they did sin itself. Rude of speech, what eloquence they possessed (and many in this respect were of no mean order) could only come of their deep sincerity.

These Protestant missionaries trod closely upon the footsteps of the pure and gentle Marquette in the descent of the Mississippi, and the visits to the Indians amid the cane-brakes of the South. Marquette's followers had been the first to ascend the Arkansas River to its source in the far distant land of the Dakotas in the Northwest. Holding aloft the cross, they boldly entered the camps of the tribes, and patiently won upon them until they laid down their drawn tomahawks and brought forth the calumet of peace. These wild children gathered around these strange beings—visitors, as they supposed, from another world, and wherever a cross was erected they regarded it with fear and awe, believing it had supreme power over them and their tribes.

He who would detract from the deserved immortality of any of these missionaries on account of their respective creeds, could be little else than a cynic whose blood is acid.

Marquette first explored the Mississippi River as the representative of the Catholic Church.

The old church baptismal records of the mission of Arkansas Post extend back to 1764, and the ministrations of Father Louis Meurin, who signed the record as "missionary priest." This is the oldest record to be found of the church's recognition of Arkansas now extant. That Marquette held church service and erected the cross of Christ nearly one hundred years anterior to the record date in Arkansas is given in the standard histories of the United States. Rev. Girard succeeded Meurin. It may be gleaned from these records that in 1788 De La Valliere was in command of Arkansas Post. In 1786 the attending priest was Rev. Louis Guigues. The record is next signed by Rev. Gibault in 1792, and next by Rev. Jannin in 1796. In 1820 is found the name of Rev. Chaudorat. In 1834 Rev. Dupuy, and in 1838 Father Donnelly was the priest in charge. These remained in custody of the first mission at Arkansas Post. The second mission established was St. Mary's, now Pine Bluff. The first priest at that point was Rev. Saulmier. Soon after, another mission, St. Peter's, was established in Jefferson County, and the third mission, also in Jefferson County, was next established at Plum Bayou. In order, the next mission was at Little Rock, Rev. Emil Saulmier in charge; then at Fort Smith; then Helena, and next Napoleon and New Gascony, respectively.

The Catholic population of the State is estimated at 10,000, with a total number of churches and missions of forty. There are twenty-two church schools, convents and academies, the school attendance being 1,600. The first bishop in the Arkansas diocese was Andrew Byrne, 1844. He died at Helena in 1862, his successor being the present incumbent, Bishop Edward FitzGerald, who came in 1867.

From a series of articles published in the Arkansas Methodist, of the current year, by the eminent and venerable Rev. Andrew Hunter, D. D., are gleaned the following important facts of this Church's history in Arkansas: Methodism came to Arkansas by way of Missouri about 1814, a company of emigrants entering from Southeast Missouri overland, and who much of the way had to cut out a road for their wagons. They had heard of the rich lands in Mound Prairie, Hempstead County. In this company were John Henrey, a local preacher, Alexander and Jacob Shook, brothers, and Daniel Props. In their long slow travels they reached the Arkansas River at Little Rock, and waited on the opposite bank for the completion of a ferry-boat then building. When these people reached their destination they soon set up a church, and erected the first Methodist "meeting-house" in Arkansas, called Henrey's Chapel. "Father Henrey," as he was soon known far and wide, reared sons, all preachers. This little colony were all sincere Methodists, and nearly all their first generation of sons became preachers, some of them eminent. Jacob Shook and three of his sons entered the ministry; Gilbert Alexander, his sons and grandsons, became ministers of God's word, as did two of Daniel Props' sons. The small colony was truly the seed of the church in Arkansas.

In 1838 two young ministers were sent from Tennessee to the Arkansas work, and came all the way to Mound Prairie on horseback.

The church records of Missouri show that the conference of 1817 sent two preachers to Arkansas—William Stevenson and John Harris. They were directed to locate at Hot Springs. It is conceded that these two missionaries "planted Methodism in Arkansas."

In 1818 the Missouri Conference sent four laborers to Arkansas, with William Stevenson as the presiding elder of the Territory. The circuits then had: John Shader, on Spring River; Thomas Tennant, Arkansas circuit; W. Orr, Hot Springs; William Stevenson and James Lowrey, Mound Prairie. What was called the Arkansas circuit included the Arkansas River, from Pine Bluff to the mouth. After years of service as presiding elder, Stevenson was succeeded by John Scripps; the appointments then were: Arkansas circuit, Dennis Willey; Hot Springs, Isaac Brookfield; Mound Prairie, John Harris; Pecan Point, William Townsend. The Missouri Conference, 1823, again made William Stevenson presiding elder, with three itinerants for Arkansas. In 1825 Jesse Hale became presiding elder. He was in charge until 1829. He was an original and outspoken abolitionist, and taught and preached his faith unreservedly; so much so that large numbers of the leading families left the Methodist Episcopal Church and joined the Cumberland Presbyterians. This was the sudden building up of the Cumberland Presbyterian Church, and nearly fatally weakened the Methodist Church. Some irreverent laymen designated Elder Jesse Hale's ministrations as the "Hail storm" in Arkansas. Fortunately Hale was succeeded by Rev. Jesse Green, and he poured oil on the troubled waters, and saved Methodism in Arkansas. "Green was our Moses."

The Tennessee Conference, 1831, sent eight preachers to Arkansas, namely: Andrew D. Smyth, John Harrell, Henry G. Joplin, William A. Boyce. William G. Duke, John N. Hammill, Alvin Baird and Allen M. Scott.

A custom of those old time preachers now passed away is worth preserving. When possible to do so they went over the circuit together, two and two. One might preach the regular sermon, when the other would "exhort." Under these conditions young Rev. Smyth was accompanying the regular circuit rider. He was at first diffident, and "exhorted" simply by giving his hearers "Daniel in the lion's den." As the two started around the circuit the second time, on reaching a night appointment, before entering the house, and as they were returning from secret prayer in the brush, the preacher said: "Say, Andy, I'm going to preach, and when I'm done you give 'em Daniel and the lions again." Evidently Andy and his lions were a terror to the natives. But the young exhorter soon went up head, and became a noted divine.

The Missouri Conference, 1832, made two districts of Arkansas. Rev. A. D. Smyth had charge of Little Rock district, which extended over all the country west, including the Cherokee and Creek Nations.

The formation of the Methodist Episcopal Church, South, occurred in 1844. This is a well known part of the history of our country. In Arkansas the church amid all its trials and vicissitudes has grown and flourished. The State now has fifteen districts, with 200 pastoral charges, and, it is estimated, nearly 1,000 congregations.

The Methodist Episcopal Church has a comfortable church in Little Rock, and several good sized congregations in different portions of the State. This church and the Methodist Episcopal

Church, South, are separate and wholly distinct in their organization.

The Baptists are naturally a pioneer and frontier church people. They are earnest and sincere proselyters to the faith, and reach very effectively people in general. The Baptist Church in Benton celebrated, July 4, 1889, its fifty-third anniversary. Originally called Spring Church, it was built about two miles from the town. The organization took place under the sheltering branches of an old oak tree. One of the first churches of this order was the Mount Bethel Church, about six miles west of Arkadelphia, in Clark County. This was one of the oldest settled points by English speaking people in the State. The church has grown with the increase of population.

Rev. James M. Moore organized in Little Rock, in 1828, the first Presbyterian Church in Arkansas. He was from Pennsylvania, eminent for his ability, zeal and piety. For some time he was the representative of his church in a wide portion of the country south and west. He was succeeded by Rev. A. R. Banks, from the theological seminary of Columbia, S. C., who settled in Hempstead County in 1835–36 and organized and built Spring Hill Church, besides another at Washington. The next minister in order of arrival was Rev. John M. Erwin. He located at Jackson, near the old town of Elizabeth, but his life was not spared long after coming. He assisted Revs Moore and Banks in organizing the first presbytery in Arkansas.

In 1839 Rev. J. M. Moore, mentioned above, removed to what is now Lonoke County, and organized a congregation and built Sylvania Church. His successor at Little Rock was Rev. Henderson, in 1840. The death of Rev. Henderson left no quorum, and the Arkansas presbytery became *functus officio.*

Rev. Aaron Williams, from Bethel presbytery, South Carolina, came to Arkansas in 1842, and settled in Hempstead County, taking charge of a large new academy at that place, which had been built by the wealthy people of the locality. He at once re-organized the church at Washington, which had been some time vacant. Arkansas then belonged to the synod of Mississippi. In 1842, in company with Rev. A. R. Banks, he traveled over the swamps and through the forests 400 miles to attend the Mississippi synod at Port Royal. Their mission was to ask the synod to allow Revs. Williams, Moore, Banks and Shaw to organize the Arkansas presbytery. They obtained the permission, and meeting in Little Rock the first Sunday in January, 1843, organized the Arkansas presbytery. The Rev. Balch had settled in Dardanelle, and he joined the new presbytery. In the next few years Revs. Byington and Kingsbury, Congregational ministers, who had been missionaries to the Indians since 1818, also joined the Arkansas presbytery. The synod of Memphis was subsequently formed, of which Arkansas was a part. There were now three presbyteries west of Memphis: Arkansas, Ouachita and Indian. In 1836 Arkansas was composed of four presbyteries—two Arkansas and two Ouachita.

Rev. Aaron Williams assumed charge at Little Rock in 1843, where he remained until January, 1845. There was then a vacancy for some years in that church, when the Rev. Joshua F. Green ministered to the flock. He was succeeded by Rev. Thomas Fraser, who continued until 1859. All these had been supplies, and in 1859 Little Rock was made a pastorate, and Rev. Thomas R. Welch was installed as first pastor. He filled the position the next twenty-five years, and in 1885 resigned on account of ill health, and was sent as counsel to Canada, where he died. About the close of his pastorate, the Second Presbyterian Church of Little Rock was organized, and their house built, the Rev. A. R. Kennedy, pastor. He resigned in September, 1888, being succeeded by James R. Howerton. After the resignation of Dr. Welch of the First Church, Dr. J. C. Barrett was given charge.

Rev. Aaron Williams, after leaving the synod, became a synodical evangelist, and traveled over the State, preaching wherever he found small collections of people, and organizing churches. He formed the church at Fort Smith and the one in Jackson County.

A synodical college is at Batesville, and is highly prosperous.

CHAPTER XIV.

NAMES ILLUSTRIOUS IN ARKANSAS HISTORY—PROMINENT MENTION OF NOTED INDIVIDUALS—AMBROSE H. SEVIER—WILLIAM E. WOODRUFF—JOHN WILSON—JOHN HEMPHILL—JACOB BARKMAN—DR. BOWIE—SANDY FAULKNER—SAMUEL H. HEMPSTEAD—TRENT, WILLIAMS, SHINN FAMILIES, AND OTHERS—THE CONWAYS—ROBERT CRITTENDEN—ARCHIBALD YELL—JUDGE DAVID WALKER—GEN. G. D. ROYSTON—JUDGE JAMES W. BATES.

> The gen'ral voice
> Sounds him, for courtesy, behaviour, language
> And ev'ry fair demeanor, an example;
> Titles of honour add not to his worth,
> Who is himself an honour to his title.—*Ford.*

NO history of Arkansas, worthy of the name, could fail to refer to the lives of a number of its distinguished citizens, whose relation to great public events has made them a part of the true history of their State. The following sketches of representative men will be of no little interest to each and every reader of the present volume.

Ambrose H. Sevier, was one of the foremost of the prominent men of his day, and deserves especial mention. The recent removal of the remains of Gen. John Sevier from Alabama to Knoxville, Tenn. (June 19, 1889), has awakened a wide-spread interest in this historic family name. The re-interment of the illustrious ashes of the first governor, founder and Congressman of Tennessee, by the State he had made, was but an act of long deferred justice to one of the most illustrious and picturesque characters in American history. He founded two States and was the first governor of each of them; one of these States, Tennessee, he had, in the spirit of disinterested patriotism, erected on the romantic ruins of the other—the mountain State of "Franklin." A distinguished Revolutionary soldier, he was the hero of King's Mountain, where he and four brothers fought. He was first governor of the State of "Franklin," six times governor of Tennessee, three times a member of Congress, and in no instance did he ever have an opponent to contest for an office. He was in thirty-five hard fought battles; had faced in bitter contest the State of North Carolina, which secretly arrested and abducted him from the new State he had carved out of North Carolina territory; was rescued in open court by two friends, and on his return to his adherents as easily defeated the schemes of North Carolina as he had defeated, in many battles, the Cherokee Indians. No man ever voted against "Nolichucky Jack," as he was familiarly called—no enemy ever successfully stood before him in battle. A great general, statesman, and patriot, he was the creator and builder of commonwealths west of the Alleghanies, and he guided as greatly and wisely as did Washington and Jefferson the new States and Territories he formed in the paths of democratic freedom; and now, after he has slept in an obscure grave for three-quarters of a century, the fact is beginning to dawn upon the nation that Gov. John Sevier made Washington, and all that great name implies, a possibility.

The name, illustrious as it is ancient, numerous and wide spread, is from the French Pyrenees, Xavier, where it may be traced to remote times. St. Francis Xavier was of this family, and yet the American branch were exiles from the old world because of their revolt against papal tyranny. Sturdy and heroic as they were in the faith, their blood was far more virile, indeed stalwart, in defense of human rights and liberty, wherever or by whomsoever assailed.

In France, England and in nearly every Western and Southern State of the Union are branches of the Xaviers, always prominent and often eminent in their day and time. But it was reserved to the founder of the American branch of the Seviers to be the supreme head of the illustrious line. He builded two commonwealths and was impelled to this great work in defense of the people, and in resistance to the encroachments of the central powers of the paternal government.

In Arkansas the Seviers, Conways and Rectors were united by ties of blood as well as by the ever stronger ties of the sons of liberty, independence and patriotism. Here were three of the most powerful families the State has ever had, and in public affairs they were as one. The political friend and worthy model of Gov. John Sevier was Thomas Jefferson. Indeed, Gen. Sevier was the fitting and immortal companion-piece to Jefferson in those days of the young and struggling republic. The Seviers of Arkansas and Missouri were naturally the admirers of Andrew Jackson champions of the people's rights, watchdogs of liberty.

Ambrose H. Sevier, was the son of John, who was the son of Valentine and Ann Conway Sevier, of Greene County, Tenn. Ann Conway was the daughter of Thomas and Ann Rector Conway. Thus this family furnished six of the governors of Arkansas.

In 1821, soon after Mr. Sevier's coming to Arkansas, he was elected clerk of the Territorial house of representatives. In 1823 he was elected from Pulaski County to the legislature, and continued a member and was elected speaker in 1827. He was elected to Congress in August, 1828, to succeed his uncle, Henry W. Conway, who had been killed in a duel with Crittenden. He was three times elected to Congress. When the State came into the Union, Sevier and William S. Fulton were elected first senators in Congress. Sevier resigned his seat in the Senate in 1848, to accept the mission of minister plenipotentiary to Mexico, and, in connection with Judge Clifford, negotiated the treaty of Guadaloupe Hidalgo. This was the last as well as crowning act of his life. He died shortly after returning from his mission. The State has erected a suitable monument to his memory in Mount Holly Cemetery, Little Rock, where sleeps his immortal dust.

How curiously fitting it was that the Sevier of Arkansas should follow so closely in the footsteps of the great governor of Tennessee, his lineal ancestor, and be the instrument of adding so immensely to the territory out of which have grown such vast and rich commonwealths. As builders of commonwealths there is no name in American history which approaches that of Sevier. A part of the neglect—the ingratitude, possibly—of republics, is shown in the fact that none of the States of which they gave the Union so many bear their family name.

William E. Woodruff was in more than one sense a pioneer to Arkansas. He was among the distinguished men who first hastened here when the Territory was formed, and brought with him the pioneer newspaper press, and established the Arkansas Gazette. This is now a flourishing daily and weekly newspaper at the State capital, and one of the oldest papers in the country. Of himself alone there was that in the character and life of Mr. Woodruff which would have made him one of the historical pioneers to cross the Mississippi River, and cast his fortune and future in this new world. But he was a worthy disciple and follower of Ben. Franklin, who combined with the art preservative of arts, the genius that lays foundations for empires in government, and the yet far greater empires in the fields of intellectual life.

He was a native of Long Island, Suffolk County, N. Y. Leaving his home in 1818, upon the completion of his apprenticeship as printer, with the sparse proceeds of his earnings as apprentice he turned his face westward. Reaching Wheeling, Va., he embarked in a canoe for the falls of the Ohio, now Louisville, where he stopped and worked at his trade. Finding no sufficient opening to permanently locate in this place, he started on foot, by way of Russellville, to Nashville, Tenn., and for a time worked at his trade in that place and at Franklin. Still looking for a possible future home further west, he heard of the Act of Congress creating the Territory of Arkansas, to take effect July 4, 1819. He at once purchased a small outfit for a newspaper office and started to the newly formed Territory, determined if possible to be first on the ground. He shipped by keel-boat down the Cumberland river, the Ohio and the Mississippi Rivers to Montgomery's Point, at the mouth of White River; thence overland to Arkansas Post, the first Territorial capital. Montgomery Point was then, and for some years after, the main shipping point for the interior points of the Arkansas Territory. From this place to the capital, he found nothing but a bridle-path. He therefore secured a pirogue, and with the services of two boatmen, passed through the cut-off to Arkansas River and then up this to Arkansas Post, reaching his point of destination October 31, 1819. So insignificant was the Post that the only way he could get a house was to build one, which he did, and November 20, 1819, issued the first paper—the Arkansas Gazette. He was the entire force of the office—mechanical, clerical and editorial. To-day his own work is his fitting and perpetual monument—linking his name indissolubly with that of Arkansas and immortality.

His genius was in the direct energy and the impelling forces which drove it with the sure certainty of fate over every opposing obstacle. Broad, strong and great in all those qualities which characterize men pre-eminent in the varied walks of life; a true nation founder and builder, his useful life was long spared to the State, which will shed luster to itself and its name by honoring the memory of one of its first and most illustrious pioneers—William E. Woodruff.

Reference having been made to John Wilson in a previous chapter, in connection with his unfortunate encounter with J. J. Anthony, on the floor of the hall of the legislature, it is but an act of justice that the circumstances be properly explained, together with some account of the manner of man he really was.

John Wilson came from Kentucky to Arkansas in the early Territorial times, 1820. His wife was a Hardin, of the noted family of that State—a sister of Joseph Hardin, of Lawrence County, Ark., who was speaker of the first house of representatives of the Territorial legislature. The Wilsons and Hardins were prominent and highly respectable people.

When a very young man, John Wilson was elected to the Territorial legislature, where he was made speaker and for a number of terms filled that office. He was a member of the first State legislature and again was elected speaker. He was the first president of the Real Estate Bank of Arkansas. Physically he was about an average-sized man, very quiet in his manner and retiring, of dark complexion, eyes and hair, lithe and sinewy in form, and in his daily walk as gentle as a woman. He was devoted to his friends, and except for politics, all who knew him loved him well. There was not the shadow of a shade of the bully or desperado about him. He was a man of the highest sense of personal honor, with an iron will, and even when aroused or stung by injustice or an attack upon his integrity his whole nature inclined to peace and good will. He was a great admirer of General Jackson—there was everything in the natures of the two men where the "fellow feeling makes us wondrous kind."

The difficulty spoken of occurred in 1836. Wilson was a leader in the Jackson party. Anthony aspired to the lead in the Whig party. At that time politics among the active of each faction meant personality. It was but little else than open war, and the frontier men of those days generally went armed, the favorite weapon being the bowie knife—a necessary part of a hunter's equipment. Unfriendly feelings existed between Wilson and Anthony.

Upon the morning of the homicide (in words the substance of the account given by the late Gen. G. D. Royston, who was an eye witness) Mr. Wilson came into the hall a little late, evidently disturbed in mind, and undoubtedly ruffled by reason of something he had been told that Mr. Anthony had previously said about him in discussing a bill concerning wolf-scalps. A seriocomic amendment had been offered to the bill to make scalps a legal tender, and asking the president of the Real Estate Bank to certify to the genuineness of the same. Anthony had the floor. When Wilson took the speaker's chair he commanded Anthony to take his seat. The latter brusquely declined to do so. Wilson left the chair and approached his opponent, who stood in the aisle. The manner of the parties indicated a personal encounter. As Wilson walked down the aisle he was seen to put his hand in the bosom of his vest. Anthony drew his knife. Gen. Royston said that when he saw this, hoping to check the two men he raised his chair and held it between them, and the men fought across or over the chair. They struck at each other inflicting great wounds, which were hacking blows. Wilson's left hand was nearly cut off in warding a blow from Anthony's knife. Wilson was physically a smaller man than Anthony. Royston held the chair with all his strength between the two now desperate individuals. So far Anthony's longer arm had enabled him to give the greatest wounds, when Wilson with his shoulder raised the chair and plunged his knife into his antagonist, who sank to the floor and died immediately. It was a duel with bowie-knives, without any of the preliminaries of such encounters.

Wilson was carried to his bed, where for a long time he was confined. The house expelled him the next day. The civilized world of course was shocked, so bloody and ferocious had been the engagement.

Wilson removed to Texas about 1842, locating at Cedar Grove, near Dallas, where he died soon after the close of the late war. Mrs. A. J. Gentry, his daughter, now resides in Clark County, Ark. The Hardins, living in Clark County, are of the same family as was Mrs. Wilson.

John Hemphill, a South Carolinian, was born a short distance above Augusta, Ga. He immigrated west and reached (now) Clark County, Ark., in 1811, bringing with him a large family and a number of slaves, proceeding overland to Bayou Sara, La., and from that point by barges to near where is Arkadelphia, then a settlement at a place called Blakeleytown, which was a year old at the time of Mr. Hemphill's location. He found living there on his arrival Adam Blakeley, Zack Davis, Samuel Parker, Abner Highnight and a few others.

Mr. Hemphill was attracted by the salt waters of the vicinity, and after giving the subject intelligent investigation, in 1814 built his salt works. Going to New Orleans, he procured a barge and purchased a lot of sugar kettles, and with these completed his preparations for making salt. His experiment was a success from the start and he carried on his extensive manufactory until his death, about 1825. The works were continued by his descendants, with few intermissions, until 1851. Jonathan O. Callaway, his son-in-law, was, until that year, manager and proprietor.

There is a coincidence in the lives of the two men who were the founders of commerce and manufacturing in Arkansas, Hemphill and Barkman, in that by chance they became traveling companions on their way to the new country.

Two brothers, Jacob and John Barkman, came to Arkansas in 1811. They worked their passage in the barge of John Hemphill, from Bayou Sara, La., to Blakeleytown, near Arkadelphia. They were a couple of young Kentuckians, full of courage, hope, and strong sense, seeking homes in the wilderness. Their coming antedated that of the first steamboat on western waters, and the history of the river commerce of this State with New Orleans will properly credit Jacob Barkman with being its founder. Considering the times and realizing what such men as Jacob Barkman did, one is constrained to the belief that among the first settlers of Arkansas were men of enterprise, foresight and daring in commerce that have certainly not been surpassed by their successors.

On a previous page the methods of this pioneer merchant in the conduct of his business have been noted. His miscellaneous cargo of bear oil, skins, pelts, tallow, etc., found a ready market in New Orleans, which place he reached by river, returning some six months later well laden with commodities best suited to the needs of the people. Indeed his "store" grew to be an important institution. He really carried on trade from New Orleans to Arkadelphia. In 1820 he purchased of the government about 1,200 acres of land on the Caddo, four miles from Arkadelphia, and farmed extensively and had many cattle and horses, constantly adding to the number of his slaves. Having filled the field where he was he sought wider opportunities, and in 1840, in company with J. G. Pratt, opened an extensive cotton commission business in New Orleans, building large warehouses and stores. Mr. Barkman next purchased the steamboat "Dime," a side-wheeler, finely built and carrying 400 bales of cotton. He ran this in the interest of the New Orleans commission house; owned his crews, and loaded the boat with cotton from his own plantation. In 1844 his boat proudly brought up at New Orleans, well laden with cotton. The owner was on board and full of hope and anticipated joy at his trip, and also to meet his newly married wife (the second), when these hopes were rudely dashed by the appearance of an officer who seized the boat, cargo and slaves, everything—and arrested Mr. Barkman and placed him in jail under an attachment for debts incurred by the commission house. His partner in his absence had wrecked the house.

To so arrange matters that he might get out of jail and return to his old home on the Caddo, with little left of this world's goods, was the best the poor man could do. He finally saved from the wreckage his fine farm and a few negroes, and, nothing daunted, again went to work to rebuild his fortune. He erected a cotton factory on the Caddo River, and expended some $30,000 on the plant, having it about ready to commence operating when the water came dashing down the mountain streams in a sudden and unusual rise, and swept it all away. This brave pioneer spent no hour of his life in idle griefs at his extraordinary losses. Though unscrupulous arts of business sharks and dire visitations of the elements combined to make worthless his superb foresight and business energy, he overcame all obstacles, and died about 1852, a wealthy man for that time.

When Arkansas was yet a Territory, among its early pioneers was Dr. William Bowie, whose name has become familiar to the civilized world, though not in the way that most men are emulous of immortality. Dr. Bowie had located, or was a frequent visitor, in Helena, Ark., and was a typical man of his times—jolly, careless and social, and very fond of hunting and fishing.

Among the first settlers in Little Rock was a blacksmith, named Black. He possessed skill in working in iron and steel, and soon gained a wide reputation for the superior hunting knives he made. When nearly every man hunted more or less, and as a good knife was a necessity, it will be seen that Black was filling a general want. The material he worked into knives consisted of old files.

One day while he was just finishing a superior and somewhat new style of hunting knife, Dr. Bowie happened to enter the shop. The moment he saw the article he determined to possess it at any price. Black had not really made it to sell—simply to gratify a desire to see how fine a blade he could make, and keep it. But a bargain was finally arranged, the blacksmith to complete it and put Bowie's name on the handle. The inscription being neatly done read: "Bowie's Knife." Its beauty and finish attracted wide attention, and all who could afford it ordered a similar one, the name of which was soon shortened into "Bowie Knife." Bowie died a patriot's death, fighting for the independence of Texas, by the side of David Crockett.

The one pre-eminent thing which entitles the Arkansas pioneer, Sandy Faulkner, to immortality is the fact that he is the real, original "Arkansaw Traveler." He was an early settler, a hunter, a wild, jolly, reckless spendthrift, and a splendid fiddler. He was of a wealthy Kentucky family, and settled first in Chicot County and then on the river only a few miles below Little Rock. By inheritance he received two or three moderate fortunes, and spent them royally. Of a roving nature, a witty and rollicking companion, he would roam through the woods, hunting for days and weeks, and then enliven the village resorts for a while. He was born to encounter just such a character as he did chance to find, playing on a three-stringed fiddle the first part of a particular tune. Now there was but one thing in this world that could touch his heart with a desire to possess, and that was to hear the remainder of the tune.

After meeting this rare character in the woods what a world of enjoyment Sandy did carry to the village on his next return! "With just enough and not too much," with fiddle in his hand, the villagers gathered about him while he repeated the comedy. His zest in the ludicrous, his keen wit and his inimitable acting, especially his power of mimicry and his mastery of the violin, enabled him to offer his associates an entertainment never surpassed, either on or off the mimic stage.

After the war Faulkner lived in Little Rock until his death in 1875, in straitened circumstances, residing with a widowed daughter and one son. Another son was killed in the war; the two daughters married and are both dead, and the son and only remaining child left this portion of the country some years ago.

When Faulkner died—over eighty years of age—he held a subordinate office in the legislature then in session, which body adjourned and respectfully buried all that was mortal of the "Arkansaw Traveler," while the little *morceau* from his harmless and genial soul will continue to travel around the world and never stop, the thrice welcome guest about every fireside.

What a comment is here in this careless, aimless life and that vaulting ambition that struggles, and wars and suffers and sows the world with woe that men's names may live after death. Poor Sandy had no thought of distinction; his life was a laugh, so unmixed with care for the morrow and so merry that it has filled a world with its ceaseless echoes.

Though there may be in this country no titled aristocracy, there are nobles, whose remotest descendants may claim that distinction of race and blood which follows the memory of the great deeds of illustrious sires. It is the nobles whose lives and life's great work were given to the cause of their fellowmen in that noblest of all human efforts—liberty to mankind. There is something forever sacred lingering about the graves, nay, the very ground, where these men exposed their lives and struggled for each and all of us. All good men (and no man can really be called good who does not love liberty and independence above everything in the world) cannot but feel a profound interest in the lineal descendants of Revolutionary fathers. "My ancestor was a soldier in the war for independence!" is a far nobler claim to greatness than is that of the most royal blue blood in all heraldry.

W. P. Huddleston, of Sharp's Cross Roads, Independence County, has the following family tree: Israel McBee was for seven years a soldier in a North Carolina regiment in the Revolutionary War. He died in Grainger County, Tenn., aged 110 years. He was the father of Samuel McBee, who was the father of Rachel McBee, who married John Huddleston, the grand father of W. P. Huddleston, Jr. The McBees were originally from Scotland.

Samuel S. Welborn, of Fort Douglas, Johnson County, was the youngest son of Elias. Samuel was born December 30, 1842. His grandfather, Isaac Welborn, was seven years a soldier in a Georgia regiment, and died at Hazel Green, Ala., in 1833, aged eighty-four years.

Samuel H. Hempstead is a name illustrious in Arkansas outside of the fact that it is descended directly from a soldier in the war for independence. The above-named was born in New London, Conn., in 1814, and died in Little Rock in 1862. He was a son of Joseph Hempstead, born in New London in 1778, and died in St. Louis in 1831. Joseph was a son of Stephen Hempstead, born in New London in 1742, and died in St. Louis in 1832. Stephen was a soldier in the American Revolution, serving under Col. Ledyard at the battle of Fort Griswold, near New London, when these towns were captured by the British under Benedict Arnold, September 6, 1781. Hempstead was wounded twice during the engagement—a severe gunshot wound in the left elbow disabling him in the arm for life. He wrote and published in the Missouri Republican in 1826, a detailed account of the battle.

Stephen Hempstead's father was also Stephen Hempstead, born in 1705 and died in 1774. The records of Connecticut, Vol. VII, show that he was made an ensign in a train band company, by the colonial council, in October, 1737, where he served with distinction through this war, known as King George's War. In May, 1740, he was made surveyor by the council. He was the son of Joshua Hempstead, born in 1678, and died in 1758. He was a representative in the Connecticut council in October, 1709; a member of the Royal council in October, 1712; ensign in train band company in 1721; lieutenant in same company in May, 1724; auditor of accounts in May, 1725. He was the son of Joshua Hempstead, Sr., born in 1649, and died in 1709; Joshua Hempstead, Sr., was a son of Robert Hempstead, born in 1600 and died in 1665. The last-named was the immigrant to America, one of the original nine settlers of New London, Conn., the founder of the town first called Hempstead, on Long Island. In 1646 Robert Hempstead built a house at New London for a residence, which is still standing, an ancient relic of great interest. It is occupied by descendants of the builder, named Caits, from the female branches. Though much modernized the old house still shows the port-holes used for defense against the Indians. A daughter of Robert Hempstead, Mary, was the first white child born in New London, March 26, 1647.

Fay and Roy Hempstead, Little Rock, are descendants of this family. Other descendants live in St. Louis, Mo.

Jesse Williams, of Prince William County, Va., enlisted under Dinwiddie's call in the French-Indian War on the English settlers in 1754, under then Lieut.-Col. Washington, of the First Virginia Regiment of 150 men. The command attempted to reach where is now Pittsburg to relieve Trent's command at that place. Two descendants of the Trents now live in Washington County. In this hard march to Fort Duquesne the men dragged their cannon, were without tents and scant of provisions, and deprived of material or means for bridging rivers. They fought at Fort Necessity. Washington cut a road twenty miles toward Duquesne. On July 3 the fight took place, and July 4 Washington capitulated on honorable terms.

In 1755 Jesse Williams again entered the service under Washington and joined Braddock at Fort Cumberland. In 1758 he was once more with Washington when Forbes moved on Fort Duquesne, being present at the capture, and helped raise the flag and name the place Pittsburg.

In the Revolutionary War he was one of the first to enlist from Virginia, and was commissioned captain, and was present in nearly all the battles of that long war.

The maternal ancestor of the Williams family was Thomas Rowe, of Virginia, a colonel in the war for independence, who was at the surrender of Yorktown.

David Williams, a son of Jesse, married Betsy Rowe. He was a soldier in the War of 1812, and served with distinction, and also in the Seminole War. He settled in Kentucky, Franklin County. His children were Jacob, Urban V., Betty, Millie, Hattie and Susan; the children of Urban V. Williams being John, Pattie and Minnie. Bettie married Jeptha Robinson, and had children, David, Owen, Austin, May, Hettie, Ruth, Sue, Jacob, Frank and Sallie. Hettie married Dr. Andrew Neat, and had children, Thomas, Estelle (Brinkley), Ella (Ford), Addis and Ben. Sue married George Poor, and had children, George, Lizzie, Sue and Minnie. Jacob Williams, the father of Mrs. Minnie C. Shinn (wife of Prof. J. H. Shinn, of Little Rock), Otis Williams and Mattie Williams, Little Rock; Joseph Desha Williams and Maggie Wells, Russellville; Lucian and Virgil, Memphis, are all of this family. Jacob Williams was a private in the Fifth Kentucky, in the late war, under Humphrey Marshall.

Among the pioneers of what is now the State of Arkansas, there was perhaps no one family that furnished so many noted characters and citizens as the Conway family. Their genealogy is traced "back to the reign of Edward I, of England, in the latter part of the thirteenth century, to the celebrated Castle of Conway, on Conway River, in the north of Wales, where the lords of Conway, in feudal times presided in royal style." Thomas Conway came to America about the year 1740, and settled in the Virginia colony. Henry Conway was his only son. The latter was first a colonel and afterward a general in the Revolutionary War. His daughter, Nellie, after marriage, became the mother of President Madison, and his son, Moncure D., was brother-in-law to Gen. Washington.

Thomas Conway, another son of Gen. Henry Conway, settled, during the Revolutionary period, near the present site of Greenville, Tenn. He married Ann Rector, a native of Virginia, and member of the celebrated Rector family. To this union seven sons and three daughters were born, and all were well reared and well educated.

In 1818, Gen. Thomas Conway moved with his family from Tennessee to St. Louis, in the Territory of Missouri, and soon after to Boone County, where he remained until his death, in 1835. Henry Wharton Conway, the eldest son, was born March 18, 1793, in Greene County, Tenn., and served as a lieutenant in the War of 1812-15; subsequently, in 1817, he served in the treasury department at Washington, immigrated to Missouri with his father in 1818, and early in 1820, after being appointed receiver of public moneys, he immigrated in company with his next younger brother, James Sevier Conway, who was born in 1798, to the county of Arkansas, in the then Territory of Missouri. These two brothers took and executed large contracts to survey the public lands, and later on James S. became surveyor-general of the Territory. During the twenties Henry W. Conway served two terms as a delegate in Congress, and received the election in 1827 for the third term, but on the 29th of October of that year, he was mortally wounded in a duel with Robert Crittenden, from the effects of which he died on the 9th of November, following. [See account of the duel elsewhere in this work.]

A marble shaft with an elaborate inscription, erected by his brother, James S. Conway, stands over his grave in the cemetery at Arkansas Post.

James S. Conway became the first governor of the State of Arkansas, upon its admission into the Union, serving as such from 1836 to 1840, after which he settled on his princely possessions on Red River in the southern part of the State. He was a large slave holder and cotton planter. He died on the 3d of March, 1855, at Walnut Hill, his country seat, in Lafayette County.

Frederick Rector Conway, the third son of Gen. Thomas Conway, was a noted character in Missouri and Illinois. John Rector Conway, the fourth son, was an eminent physician, who died in San Francisco in 1868. William B. Conway was born at the old homestead in Tennessee, about 1806. He was thoroughly educated, read law under John J. Crittenden, of Kentucky, and commenced the practice at Elizabethtown in that State. He moved to Arkansas in 1840, and in 1844 was elected judge of the Third circuit. In December, 1846, he was elected associate justice of the supreme court. He died December 29, 1852, and is buried by the side of his noble mother, in Mount Holly Cemetery, Little Rock. The sixth son, Thomas A., died in his twenty-second year in Missouri.

The seventh and youngest son, Gov. Elias N. Conway, was born May 17, 1812, at the old homestead in Tennessee, and in November, 1833, he left his parents' home in Missouri, and came to Little Rock, and entered into a contract to survey large tracts of the public lands in the northwestern part of the State. Having executed this contract, he was, in 1836, appointed auditor of State, a position which he held for thirteen years. In 1852 and again in 1856, he was elected on the Democratic ticket as governor of the State, and served his full two terms, eight years, a longer period than any other governor has ever served. Much could be said, did space permit, of the eminent services this man has rendered to Arkansas. Of the seven brothers named he is the only one now living. He leads a retired and secluded life in Little Rock, in a small cottage in which he has resided for over forty years. He has no family, having never been married.

Robert Crittenden, youngest son of John Crittenden, a major in the Revolutionary War, was born near Versailles, Woodford County, Ky., January 1, 1797. He was educated by and read law with his brother, John J. Crittenden, in Russellville, that State. Being appointed first secretary of Arkansas Territory, he removed to Arkansas Post, the temporary seat of government, where on the 3d day of March, 1819, he was inaugurated and assumed the duties of his office. On the same day James Miller was inaugurated first governor of the Territory. It seems, however, that Gov. Miller, though he held his office until succeeded by Gov. George Izard, in March, 1825, was seldom present and only occasionally performed official duties. This left Crittenden to assume charge of the position as governor a great portion of the time while Miller held the office. Crittenden continued as secretary of the Territory until succeeded by William Fulton, in April, 1829, having served in that capacity a little over ten years. In 1827 he fought a duel with Henry W. Conway, the account of which is given elsewhere. According to Gen. Albert Pike. with whom he was intimately associated, "he was a man of fine presence and handsome face, with clear bright eyes, and unmistakable intellect and genius, frank, genial, one to attach men warmly to himself, impulsive, generous, warm hearted." He was the first great leader of the Whig party in the Territory, and continued as such until his death, which occurred December 18, 1834, at Vicksburg, Miss., whither he had gone on business. He died thus young, and before the Territory, which he had long and faithfully served, became a State.

Archibald Yell, not unfamiliar to Arkansans, was born in North Carolina, in August, 1797, and while very young immigrated to Tennessee, and settled in Bedford County. He served in the Creek War as the boy captain of the Jackson Guards, under Gen. Jackson, also under the same general in the War of 1812–13, participating in the battle of New Orleans, and also in the Seminole War. He was a man of moderate education, and when the War of 1812 closed, he read law and was admitted to the bar in Tennessee. After the close of the Seminole War, he located at Fayetteville, Lincoln County, Tenn., and there practiced law until 1832, when President Jackson gave him the choice to fill one of two vacancies, governor of Florida or Territorial judge in the Territory of Arkansas. He chose the latter and in due time located at Fayetteville, in Washington County. He was a man of fine personal appearance, pleasant and humorous, and possessed the faculty of making friends wherever he went. He was elected and served as grand master of the Masonic fraternity in the jurisdiction of Arkansas; was a Democrat in politics, and the first member of Congress from the State of Arkansas; was governor of the State from 1840 to 1844; was elected again as a member of Congress in 1844, and served until 1846, when he resigned to accept the colonelcy of an Arkansas regiment of volunteers for the Mexican War. He was killed in the battle of Buena Vista, February 22, 1847.

In his race for Congress in 1844, he was opposed by the Hon. David Walker, the leader of the Whig party, and they made a joint canvass of the State. Yell could adapt himself to circumstances —to the different crowds of people more freely than could his antagonist. In 1847 the Masonic fraternity erected a monument to his memory in the cemetery at Fayetteville. Gov. Yell was a man of great ability, and one of the great pioneer statesmen of Arkansas.

The eminent jurist, Judge David Walker, descended from a line of English Quakers, of whom the last trans-Atlantic ancestor in the male line was Jacob Walker, whose son George emigrated to America prior to the war of the Revolution, and settled in Brunswick County, Va. Here he married a lady, native to the manor born, and became the first American ancestor of a large and distinguished family. One of his sons, Jacob Wythe Walker, born in the decade that ushered in the Revolution, early in life removed to and settled in what is now Todd County, Ky. Here, on the 19th day of February, 1806, was born unto him and his wife, Nancy (Hawkins) Walker, the subject of this sketch—David Walker. Young Walker's opportunities for obtaining a school education in that then frontier country were limited, but, being the son of a good lawyer, he inherited his father's energetic nature, became self-educated, read law and was admitted to the bar in Scottsville, Ky., early in 1829, and there practiced until the fall of 1830, when he moved to Little Rock, Ark., arriving on the 10th of October. Soon after this he located at Fayetteville, Washington County, and remained there, except when temporarily absent, until his death. From 1833 to 1835 he was prosecuting attorney in the Third circuit. He was one of the many able members of the constitutional convention of 1836. In 1840 he rode "the tidal wave of whiggery" into the State senate, in which he served four years. In 1844 he led the forlorn hope of his party in the ever memorable contest with Gov. Yell for Congress. In 1848, while on a visit to Kentucky, and without his knowledge, a legislature, largely Democratic, elected him associate justice of the supreme court over strong Democratic opposition, embracing such men as Judges English and William Conway, both of whom afterwards succeeded to the office.

He had always been a lover of the Union, but when the Civil War came on, having been born and reared in the South, and having become attached to its institutions, he finally chose rather to cast his fortunes with the proposed Confederacy than with the Federal Union. In February 1861, he was elected a delegate to the State convention which convened on the 4th of March, and finally, at its adjourned session, passed the ordinance of secession. He and Judge B. C. Totten were candidates for the chairmanship of this convention, the former representing the Union strength, and the latter the disunion element as it was then developed. Walker received forty out of the seventy-five votes cast, and thereupon took the chair; but owing to the rapid change of sentiment all of the majority, save one, finally voted with the minority, and Arkansas formally withdrew from the Union, with Judge Walker as a leader. In 1866 he was elected chief justice of the State, but in less than two years was removed from the office by military power. At the close of the reconstruction period he was again elected to the supreme bench and served thereon until September, 1878, when he resigned at the age of seventy-two, and retired to private life. He died September 30, 1879. He was a pious and conscientious man, an able jurist, a pioneer of Arkansas, highly respected by its citizens.

Gen. Grandison D. Royston, a son of Joshua Royston and Elizabeth S. (Watson) Royston, natives, respectively, of Maryland and Virginia, and both of pure English descent, was born on the 9th of December, 1809, in Carter County, Tenn. His father was an agriculturist and Indian trader of great energy and character, and his mother was a daughter of that eminent Methodist divine, Rev. Samuel Watson, one of the pioneers of the Holstein conference in East Tennessee. He was educated in the common neighborhood schools and in a Presbyterian academy in Washington County, Tenn. In 1829 he entered the law office of Judge Emerson, at Jonesboro, in that State, and two years after was admitted to the bar. Subsequently he emigrated to Arkansas Territory, and in April, 1832, located in Fayetteville, Washington County, where he remained only eight months, teaching school five days in the week and practicing law in justices' courts on Saturdays. He then moved to Washington, in Hempstead County, where he continued to reside until his death. In the performance of his professional duties he traveled the circuits of the Territory and State in that cavalcade of legal lights composed of such men as Hempstead, Fowler, Trapnall, Cummins, Pike, Walker, Yell, Ashley, Bates, Searcy and others.

In 1833 he was elected prosecuting attorney for the Third circuit, and performed the duties of that office for two years. In January, 1836, he served as a delegate from Hempstead County in the convention at Little Rock, which framed the first constitution of the State; and in the fall of the same year he was elected to represent his county in the first legislature of the State. After the expulsion of John Wilson, speaker of the house, who killed Representative John J. Anthony, Royston was on joint ballot elected to fill the vacant speakership but declined the office. In 1841 President Tyler appointed him United States district attorney for the district of Arkansas, which office he held a short time and then resigned it. In 1858 he represented the counties of Hempstead, Pike and Lafayette in the State legislature, and became the author of the levee system of the State. In 1861 he was elected to the Confederate Congress, serving two years. In 1874 he was a delegate from Hempstead County to the constitutional convention, and was elected president of that body. In 1876 he represented the State at large in the National Democratic convention at St. Louis, and voted for Tilden and Hendricks. He was always a Democrat, a man of culture, refinement and winning manners, and enjoyed in a large degree the confidence of the people. He obtained his title as general by serving on the staff of Gov. Drew with the rank of brigadier-general. He died August 14, 1889, in his eightieth year. He, too, was one of the last prominent pioneers of Arkansas, and it is said he was the last surviving member of the constitutional convention of 1836.

Judge James Woodson Bates was born in Goochland County, Va., about the year 1788. He was educated in the Yale and Princeton Colleges, graduating from the latter about 1810. When quite young he attended the trial of Aaron Burr, for treason, at Richmond. Soon after graduating he read law. In the meantime his brother, Frederick Bates, was appointed first secretary of Missouri Territory, and was acting governor in the absence of Gov. Clark. About 1816 he followed his brother to the West, and settled in St. Louis. In 1820 he removed to the Post of Arkansas and there began the practice of his profession, but had scarcely opened his office when he was elected first delegate to Congress from Arkansas Territory. In 1823 he was a candidate for re-election, but was defeated by the celebrated Henry W. Conway, an able man, who commanded not only the influence of his own powerful family, but that of the Rectors, the Johnsons, Roanes and Ambrose H. Sevier, and all the political adherents of Gen. Jackson, then so popular in the South and West. The influence and strength of this combined opposition could not be overcome.

After his short Congressional career closed, he moved to the newly settled town of Batesville, and resumed the practice of his profession. Batesville was named after him. In November, 1825, President Adams appointed him one of the Territorial judges, in virtue of which he was one of the judges of the superior or appellate court organized on the plan of the old English court in banc. On the accession of Gen. Jackson to the presidency, his commission expired without renewal, and he soon after removed to Crawford County, married a wealthy widow, and became stationary on a rich farm near Van Buren. In the fall of 1835 he was elected to the constitutional convention, and contributed his ability and learning in the formation of our first organic law as a State Soon after the accession of John Tyler to the presidency, he appointed Judge Bates register of the land office at Clarksville, in recognition of an old friend. He discharged every public trust, and all the duties devolved on him as a private citizen, with the utmost fidelity. Strange to say, whilst he possessed the most fascinating conversational powers, he was a failure as a public speaker. He was also a brother to Edward Bates, the attorney-general in President Lincoln's cabinet. He was well versed in the classics, and familiar with the best authors of English and American literature. He died at his home in Crawford County in 1846, universally esteemed.

Index Prepared By:
Mrs. Leister E. Presley
Searcy, Arkansas

Abbott, Clara 62
Abernathy, J. L. 71
Abrams, James 31
Adams, A. 31
  C. W. 70
  Jesse 31
  John 31
  John D. 63
  John Quincy 53, 112
  Mathew 31
  Samuel 42, 43, 58
  William 31, 43
Ainsworth, Harrison 31
Akin, James 29
  John 32
Alexander, Gilbert 100
  Mark W. 70
Allen, Sam 31
  W. O. 37
Anderson, John 30
  Samuel 32
  W. A. 31
Anthony, J. C. 32
  J. J. 38
  John J. 104, 105, 111
Archer, G. W. 30
Armstrong, H. 32
  W. E. 30
Arnett, S. F. 71
Arnold, J. 32
  Newton 31
  S. 32
  Thomas 32
Arrington, A. W. 97
Ashley 111
  Chester 70, 87
Askew, B. F. 72
  Emer 31
Atchinson, William 32
Atkinson, J. L. 30
  W. E. 43
Augspath, L., Dr. 44
Avery, B. F. 43
Ayers, E. D. 43
Babcock, E. F. 60
Baber M.D. 71
Bacon, H. 30
Badgett, W. 32
Badham, H. A. 70
Bagwell, Aaron 30
Bailey, De Ross 72
  W. W. 59
Bain, R. 32
Baird, Alvin 100
  J. M. 32
Baker, Colbert 30
  Elijah 32
  Isaac 70
Balch, Rev. 101

Ball, B. B. 30
  E. B. 69
Bancroft 35
Bandy, H. W. 31
Banks 79
  A. R. 101
Bankson, J. 30
Barber, David 30, 37
  James 30
  L. E. 69
Barfield, G. C. 31
Barker, D. E. 42
Barkman, Jacob 30, 37, 84, 105, 106
  John 105
Barnes, James 32
  Thomas 71
Barrett, J. C. 101
Barrow, J. C. 72
Bartholomew, W. S. 59
Bartlett, Liberty 71
Bartley, E. 31
Basham, Oliver 43
Bates 111
  Edward 112
  J. W. 69
  James W. 38
  James Woodson 112
Batson, F. J. 69, 71
  J. McL. 72
Battle, B. B. 69
Baxter, E. 42, 69
  Elisha 40, 41, 54, 55, 71, 72, 76
  John B. 58
Bean 29
  John 31
  Robert 31, 37, 61
Beane, Mark 30
Beard, Alexander 32
Bearden, J. T. 69
Beasley, George W. 70
Beattie, Mrs. M. M. 62
Beavers, B. B. 42
Bedford, Robert 58
Beebe, Roswell 32
Beeler, Samuel 32
Belden, L. D. 73
Bell 29, 44
  Durant H. 32
  R. S. 31
Bellah, Richard W. 16
Beller, William 30
Bennett, J. E. 69
  John E. 70
Bentley, Edward 62
Benton, Thomas H. 87
Berry, J. H. 42, 71
  J. R. 40, 42

Bertrand, Charles P. 38
Bettis, R. S. 32
Bettiss, W. 31
Bevins, W. C. 71
Bienville 34
Billingsley, James 30, 61
Bird, James 32
Birney 44
Biscoe, H. L. 31
Bishop, Moses 31
Bizzell, D. W. 59
Black, A. L. 31
  J. D. 71
  (James) 106
  John 32
  John, Sr. 32
  R. H. 71
  Thomas 31
  William 32
Blackmore, A. G. 31
  Charles 30
Blaine, James 30
  (James G.) 44
Blair, W. P. L. 30
Blakely, Adam 29, 105
Blanchard 70
Blane, Robert 31
Blevins, A. W. 71
Blocher 76
Blue, M. H. 32
Blunt, 78
  Reuben 30
Blyeth, J. 31
Blythe, S. K. 32
Bocage, J. W. 70
Bogy 29
  Lewis 30
Boileau, A. 42
  Alexander 42
Boisbriant, 34
Boles, Thomas 59, 71
Bond, J. W. 32
  John B. 57
Boon, Squire 71
Boone, Daniel 29, 87
  J. W. 30
Boswell 97
  Hartwell 31
Boudinot 23
  E. C. 23
  Elias C. 23
Bowen, J. C. 31
  John 31
  T. M. 69
  Thomas M. 39
Bowie, William 106
Boyce, William A. 100
Bozeman, W. G. 32
Braddock, (Gen. Edward) 108
Bradford, H. 31
  Henry 30
  R. 32

Bradley, J. M. 72
  W. L. 32
Bragg, Richard 57
Brannon, Moses 30
Brauner, John C. 43
Brazil, R. 32
  V. 32
Breckenridge (John C.) 44
Brewer, Henry 31
Breysacher, Dr. A. L. 44, 62, 63
Bridewell, C. A. 58
Bridgeman, Benton J. 71
  Martin 31
Bright, S. C. 62
Brinkley, Estelle 108
Broadway, Yancy 30
Bronough, E. C. 70
Brookfield, Isaac 100
  L. 30
Brooks, H. W. 58
  Joseph 40, 41, 55
Brown, 76
  B. C. 70
  B. J. 71
  Benton J. 71
  E. F. 71
Brown, George R. 59
  H. B. 31
  H. H. 77
  Henry 31, 32
  Isaac 32
  J. B. 31
  James 30
  Joe 32
  Kate P. 62
  R. C. S. 69, 72
  Richard C. S. 58, 70
Brugman 79
  Peter 57
Brundidge, S. 70
Brunson, V. 42, 62
Buchanan (James C.) 44, 53
  S. H., Rev. 60
Buckley, N. H. 30
Buford, Elijah 31
Bunn, H. Y. 77
Burkem, Charles 31
Burress, B. 31
Bush, John 30
Butler, J. W. 71
  James W. 71
Buzzard, Jacob 31
Byers, J. H. 71
  J. P. 71
  William 71, 72
Byington, Rev. 101
Byrd, R. C. 42
  Richard C. 38, 42
Byrne, Andrew 99
  L. A. 72
Cabeen, John T. 32
Cadillar, Lamothe 34

Cain, W. R. 71
Caldwell, Charles 37, 38, 69
  J. H. 31, 32
  John 37
  Samuel 32
Calhoun, John C. 88
Callaghan, D. 32
Callaway, John 30
  Jonathan O. 30, 105
  R. H. 32
Callen, Thomas 30
Calvert, W. H. 31
Campbell, George 30
  J. 32
  James 30, 31, 32
  W. B. 69
  W. P. 43
Cantrell, A. C. 30
  W. A. 44, 62
Carlton, James 31
Carothers, H. M. 32
Carpenter, A. M. 31
Carr, W. B. 31
  W. H. 31
Carrick, A. 32
Carringan, Robert 71
Carroll, (Charles) 88
  D. W. 71, 72
  Gray 72
  I. H., Mrs. 62
  Rosey 76
Carter, H. S. 71
Caruth, George W. 69
Caruthers, A. 32
  V. 32
Case, W. A. 70
Cass, (Lewis) 44
Cate, W. A. 71
Cauthorn, W. 32
Chamberlain, J. 37
Chapman, J. 30
Chaudorat, Rev. 99
Cherry, S. A. 30
  S. R. 30
  William 30
Childress, S. W. 70
Chism, B. B. 42, 43
Choate, J. R. 32
Choiseul 35
Chopart 26
Chouteau, Pierre 21
Chrisman 76
Churchill, Gen. 76
  J. C. 58
  T. J. 42, 43
Clark, Gov. 21
  Adam 57
  Benjamin 30
  David 31, 37
  E. T. 37, 69
  G. 32
  J. 30

Clark, Cont.
  Jeff 17
  John 30, 32, 37
  T. H. 30
  William 36
  (William) Gov. 88
Clarke, Francis D. 62
  T. P. 62
Clarkson, Wiley 30
Clay, (Henry) 44, 52, 53, 88
Clayton, P. 42
  Powell 40, 78, 79
  W. H. H. 70
Cleburne, P. H. 76
  Patrick A. 75, 76, 88
Clement, W. A. 58
  William 31
Clendening, J. H. 59
  J. J. 69, 71, 72
  John J. 70
Cleveland (Grover) 44, 88
Clifford, Judge 103
Coarser 76
Cobbs, P. M. 32
  Paul M. 43
Cocke, J. H. 32
  John W. 70
Cockrell, Sterling R. 69
Coffee, Col. 79
Coffin, Charles 71
Cohen, Albert 57
Coleman, H. S. 57
Collins, Samuel 32
Collum, George 21
Compton, F. W. 69
Conway 53, 58, 103, 109
  Ann 103
  E. N. 42
  Elias 38
  Elias N. 42, 109
  Frederick Rector 109
  George 69, 71
  Henry 109
  Henry W. 38, 103, 110, 112
  Henry Wharton 109
  J. R. 32
  J. S. 42
  J. T. 31
  James Sevier 109
  John Rector 109
  Moncure D. 109
  Nellie 109
  Thomas 103, 109
  Thomas A. 109
  W. B. 31
  W. H. 31
  William 69, 71, 111
  William B. 109
Coody, W. R. 72
Cook, John 72
  William 32
Cooper, J. M. 32

Copeland, N. 31
　Singleton 30
Corbin, J. 44
　J. C. 43, 95
cornish, John 32
Couch, S. 32
Coulter, James 32
Counts, George 32
Cousin, G. N. 69
Cox, N. W. 59, 69
Craig, J. B. 32
　John B. 29
Cravens, A. J. U. 44
　J. E. 71
　J. L. 31, 44
Crawford 76
　James 32
　John 42
Craycraft, A. T. 72
Crease, J. H. 43
　John H. 43
　Robert P. 32
Creswell, A. 31
Crittenden, J. J. 43
　John 110
　John C. 109
　John J. 110
　N. Y. 31
　Robert 23, 36, 38, 42, 52,
　　53, 68, 70, 88, 103, 109,
　　110
Crockett, David 106
Cromwell, G. W. 31
Cross, D. C. 76
　Edward 30, 58, 69
Crow, A. M. 59
Crowley, Benjamin 30
Culberhouse, T. D. 59
Cummins 111
　William 70
Cunningham, G. S. 71
　L. B. 43
　M. 32
Cureton, John 32
Curl, H. H. 32
　J. T. 32
Curran, I. 31
　John Philpot 29
　L. R. 32
　T. 31
　Thomas 29
Curtis, Gen. 75, 77, 78
Curry, R. S. 59
D'Abbodie 34
Dale, L. D. 32
Daniel, George 30
　J. L. 31
　T. L. 31
Danley, C. C. 42
Dardenne, S. 31
Daugherty, H. C. 31
　N. 32

Davidson, J. W. 78, 79
Davis, A. D. G. 69
　David 32
　Hiram 30
　J. G. 31
　William 30, 72
　Zack 29, 105
Dawson, Col. 76
Deadman, R. H. 43
Dedman, R. H. 71
Dengler, Fred 60
Dennis, John 32
Denton, J. L. 43, 95
　W. F. 69
Desha 76
　Ben 88
　F. W. 71
DeSoto, Ferdinand 13, 24, 25
Dewitt, J. W. 31
D'Iberville, Lemoine 27
Dibrill, Dr. J. A. 43, 44, 62
Dickenson, T. 69
　Townsend 69
Dickinson, D. S. 31
　J. W. 31
Dinsmore, H. A. 71
Dinwiddie 108
Dobbins 76
Dockery, Col. 76
Dodge, George E. 62
Donnelly, Father 99
Dooley, George 31
　P. C. 72
　Thomas 30
Dorr, J. M. 31
Dorsey, Stephen W. 40
Dougherty, William 32
Douglas, Jesse 31
　(Stephen A.) 44
Drew, (Thomas S.) Gov. 32, 112
　T. S. 42
　Thomas 30
Dudley, J. G. 30
Duke, William G. 100
Duncan, W. B. 30
Dunham, W. 31
Dunlap, W. S. 42, 43
Dunn, U. G. 62
DuPoisson 26
DuPuy, Rev. 99
Durham, W. 30
Dye, J. R. 31
　John H. 63
Dyer, M. N. 71
Eagan, James 31
Eagle, J. P. 42, 44, 76, 77
Eakin, J. R. 69
Earl, T. R. 59
Earle, E. J. 72
Edgington, H. 31
Edmondson, J. T. 32
Edrington, J. P. 31

Edrington, Cont.
  W. B. 71
Edward I. 109
Ehrenbers, H. 57
Elliott, J. M. 72
  J. T. 71, 72
Ellis, E. A. 59
  Radford 37
  William 30
Elvin, Samuel 29
Embry, Col. 77
  B. T. 42
Emerson, Judge 111
Engleman 79
Engles, Henry 31
English, Judge 111
  B. 31
  E. H. 69
  J. 37
  Stephen 32
  Eno. Amos F. 78
Enos, William 32
Eolsom, Isaac 57
Erwin, John M. 101
Eskridge, T. P. 68
  Thomas P. 38
Etter 76
Evans, Lewis 32
  Onesimus 58
  S. J. 59
Ewing, Finis 98
  J. 31
Fagan, Col. 76
Fairchild, H. F. 69
Farr, Z. P. H. 70
Farrelley, C. C. 69
Farrelly, T. 30, 37
Faulkner, Sandy 106, 107
Featherstone, L. P. 60
  Lincoln 70
Ferebee, G. W. 37
Fereby, G. W. 31
Feguson, W. D. 30
Ferribee, George W. 30
Ficklin, John S. 31
Fields, J. P. 32
  John 32, 71
  W. H. 71
Files, A. W. 42
Fillmore (Willard) 44
Fish, Thomas 37
Fishback, W. M. 43
Fisk 44
  David 30
Fiske, Gen. 78
FitzGerald, Edward 99
Fitzpatrick, C. B. 70, 71
Fitzwilliam 76
Flannagin, Col. Gov.
  (Harris) 77
  H. 42, 78
Fletcher, George 30
  John G. 63
  T. 42
  W. P. 59
Flourney, T. B. 76

Floyd, John B. 70
  W. W. 71
Flynn, P. O. 31
Folsom, I. 64
Fones, D. G. 63
Foran, David 32
Forbes 108
  Isaac 32
Ford, Ella 108
  J. B. 31
Foster, N. M. 70
Fowler, 111
  Judge 70
  A. S. 59
  Absalom 37, 69, 70
  J. H. 31
Fox, J. W. 72
Franklin, Ben 103
Fraser, Thomasson 101
Frierson, J. G. 70
Fritz, William 31
Frolich, Jacob 42
Fuller, R. C. 72
Fulton, John 30
  (Robert) 84
  William 38, 42
  William S. 103, 110
Fultony, William 30
Gainer, J. C. 32
Gallagher, George A. 69
Galvez, Bernardo 34
Gamble, W. T. 30
Gantt, E. W. 71, 72, 76
  R. S. 43
Gardner, A. E. 60
Garfield, (James A.) 44
Garland, A. H. 42, 89
Garner, John C. 32
  T. J. 32
Garrott, W. 32
Gayarre 35
Gentry, Mrs. A. J. 105
German, Peter 31
Gibault, Rev. 99
Gibson, James A. 57
  L. P. 62
  Lorenzo R. 44, 62
  T. B. 72
Gilchrist, William 58
Girard, Rev. 99
Glass, Dudley 32
  Hiram 31
Glenn, W. J. 57
Godden, C. C. 71
Gooch, Benjamin 32
Gorman, W. A. 78
Goshen, W. 30
Gould, J. 32
  Josiah 70
Grace, W. P. 71
Graham, Moses 30
Grant, J. T. 30
  Gen. (U.S.) 40, 41, 44, 80, 81
Graves, R. 32

Gray, C. S. 62
  Isaac 31
  John 31
  Rolla 32
  William J. 32
Greathouse, G. 32
Greeley, (Horace) 40, 44
Green, J. J. 71
  Jesse 100
  Joshua F. 101
  Len B. 71
  W. W. 72
Greenwood, A. B. 71
Greer, A. J. 38, 70
  D. B. 42
Gregg, L. 69, 71
  Lafayette 72
Grey, W. H. 43
Griffin, John J. 32
  L. C. 30
  Dr. Theophilus 31
  William 29
Griffith, S. L. 62
Guigues, Rev. Louis 99
Gunter, T. M. 72
Guthrie, Samuel 32
Hackett, W. P. 31
Hadley, O. A. 42
Haggard, N. 69, 71
Haggerdon, Michael 32
Haggerton, Joseph 31
Halbrook, George 32
Hale, E. M. 32
  Jesse 100
  T. S. 32
Hall, G. 30
  Richard 31
  S. S. 32, 69
  Samuel S. 69, 70
Hallum, John 97
Ham, E. D. 71
Hamby, C. C. 58
Hamilton, John 30
Hammill, John N. 100
Hampton, J. R. 42
Hancock, 81
  (Winfield S.) 44
Hane, W. 30
Hanks, F. 31
Hanley, Thomas B. 69, 70
Haralson, H. 69
Hardin 104, 105
  Ben 29
  George 32
  Joab 29, 37
  John P. 31
  Joseph 31, 37, 104
Hargrave, W. N. 72
Hargrove, John 31
  R. H. 32
Harley, Amanda 32
Harrell, Elias 71
  J. M. 72
  John 100
Harrig, D. H. 30

Harrington, S. H. 69
Harris, Benjamin 31
  J. A. 31
  John 100
  William 31
Harrison, D. 30
  M. LaRue 76
  W. M. 69, 70
  (William Henry) 36, 44
Hart, W. P. 64
Hartfield, A. 32
  R. 32
Harwood, Susan B. 62
Hatch, George 32
  William 30
Hatchet, B. 62
Hawkins, B. 31
  M. L. 30, 72
  Nancy 110
Hawley, L. B. 57
Hayden, 79
Hayes, Dr. N. N. 44
  (Rutherford B.) 44
  S. M. 32
  S. S. 32
Haynes, T. S. 30
Hazeldine, W. C. 70
Hearn, R. D. 72
  Rufus D. 72
Hemingway, W. E. 69
Hemphill, John 29, 105
Hempstead 111
  Fay 58, 108
  Joseph 107
  Joshua 108
  Joshua, Sr. 108
  Mary 108
  Robert 108
  Roy 108
  S. H. 38, 69, 71
  Samuel H. 70, 107
  Stephen 107, 108
  Stephen, Sr. 108
Henderson, Rev. 101
  J. 32
  J. P. 72
  M. J. 72
  W. F. 43, 70
Hendricks 112
  Austin 31
Hennepin, Louis 25
Henrey, John 99, 100
Henry, James A. 57
  John 32
Heron, F. 32
Herron 78
Hester, W. W. 32
Hicks, J. A. 30
Highnight, Abner 105
  Adam 29
Hilger, Philip 32
Hill 76
  B. W. 95
  G. W. 43
  W. H. 62

Hindman 75
  T. C. 76-78
Hipolite, W. W. 64
Hively, Daniel 31
Hobbs, Mrs. 20
Hodges, W. E. 31
Hogan, Col. 29
Hoge, Judge 70
  J. M. 32, 71
Hogg, John 32
Holdernist, J. I. 14
Holland, N. 31
Hollowell, J. L. 43, 71
Holmes, James S. 57
Holt, H. L. 30
  R. P. 57
Hooper, P. O. 57, 63
Horner, Col. 70
  John J. 57
  W. B. R. 31, 37, 69
Hortu, Francisco Luis 34
Hough, Thomas 32
Houks, Jesse M. 70
House, J. W. 63
Houston, J. P. 31
  John 30
Howard, B. F. 30
  H. C., Dr. 44
  J. H. 72
  R. A. 69
Howell, W. C. 32
Hubbard, Thomas 69-71
Hubbins, A. B. 30
Hubble, Daniel 30
Huckleberry, J. 71
Huddleston, John 107
  W. P. 107
  W. P., Jr. 107
Hudson, William J. 31
Hudspeth, Solomon 32
Huey, A. S. 42
Hughes, G. B. 30, 32
  John 31
  S. P. 42
  Simon B. 69
  Simon P. 43, 59
Hughey 76
Humphrey, Charles 32
Hunt, William 30
Hunter, Andrew 99
  Enos C. 30
Hurley, George W. 57
Huson, R. 30
Hutchinson, T. S. 32
Hutt, John 43
Hutton, H. N. 72
Hynson, H. R. 31
Ingram, William 31
Inman, W. A. 71
Irvin, M. 31
Izard, George 38, 42, 110

Jackson, Andrew 22, 52, 53,
    103, 104, 110, 112
  R. E. 59
  (Stonewall) 80, 81
  T. V. 31
  Jacobs, J. 31
Jacoway, W. D. 71
Jameson, George 31
Janes, John 32
Jannin, Rev. 99
Jefferson, Thomas 28, 53, 93,
    103
Jeffery, Daniel 31
  J. 31
Jeffries, Charles L. 58
Jenette, Thomas 31
Jennings, Orville 71
Jett, A. S. 57
  J. P. 31
  W. A. 57
Johnson 112
  Abner 30
  B. H. 31
  B. W. 72
  Benjamin 38, 70
  J. J. 76
  J. M. 42
  John 32
  P. M. 31
  R. W. 71
  Robert 57
  Robert W. 43
  S. M. 71
  T. W. 30
  Thomas 43, 69, 71, 81
Johnston 81
Joiner, J. J. 32
Joliet 25, 98
Jones, D. W. 43
  Dan W. 72
Jones, Edwin 31
  John T. 70
  Lafayette 31
  Martin 32
  S. B. 71
Joplin, Henry G. 100
Jordan, Pleasant 71
Jordon, C. T. 43
  P. 43
Jouett, C. 52
  Charles 36, 68
Joyner, L. J. 72
Karns, John P. 58
Kavanaugh, William 32
Keats, James B. 38
Kelerec, Baron De 34
Kellam, James 30
Keller, J. M. 64
Kelley, Charles 31
Kellums, William 31
Kelly, Elijah 36
  W. 31

Kennedy, A. R. 101
Kenner, W. 32
Kent, M. D. 72
Kessee, J. W. 43
Kessie, J. P. 31
King, James 32
  John 32
  William 30
Kingsbury, Rev. 101
Kingston, George A. 72
Kinkead, William 31
Kinney, E. C. 61
Kirkhan, J. H. 31
Kirkland, Lottie 62
Knapp, Gilbert 19, 20
Kuykendall, Gilbert 19, 20
Lacey, Thomas J. 69
L'Epiney, de 34
Laferty, J. L. 32
Lamar, G. W. 76
Lane, William Q. 30
Langford, W. C. 72
Langham, A. L. 32
LaSalle, 25, 26, 34
La Suer 27
Latting, Richard 30
Law, John 27, 82
Lawrence, W. B. 64
  William, Dr. 43
Lawson, G. F. 31
Lawton, G. F. 31
  I. B. 59
Lea, R. J. 72
Leach, D. D. 58, 70-72
Lear, D. W. 43
Ledyard, Col. 107
Lee, (R. E.) 80, 81
Leeper, Mathew 58
Lefevre, Akin 29
  Ambrose 29
  Enos 29
  Francis G. 29
  John B. 29
  Leon 29
  Mary Louise 29
  Peter 29
  Peter L. 29
Lemos, Gayoso de 34
Letcher, Robert P. 36, 52, 68
Lewers, A. C. 72
Lewis, Eli 30
  J. M. 43
  (Meriwether) 36
  William 32
Linceum, G. B. 32
Lincoln, Abraham 38, 39, 73
  L. R. 32
  Louis C. 57
Lindsey, C. 32
  W. H. 31
Linton, John 70
Little, Cyrus 32

Little, Cont.
  J. F. 32
  J. P. 32
  John S. 72
  N. O. 32
  P. 32
  Philander 70
  William J. 63
Livingston 28, 84
  J. 30
Locke, M. F. 59
Logan, James 32
  Mathew 30
Lorance, Joseph 31
Lott, Robert 32
Lotta, G. G. 73
Louis XIV 26, 27
Lowe, D. W. 31
  E. M. 31
  H. C. 32
Lowery, J. F. 70
  James 100
Loyd, D. K. 31
  E. F. 31
Lubbock, G. W. 76
Lucas, James H. 30
Lyle, C. P. 32
Lyon, Col. 76
  Richard 72
McAllister, J. 32
McAmy, Robert 32
McBee, Israel 107
  Rachel 107
  Samuel 107
McCabe, J. D. 72
McCall, Robert 30
McClellan, John 32
McClernand, Gen. 78
McClung, S. 31
McClure, (Chief Justice) 40
  John 69
McCowan, G. W. 72
McCoy, John 38
McCracken, Isaac 60
McCuiston, T. 31
McCulloch, P. D. 70
McDaniel, George 32
  W. W. 31
McDonald, A. B. 31
  Edward 37
  William 30
McDonough, J. B. 72
McElmurry, John 37
McElroy, Samuel 32
McGehee, M. 72
McHenry, A. 32
McIntosh, James 76, 77
McKeal, J. H. 31
McKean, Joseph W. 58
McKennon, A. S. 71
McKenzie, J. H. 31
McKinney, D. E. 32, 37

McKissick, James 58
McLean 79
McMiken, R. S. 31
McMillan, John 30
McRae, Dandridge 59, 76
McRains, A. W. 32
Mack, L. L. 70, 71
  William H. 30
Mackey, Elias 30
Macklinin, Sackfield 69
Maddox, John 31
Madison (James) 109
  Nellie 109
Magness 29
Magruder, B. 30
Mansfield, W. W. 69, 71
Manville, M. W. 59, 60
Marquette 98, 91
  Jacques 29
Marriott, James 76
Marrs, James 32
Marshall 76, 108
  G. 32
  Gilbert 32
  M. C., Dr. 44
  S. M. 63
  William B. 31
Martin, A. 32
  Allen 32
  Bennett 69
  Bennett H. 70
  Betty 53
  G. L. 30
  G. M. 31
  J. W. 71
  Jared C. 43
  John C. 43
  T. B. 72
  W. A. 76
  W. H. 71
  William 29
Mason, D. D. 30
  S. F. 31
Matheny, William G. 32
Mathers, Thomas 30
Mathews, Sam 31
Mattix, Edward 32
Maxwell, James 30
May, A. F. 69
  W. N. 71
Meade, George H. 58, 62
Merrick, T. D. 76
Metcalf, Ed 58
Meurin, Father Louis 99
Michaels, John W. 62
Micham, James 31
Miles, James 30
Miller 76
  Fred 31
  James 29, 36, 38, 42,
    52, 68, 84, 110

Miller, Cont.
  Samuel 29, 31
  T. G. 59
  W. R. 42
  William R. 29, 42
Mills, Jack 30
Mills, Thomas J. 31
Miro, Estevar 34
Mitchell 72
  C. E. 72
  C. F. 72
  Isaac 32
  James 43
  John 30
  M. 31, 59
  W. 32
  W. C. 30, 76
Mobley, C. H. 30
Monroe, James 28
  (James, President) 36, 53, 68
Montgomery, J. C. 31
  J. R. 43
Mooney, Daniel 31
Moore, C. B. 43, 69
  Charles 32
  E. B. 42. 57
  J. M. 69
  J. R. 32
  James M. Rev. 101
  John 29
  Thomas O. 78
Morehead, R. H. 60
Morgan, William 32
Morrell, Hiram 30
Morris, Henry 32
  Isaac 31
  John 58
Morrison, A. 32
  J. 31
  Joshua 31
Morse, B. B. 69
  H. P. 72
  J. J. 32
Morton, John 31
Mosby, William 57
Mosley, W. S. 70
Moss, James 31
Mount, Joseph 62
Murfree, E. H. 44
Murphy, I. 42
  Isaac 32, 39, 54, 67, 73
Murray, James 30
  John C. 70
  Thomas 32
Napoleon 28, 81
Nations, Lucinda 62
Neal, J. W. 30
Nealy, R. H. 71
Newton, 76
  L. 32
  R. C. 43

Newton, Cont.
  Thomas W. 37
  W. M. H. 30
Nichols, John 30
Nooner, William 30
Norris, Nicholas 32
North, Lord Kit 96, 97
Nowlin, S. H. 60
Nunn, A. H. 32
Nutall, (Thomas) 97
Oakley, A. M. 30
  Allen M. 58
Oates, O. H. 42, 70
Oden, 70
  R. C. 32, 69
Oders, H. O. 30
O'Farrell, Sebastian de Coso
  Calvoy 34
O'Guinn, Daniel 30
Oldham, W. S. 69
  Williamson S. 58
O'Neal, Thomas 31, 32
O'Reilly, Alexander 34
Orr, W. 100
Orts, Z. 62
Otey, C. A. 70
Owen, D. D. 13, 14, 16,
    18, 50
  E. M. 32
  E. W. 30
  John F. 59
  Michal 32
  Thomas 32
Pace, A. E. 32
  Twitty 32
Padgett, W. B. 71, 72
Page, Henry 43
  J. R. 72
Palmer 76
Parham, Maj. R. H., Jr. 62
Parker, J. G. 57
  R. C. 72
  Samuel 29, 105
Parks, W. J. 31
Parrott, 70
  W. H. 69
Parsel, Thomas 58
Paschal, George W. 69
Pate, L. 32
Patterson, N. W. 72
  W. K. 71, 76
Patton, William B. 30
Pearcy, Charles 31
Peay, G. N. 32
  John C. 32
  Nicholas 58
Peel, James 29
  Richard 29
  S. W. 71
  Thomas 29
Peete, Samuel 58
Pelham, C. H. 31

Pelham, Cont.
  William 38, 42
Perryman, M. 30, 31
Pevehouse, William 30
Peyatte, Jacob 32
Phillips, S. 31
  Sylvanus 37
Pickering, G. H. 31
Pickett, G. C. 30
Pierce, (Franklin) 44
  N. B. 76
Pierson, J. G. 31
Pike 111
  Albert 23, 53, 69, 70, 80,
    96, 97, 110
Pindall, L. A. 69
  X. J. 72
Pinkston, P. 31
Pittman, J. M. 71
  P. R. 72
Pleasants, L. C. 32
Polk, (James K.) 44
  Thomas 31
Poor, George 108
  Lizzie 108
  Minnie 108
  Sue 108
Pope, Dunbar H. 43
  John 38, 42
Porter, A. R. 71
Pound, Thomas W. 71
Powell, Henry 30
  P. O. 32
  R. H. 71, 72
  William 31
Pratt, J. C. 72
  J. G. 106
Price, John J. G. 39
  Gen. (Sterling) 79, 80
Props, Daniel 99, 100
Prudden, H. 32
Pucket, Asa 30
Pullen, J. T. 31
  John W. 58
Quarles, Eli 30
  Greenfield 70
Quayle, W. H. 60
Quillin, John 71
Quindley, John 42
Rainy, O. F. 71
Ramsey, W. K. 58
Randolph, Lewis 38, 42, 53
Ranger 76
Rankin, W. W. 32
Ratchford, James 30
Ratcliff, T. J. 71
Ratcliffe, W. C. 69
Rea, Joseph 32
Read, F. B. 30
  Opie 97
Reagan, C. G. 72
Rector 53, 103, 109, 112

Rector, Cont.
  H. M. 42, 77
Redmon, J. 31
Reed, John 29, 31
Reeves, Peter G. 31
Reid, Charles C. 72
Remmel, H. L. 59
Renick, A. H. 32
Renner, R. E. 59
Reyburn, Gen. 79
  "Diamond Joe" 86
  Thomas C. 78
  W. P. 30
Reynolds, H. N. 30
Rice, Dorsey 75, 76
Richardson, John R. 57
  Josiah 32
  R. 31
  Thomas 31
Riddick, J. E. 70. 71
Ridges 23
Ridley, R. 31
Righton, N. 31
Rightsell, J. R. 63
Riley, James 32
Ringo, A. H. 70
  Daniel 30, 37, 69, 70
Ringgold, John H. 31
Ritchie, J. F. 72
Roane, 112
  Andrew 32
  E. H. 31
  J. S. 42, 70
  John 76
  Sam C. 31, 37, 38, 69
  Samuel C. 61
Roberts, Abraham 30
  H. C. 31
  L. G. 44
  P. W. 32
Robertson, Charles 30
  J. W. 69
  V. 32
  W. H. 30
Robinson, Austin 108
  David 108
  Frank 108
  Hettie 108
  Ira 30
  J. H. 30
  Jacob 108
  Jeptha 108
  John 31
  May 108
  Owen 108
  Ruth 108
  S. K. 59
  Sallie 108
  Sue 108
Roddy, Hall 31
Rodney, John 31
Rogers 23

Rogers, Cont.
  G. W. 30
  J. H. 72
Roosevelt, Capt. 32, 83
Roots, Logan H. 59
Rorer, David 32
Rose, M. 31
Ross, Chief (John) 23
  Nathan 31
Rowe, Betsy 108
  Thomas 108
Rowland, R. N. 32
Royston, D. L. F. 69
  Elizabeth 111
  G. D. 69, 71, 105
  Gradison D. 38, 41, 43, 111
  Joshua 111
Rudd, N. 30
Ruddell, John 31
Rumbrough, P. C. 60
Runyan, L. 30
Russell, James 32
  Uriah 31
  William 32, 60
Rutherford, A. H. 43
  R. B. 72
  S. M. 31, 32, 38
Ruttes, William 32
Rycroft, Francis 30
Sabin, A. N. 30
  C. S. 30
Safford, Judge 30
St. Denys 27
Salcedo, Juan Manuel 34
Sandels, Mont. H. 69
Sanders, S. T. 38
Sandford, H. 31
  J. K. 31
Sanville, Marquis De 27, 34
Saulmier, Rev. Emil 99
Saunders, M. T. 70
  Milton 32
Savage, Mr. 20
Saylors, J. C. 31
Schofield, J. M. 78
Scott, Gen. 22
  Allen M. 100
  Andrew 31, 36, 52, 57, 68-70
  C. C. 69, 72
  George W. 38, 42
  R. H. 32
  W. C. 71
  William C. 70
  (Winfield) 44
Scripps, Joseph 100
Scull, Henry 30
  Hewes 30
  James 38, 43
Seaborn, George 31
Searcy, 111
  R. 31
  Richard 37, 69

Searle, E. J. 69, 72, 76
Sears, Thomas 31
Seay, Charles H. 32
Sebastian, W. K. 69, 70
Sevier 53
  A. H. 37, 69
  Ambrose H. 38, 102, 103, 112
  Ann Conway 103
  John 53
  John, Gen. 102, 103
  Valentine 103
Seymour, (Horatio) 44
  William 31
Shader, John 100
Shaver, Col. 76
Shaw, Rev. 101
Shelly, Abraham 30
Sheppard, V. B. 73
  Y. B. 71
Sheridan, Gen. 81
Sherman, Gen. 81
Shinn, Prof. J. H. 108
  Minnie C. 108
Shook, Alexander 99, 100
  Jacob 99, 100
Shreve, Capt. 84
Simmons, J. I. 30
Simpson, B. M. 32
Sinclair, A. 31
Skelton, John 32
Skinner, J. 31
Slemmons, W. F. 71
Smead, H. P. 72
Smith, A. B. 71
  A. J. 30
  C. P. 31
  C. W. 72
  E. Kirby 78
  H. S. 30
  Hiram 32
  J. T. 76
  Jabez M. 72, 76
  Reuben 30
  S. S. 31, 32
  Thomas 95
  W. W. 69
Smithee, J. N. 43
  R. P. 32
Smithson, B. H. 32
Smyth, A. D. 100
  Andrew D. 100
Sneed, Judge 70
  Charles 30
  S. G. 69, 71
Snoddy, Rufus 30
Solomon, S. 58
Sorrels, J. W. 58
  T. F. 70-72
  W. 31
Spotts, John 31
Sprague, Alden 58

Stanton, W. N. 70
Stark, Dent D. 76
Staunton 78
Stayton, J. W. 42
Steele, D. C. 31
  Frederick 78-80
  T. G. T. 72
Stephens, Reuben 32
Stephenson, A. G. 69
  Eugene 70
  M. L. 69, 71
  William 37
Stevenson, W. 37
  William 100
Steward, J. M. 30
  Moses 30
Stinnett, S. 32
Stirman, E. J. 71
  John I. 42
Stokes, Holloway 31
Stokeley, John 32
Stone, H. 59
  Robert H. 31
Story, William 69, 70, 72
Stotts, J. 30
Strain, Isaac 69
Strong, William 32
Stroud, A. 30
Stuart, H. B. 72
  William 31
Sullivan, R. F. 31
Sumner, J. C. 30
Sumpter, J. J. 99
Sutfin, J. 30
Sutton, W. H. 30. 70
Tabor, Elijah 30
Tappan, J. C. 76
Tarlton, Miss 76
Tate, W. L. 59
Taylor, C. M. 43
  Creed 31
  Dick 79
  J. K. 32
  R. H. 58
  Sam 31
  Samuel 32
  (Zachery) 44
Teague, John 32
Tebbetts, J. M. 72
Tell, William 42
Temple, A. J. 72
  N. J. 71, 72
Tennant, Thomas 100
Thetford, A. B. K. 30
Thomas 76
  Alonzo 70
  O. H. 30
Thomasson, H. F. 71
  Henry F. 39
Thompson, Duane 72
  L. 30

Thompson, Cont.
 W. E. 43
 William 43
 Woodville E. 95, 96
Throckmorton, William A. L. 80
Thweat, P. O. 70
Tilden, (Samuel J.) 44, 112
Tindall, T. H. 39
Tolleson, I. C. P. 31
 J. C. P. 69, 70
Tonti, (Henri de) 25, 26
Tory, John 30
Totten, B. C. 39, 75, 111
Townsend, William 100
Trapnall 111
 Frederick W. 70
Trent 108
Trigg, James 58
Trimble, Alden 29
 James 31
 T. C. 72
 W. W. 32
 William 37, 38, 70
Troy, John 31
True, James M. 76
Tucker, S. S. 70, 71
Tully, L. B. 38
Tupper, Isaac T. 71
Turner, B. D. 69
 Benton 59
 H. 31
 Jesse 69, 70
Tyler, (John) 112
Ulloa, Antonio de 34
Unzaga, Louis de 34
Van Buren, (Martin) 44
Vance, A. J. 62
Van Dorn 77
Vanhoose, J. H. 59
Van Patten, P. 44, 62
Vaughan, C. M. 58
 F. T. 71, 72
 John 59
Villiere, De La 99
Von, Moltke 81
Wail, Philip 32
Waitie, Stand, Gen. 23
Walker, A. S. 30, 32
 David 39, 69, 70, 110, 111
 Davis 76
 George 110
 J. W. 71
 Jacob 110
 Jacob Wythe 110
 James 32
 James D. 72
 James H. 58
 John 32
 Nancy 110
 R. K. 63
 S. B. 32
 S. C. 71

Wallace, J. G. 71
 L. W. 32
 O. W. 30
 W. F. 72
 W. L. 32
Walrath, A. 59
Ward, A. M. 31
 Augustus 31
 I. W. 31
 Isaac 30
 James 30
 Zeb 59
Warner, E. A. 71
Warren, D. B. 58
Warwick, W. I. 69
Washington, (George) 108, 109
Waters, C. C. 70
 D. C. 31
Wathen, J. H. 30
Watkins, George C. 43, 58, 71
 Robert A. 42
Watson, Elizabeth 111
 James 30
 Samuel 111
 Shelton 69, 71
Weaver S. M. 42
Webb . W. 30
 W. 32
Webbe T. F. 72
Webster, Daniel 93
Welborn, Elias 107
 Isaac 107
 Samuel S. 107
Welch, Thomas R. 101
 W. B. 43
Wells, Emma 62
 George 77
 William 30
West 76
 L. N. 30
Wetmore, G. C. 31
 George 31
Wheeler, Amos 37
 S. 58
 Stephen 42, 58, 59
Whinnery, Abraham 58
Whissen, A. A. 59
White, H. King 72
 Isaac 31
 J. T. 30
 R. J. T. 42
 Robert J. L. 40
 Robert J. T. 42
 William 32
Whittington, G. 30
 H. A. 30
Whitworth, J. W. 31
Whytock, John 40, 69, 71, 72
Wideman, John 31
Wilburn, D. 30
Wiley, B. J. 32
Willey, Dennis 100

Williams, (Attorney General) 41
  A. B. 69, 71, 72
  Aaron, Rev. 101
  B. D. 59
  Betty 108
  David 108
  E. K. 31
  Hattie 108
  J. A. 72
  Jacob 108
  James 31
  Jesse 108
  John 108
  John A. 72
  Joseph Desha 108
  L. 32
  Lucian 108
  Maggie 108
  Mattie 108
  Millie 108
  Minnie 108
  Minnie C. 108
  Otis 108
  Pattie 108
  Samuel 41
  Sam W. 43, 69-71, 75, 76
  Urban V. 108
  Virgil 108
Williamson, J. 42
  James 77
  John 38
  R. C. 32
Williford, William 32
Wilshire, W. W. 69
Wilson, A. M. 30
  Alfred M. 71
  Alfred W. 70
  Emzy 38, 42
  Frank 71
  J. M. 71
  John 32, 37, 38, 104, 105, 110
  John M. 70, 72
  T. A. 58
  Thomas 32
  Washington L. 58
Winfrey, John 42
Witherspoon 76
  J. L. 43, 69
Witt, A. R. 62
  R. S. 32
Witter, D. T. 30
Wise, Z. L. 72
Wood, C. D. 72
  James B. 72
  William 32
Woodruff, W. E. 43, 62
  William E. 103, 104
  William E., Jr. 43

Woodson, James 38
Woody, W. B. 32
Woolsey, J. P. 57
Wooly, Samuel 70
Wright, C. 31
Wyatt, Thomas 29
Xavier, St. Francis 103
Yarberry, Milton 30
Yell 75, 111
  Archibald 70, 80, 110, 111
  James 76
Yoemans, William F. 38
Yonley, T. D. W. 39, 43, 69
Young, Arch 71
  J. K. 72
  J. O. 32
  James K. 71

www.ingramcontent.com/pod-product-compliance
Lightning Source LLC
Chambersburg PA
CBHW020658300426
44112CB00007B/427